)03

DIMENSIONS OF JAPANESE SOCIETY

Also by Kenneth G. Henshall and from the same publishers

A HISTORY OF JAPAN: From Stone Age to Superpower

Dimensions of Japanese Society

Gender, Margins and Mainstream

Kenneth G. Henshall
Professor of Japanese Studies
Department of East Asian Studies
University of Waikato
New Zealand

First published in Great Britain 1999 by
MACMILLAN PRESS LTD
Houndmills, Basingstoke, Hampshire RG21 6XS and London
Companies and representatives throughout the world

A catalogue record for this book is available from the British Library.

ISBN 0–333–74478–0 hardcover
ISBN 0–333–77239–3 paperback

First published in the United States of America 1999 by
ST. MARTIN'S PRESS, INC.,
Scholarly and Reference Division,
175 Fifth Avenue, New York, N.Y. 10010

ISBN 0–312–22192–4

Library of Congress Cataloging-in-Publication Data
Henshall, Kenneth G.
Dimensions of Japanese society : gender, margins and mainstream /
Kenneth G. Henshall.
p.   cm.
Includes bibliographical references and index.
ISBN 0–312–22192–4 (cloth)
1. Social values—Japan.   2. Marginality, Social—Japan.   3. Sex
role—Japan.   4. Minorities—Japan.   5. Japan—Social
conditions—1945–   I. Title.
HN723.5.H48   1999
306'.0952—dc21   98–43697
                                                              CIP

This book is printed on paper suitable for recycling and made from fully managed and
sustained forest sources.

10   9   8   7   6   5   4   3   2   1
08   07   06   05   04   03   02   01   00   99

Printed and bound in Great Britain by
Antony Rowe Ltd, Chippenham, Wiltshire

To the memory of Alex French (1960–94), whose achievements in Japan were inspiring, and whose courage and determination in the face of adversity were humbling

Contents

List of Tables

Preface

Dimensions aims to present a fair and balanced account of Japanese society. Early western works on the topic were coloured by prevailing images of Japan as a quaint and exotic land. Postwar works continued a focus on differences between Japan and the west. This was particularly the case during the 1970s and 1980s, when they often reflected Japanese attempts to explain their economic success by ascribing to themselves immutable attributes of Japaneseness such as harmony and homogeneity. Japan was portrayed as something special, unique, monolithic, and unchanging. By contrast, recent works during the late 1980s and 1990s have over-reacted against this holistic simplification and exaggeration by an excessive focus on diversity and conflict. They have also tended to water down the particularity of Japan by overly stressing elements of universality, in their cause of proving that Japan is really nothing special.

There is truth on both sides, but it has been obscured by all the exaggeration. What is needed—certainly for the reader approaching Japanese society for the first time—is a balanced account that recognises both diversity and uniformity, both harmony and conflict, both the particular and the universal. This is what *Dimensions* tries to achieve.

The book's three-part structure reflects this attempt to achieve balance. One of the most universal matters in human society is that of relationships between men and women. It is self-evident—yet often overlooked—that these are essential not only to the survival of any particular society, but also to the survival of humankind as a whole. Since male–female relationships are so fundamental, yet seem to form such a distinctive pattern in Japan, the first part of the book focuses on gender issues. This discussion of the essential basis of society 'sets the scene', as it were, for further discussion. The fact that gender is treated as a part of the book in its own right, and not incorporated into a more general discussion, also reflects the growing recognition of Gender Studies as a discipline.

The second part discusses marginals, who largely represent key elements of the diversity in Japanese society that has been made so much of in recent years. However, discussion is broadened beyond the minority groups typically found in studies of Japanese diversity, such as the indigenous Ainu of Hokkaidō or ethnic Koreans. Because marginalisation is an important means of understanding mainstream values, discussion includes non-minority marginalised groups such as the sick and the mentally disabled. There is a particular focus on how and why such people are marginalised.

The third part discusses the mainstream, who are overwhelmingly the substantial part of the very normative society of Japan. They are discussed after marginals, and not before them, for a number of reasons. It makes sense to approach the centre from the periphery. Among other things this permits a better appreciation of that centre and its values. Moreover, however much on the fringe, marginals are nevertheless a part of society and need to be taken into account. To discuss them after the mainstream would seem somehow to perpetuate their 'tag on' status, and I believe they are worth more than that—though not to the extent of dominating the book. Discussion of mainstream society follows the life-cycle of youth, adulthood, and old age. It then proceeds to consider how the individual self relates to the group and to society as a whole, and finishes with a consideration of how Japanese derive and perceive a national identity.

The Introduction briefly discusses western perceptions of Japan, particularly the view of Japan as an opposite of the west, and considers how we might best approach the study of it. The Conclusion draws together the various parts, and tries to identify what we might genuinely consider to be distinguishing characteristics of Japanese society. It draws particular attention to the ideal of purity.

Again in the interests of balance, I have tried to use a wide variety of both primary and secondary sources, ranging from often esoteric scholarly works to reference books to popular commentaries to newspapers and magazines, as well as novels, videos, comic books, and song lyrics. Where possible I have tried to confine my sources to English, for a further aim of *Dimensions* is to make Japanese society accessible. Realistically, few readers will be willing or able to read material in Japanese. This can still be something of a problem when it comes to primary material, such as *manga* (comics), but so much secondary material—and, thanks to numerous translations, not a little primary material—is now available in English that a command of Japanese is nowhere near as important as it was thirty years ago, when I first started my own study of Japan. I have used plentiful references for those readers wishing to follow up particular points—which

I hope they will—and in the vast majority of cases they will not have to read Japanese to do so. The References likewise include English-language works only.

Acknowledgements

I am indebted to a number of colleagues around the globe for assistance in one form or another. Some have commented on parts of the manuscript, others have given overall guidance, still others have provided specific information. They include, alphabetically, John Bowen, Ron Caseley, Ken Coates, Marion De Ras, Kenichi Harada, Carin Holroyd, Arne Kalland, Gavan McCormack, Brian McVeigh, Kim McWilliams, Akiko Nakayama, Tsutomu Nishigaki, Fumiko Nishimura, Yoshio Sugimoto, and Tadashi Uda. The shortcomings of this book are in no way a reflection of their advice or input, and any conclusions drawn or views asserted in it do not necessarily reflect their own views.

My thanks are also due to Harlequin Publishers, the staff at Macmillan Press (especially Tim Farmiloe, Aruna Vasudevan, John Smith and Vicki Johnson), Jo North and the University of Waikato.

Glossary of Key Japanese Terms

Ainu: indigenous inhabitants of Japan, now confined to Hokkaidō
amae: child-like dependence on others
amayakashi: spoiling or indulging, allowing *amae*
awase: synthesising opinions, compromise
burakumin: 'hamlet people', social outcasts
bishōnen: 'beautiful young man', embodying youthful purity
daimyō: feudal lord, esp. in Tokugawa period
dōwa: 'integration', euphemistic reference to *burakumin*
enjo kōsai: 'financially assisted relationship', often euphemism for paid sex with a young girl
enryo: reserve or restraint
eta: 'great filth', nowadays *burakumin*
furōsha: vagrant
gaman: endurance
giri: duty
Heian: Kyōto (capital 794–1868), period name 794–1185
hinin: 'non-person', nowadays *burakumin*
honne: true inner feelings
ie: old-style extended family
Jōmon: period name to c.300 BC
juku: after hours 'cram' school
Kamakura: former shōgunal base, period name 1185–1333
kami: Shintō god(s)
kanjin: contextual (Japanese-style) individual
karōshi: death through overwork
kata: form, normative ideal
kawaii: cute
kegare: impurity
ko: child or junior in relationship
kōha: 'hard school' male
kojin: (western-style) independent individual
mai-hōmu taipu: male who prefers family over work
Meiji: period name 1868–1912

mōretsu-gata: 'fiercely determined type', used of hard workers of postwar period committed to rebuilding nation

Nara: ancient capital, period name 710–794

nenkō-sei: seniority system for pay and promotions

Nihonjinron: 'theories about the Japanese', type of self-congratulating and usually simplistic literature of 1970s and 1980s seeking to explain Japan's success, often stressing uniqueness and superiority

obasute: abandoning granny/one's parents (*oyasute*)

omote: front or surface appearance, often 'face'

on: indebtedness, obligation

oya: parent or senior in relationship

risshishugi: successism, achievement-orientation, self-help

ryōsai kenbo: 'good wife, wise mother'

samurai: retainer, later warrior

shakaijin: adult defined by social responsibility, esp. productive work

shi-nō-kō-shō: 'warrior-peasant-artisan-merchant', hierarchical social structure in Tokugawa period

shōgun: military ruler

shūshin-koyō: 'lifetime employment'

soto: outside

tatemae: front or pretext or outer form, often 'lip service'

tate-shakai: vertical society

Tokugawa: shōgunal dynasty 1600–1868, name for same period

uchi: home or inside or inner group

ura: rear or that below surface

Yamato: old Japan, 'mainland' Japan, period name c.300–710

Yayoi: period name c.300 BC–AD 300

yuzuriai: 'give and take', tolerance, accommodation

Introduction: Japan as Other, and the Other Japan

Japan has 'vast numbers of cattle of all sorts', and is 'well stocked with elephants, oxen, buffaloes, and sheep'.... Japanese costumes 'have not been altered for at least 2,444 years. They universally consist of night-gowns'.... 'Such is the simplicity of their habit, that they are soon dressed.'

Such are some of the pearls of wisdom passed on to us by the *Encyclopaedia Britannica* of 1797. Two hundred years later, our knowledge of Japan has improved somewhat. In those intervening years Japan has changed from a remote and obscure land to an international superpower. The isolated country has been forced on more than one occasion to open up by western powers, first in the mid-nineteenth century and then again after its defeat in World War Two, when for seven years it was occupied by Americans. Japanese people and products are now commonplace around the world.

And yet, for all our contact with Japan, our knowledge of it is still far from perfect. We may even prefer it that way, for Japan continues to play for many of us the role of Other. It is a mysterious Other, an imprecise Other whose very vagueness allows us to make of it what we will. We are intrigued by it, and like to learn about it, but the more we do, the more we risk losing that convenient Other. If you have no Other, how can you define the Self? And how dull life would be without an element of mystery such as Japan provides.

We still like to think of Japan in many ways as a Topsy-Turvy Land, a Back-to-Front Land where everything is the opposite to our own cosy ways. That fictional hero of the western world, James Bond, tells us that 'the bloody Japs do everything the wrong way around'. The word 'wrong' is particularly telling, for it confirms the rightness of our own ways. We do like to see the Other as wrong. Japan is a particularly convenient Other here, not only because so much about it is still rather unclear to us, but also because of its defeat in the war. Victory has given us a sort of licence to criticise it with impunity.

As one example, holier-than-thou western fingers were wagged at Japan recently when it was found to have been sterilising mentally handicapped women to preserve the quality of the race. Then it was discovered that the French had been doing the same thing. So too had the Swedes, who were supposed to have a model caring society. The fingers abruptly stopped wagging. The French and the Swedes are Us, our western Self, not the Other. (And it was not the 'Germans' who were responsible for the Holocaust, but the Nazis. Germans are Us, Nazis are Other.)

Even those who genuinely wish to learn about Japan have not always had the means to do so. It can be a difficult place to gain first-hand knowledge of. And while scholarly writers on Japan usually try their best to present what they see as the truth, they are only human. They too are swayed by prevailing paradigms and images—mostly going with the flow, but sometimes actively going against it. In partic-ular, scholars have been swayed by the dialectics of difference. The respected anthropologist Ruth Benedict, who briefed the wartime US government about Japan, opened her report—later published as the classic study *The Chrysanthemum and the Sword*—with a reference to Japan as 'the most alien enemy the United States had ever fought'. 'Alienness' had dominated western perceptions of Japan long before that, and, now seemingly legitimised by such a respected scholar, it continued to do so for a long time after.

Presently the focus on difference became extreme. Japan had become an economic superpower by the late 1960s, and a genre of supposedly scholarly works emerged that tried to explain the reasons for Japan's success. Known as *Nihonjinron* ('Theories about the Japanese'), and largely but not entirely written by Japanese, the liter-ature stressed qualities such as loyalty, harmony, homogeneity, diligence, and group-orientedness. That in itself was not so bad, for such qualities undeniably have a strong presence in modern Japan. However, carried away by enthusiasm for the cause, *Nihonjinron* writers grossly exaggerated fact, sacrificed academic authority, and portrayed these qualities as if they were immutable attributes of some fixed Japaneseness. The stress on the uniqueness and specialness of the Japanese reached extraordinary levels, with one *Nihonjinron* writer even claiming of the Japanese that 'the peculiarity of their background makes it impossible to judge them on the basis of the criteria suitable to the evaluation of other peoples'.

This was throwing down the gauntlet to many academics. Works soon started to appear that challenged this claim, works that focused on the universality of Japanese behaviour rather than its particularity. More specifically, a stress came to be placed on the opposite to each of the qualities asserted by the *Nihonjinron* writers. Whole books were dedicated to diversity and conflict and minorities. The monolithic Japan of *Nihonjinron* literature was deconstructed with an enthusiasm not unlike that of the *Nihonjinron* writers themselves.

However, the pendulum has now swung too far. Deconstructionist literature, while valuable as a counter-balance, has come to occupy a disproportionate role in recent studies of Japan. You cannot properly understand English society by concentrating on French-speakers in the Channel Islands, or on recently arrived Chinese immigrants running fish-and-chip shops in the East End of London. The equivalent is true of Japan and its minorities.

This does not mean that such people, such minorities, can be ignored. They are undoubtedly a part of society, however marginal they might be, and they need to be taken into the reckoning. In fact, the attitude of any mainstream society towards its marginals and minorities is a very important indicator of the nature of that society. Moreover, marginalised minorities help define the values of the mainstream by acting as a domestic Other—for Otherness is not just defined at international level. They are, as it were, the 'other side' of a society.

And yet, in any society the vast majority of people generally conform to a range of accepted norms, however much they might differ in gender, age, occupation, and personality profile. There is usually a set of norms tailored to fundamental groupings such as those based on age and gender, and these norms in turn belong to a larger set of 'national norms'. Japan is no exception, and is indeed very much more normative than most societies.

What is needed is a balanced approach, balance between mainstream and marginals, between 'normalcy' and 'non-normalcy', between type and individual, between the universal and the particular. This is no easy matter, especially for non-native researchers and especially so in an age of cultural sensitivity. When generalising, as one must, one immediately risks the criticism of stereotyping—a criticism that often conveniently overlooks the fact that nations generalise about themselves and even produce self-stereotypes, as is clearly demonstrated in Japan's case by *Nihonjinron*. If it is a negative generalisation, then one can all too readily draw the dreaded accusation of racism, or at least cultural chauvinism. If one errs too much towards a stress on the particular, then one is accused of cultural relativism. If one errs too much towards a stress on the universal, then one is usually safe from criticism, but the particularity of the object being studied is in danger of being rendered bland and characterless.

It is clear that common sense must prevail. *Nihonjinron* literature undoubtedly errs very much towards stereotyping, yet, however poor the scholarship, it should not be totally dismissed, for it tells us much about Japanese ideals and self-perception. Common sense also tells us that, however much we respect the ideal of perfect balance, we must in practice incline towards difference, for how else can one define anything except by contrast? Nothing is absolutely unique, and all things are found in all societies. But there is considerable room for difference in the matter of degree, in the matter of priorities and preferences, in relativities rather than absolutes. It is here that Japan differs more from us in the west—a necessarily generalised 'west'—than western nations differ among themselves.

A major area of interest is where the axes of universality and particularity meet. Like every other nation on the planet, Japan has had to put in place systems and conventions to accommodate the universal needs of human society, such as to procreate, to protect and socialise the young, to cope with sickness, to find shelter and security, to relate constructively to others, to preserve order and avoid anarchy, and so forth. The relationships between men and women are particularly fundamental, for without them there would be no society, no humankind at all. Yet societies do not necessarily devise the same methods to achieve these aims. As so many commentators have remarked, Japan has organised its society with ways and means that often seem strange and paradoxical to westerners.

To many westerners the Japanese do still seem a confusing people. They are both polite and impolite, self-effacing yet assertive, honourable yet duplicitous, and so on. These sorts of paradox are quite easily explained once one understands the concept of the situational ethic, whereby behaviour is regulated by rules of conduct specific to certain types of situation rather than by a universal moral code. This is what usually applies in Japan, but it is still something that eludes many westerners accustomed to the Ten Commandments and a clear division between Good and Evil.

Other paradoxes are less easily explained. How can a Confucianist society, which supposedly respects its elderly and shows filial piety towards parents, have legends of abandoning aged parents on hillsides? In more recent times, how could it justify trying to dump them overseas, or the 'rent-a-family' in which actors are paid to visit aged relatives on behalf of real sons too busy to see them? How can a society that supposedly respects nature have polluted it so badly at one stage? And how can it have such respect for the artificial and for role-playing, not just of sons, but to such an extent that the ultimate portrayal of one gender is felt best achieved through impersonation by the other? How can a society that has a female for its principal deity treat its women as inferior? How can men be so dominant over women yet so dependent on them? How can a society that supposedly adores children have traditions of infanticide and of selling 7-year-olds into prostitution, and even now still turn a blind eye to child prostitution?

Yet, even such paradoxes as these can to a very large extent be explained, as these pages attempt to do. Some are the result of misunderstanding, but some indicate methods of social organisation, patterns of behaviour, and concepts of the self and others that are not necessarily familiar to us in the west. As Benedict herself also said (though it was largely overlooked), what might appear as paradoxes to a foreign observer are very probably not paradoxes to the people observed. If we start from a premise that the Japanese themselves do not see their behaviour as strange and paradoxical, but as an outcome of the way in which they have chosen to organise their society and their lives, then we can learn much about not only the particularity of Japan, but about ourselves, and about the universality of the human condition. This will go a long way towards compensating for the loss of Japan the Mysterious Other.

Part One

The Essentials of Society: Men and Women

1.1 HARD MEN, SOFT MEN, IDEAL MEN, REAL MEN: THE CONSTRUCTING OF MALENESS

In many ways Japan is a male-dominated society. Though attitudes towards traditional gender roles are slowly changing, men still occupy around 95 per cent of positions of authority in business and politics, as opposed to the 60 to 70 per cent common in many western countries. They earn more, have better promotional opportunities, and are better educated.[1] Outside the home, they make almost all the major decisions.

Demographically, however, it is women who prevail, and increasingly so. Since the late 1930s men have steadily been outnumbered by women in the population as a whole. There are now 61.7 million males in Japan, and 64.2 million females.

But figures can be notoriously misleading. The male species is certainly not in decline, for the female majority is made up entirely of the elderly. In every age bracket up until the late 50s, men are in the majority. In the under-5 category, there are only nine girls for every ten boys.[2] Among those over 80 years of age, by contrast, women outnumber men almost two-to-one. In 1997 Japanese women had a life expectancy of 83.0 years, outliving their men (76.6) by more than six years. Both genders are the longest-lived in the world, or very close to it. However, a basically similar pattern is seen in many advanced nations in the twentieth century. This suggests that, in conditions where few women die in childbirth and there are few major diseases, men may naturally be shorter-lived than women. In other words, the more aged a society's population becomes, the more women prevail numerically. In Japan's case, this process is outweighing the prevalence of males in pre-elderly age groups.

Though younger males in Japan may not be in decline numerically, they are in serious decline spiritually in the view of many older

1

Japanese males. The disciplined hardworking types of the immediate postwar period, the supposed latter-day samurai whose selfless efforts helped Japan rise to superpower status, despair that they are being succeeded by a generation of weak and selfish wimps.[3] Women, for their part, seem to send out mixed signals to the new male.

What sorts of male images, then, prevail among Japanese males themselves, among Japanese females, and among non-Japanese? What sort of ideals and expectations are associated with being a male in Japan?

For better or for worse the recorded history of Japan, like most nations, is overwhelmingly a record of the deeds of its men. It follows therefore that much of the respect and disrespect Japan has earned internationally is directed largely at its males. Broadly generalising, on the positive side, the popular (though not necessarily accurate) image of the samurai from Japan's past has brought respect for the Japanese male's perceived courage and loyalty. The economic success of Japan has also meant the Japanese male is respected for his determination and resilient hardworking nature, as well as a high degree of intelligence and capability. On the negative side, he is not respected for a perceived aggressiveness, arrogance, chauvinism, and narrowness of vision, and at times for tactics considered unethical. He is often called an 'economic animal' or a 'worker ant'. Memories of the war and acts of brutality and fanaticism still also continue to colour international perceptions of the Japanese male, particularly in Asia.

Japanese males themselves naturally have their own preferred self-images, which are not always the same as overseas images. One widely held image in postwar times—though it is weakening of late—has been that of the corporate warrior or latter-day samurai, committed to serving his company and his country. Until quite recently a true man was expected as a matter of course to sacrifice his family life and any personal wishes in order to concentrate on the all-important duty of selflessly serving his master. In the modern age this meant his boss at the office, through whom he served the company, and in turn the nation.[4] This ideal was based largely on the *kōha* ('hard school') male, supposedly represented by the samurai of old.[5]

The idealised *kōha*/samurai male should show selfless *gaman* (endurance), *makoto* (sincerity), and *isshin* (single-minded commitment) in the carrying out of his duties. Traditionally he was supposed to be a man of Zen-like austerity who endured hardship without complaint, a man of action not words or finer thoughts, a man who set about his duties without asking questions. Such an ideal image was not entirely of his own making. In early and medieval history samurai retainers were in actual fact rarely characterised by loyalty, and to prevent treachery and minimise defections their warlord masters deliberately encouraged the ideal of selfless and unquestioning execution of duty. Similarly the Tokugawa shōguns, military rulers of Japan from the seventeenth to the nineteenth centuries, promoted such an image to lessen the possibility of heterodoxy and subversion.[6]

A *kōha* male—at least in the old days—ought never to give any importance to romance or other similar matters seen as soft and unmasculine, like food or personal comfort. To actually be in love with one's wife was considered demeaning, for manhood was sullied by any admission of affection.[7] One major distinction between the Japanese samurai and the European knight is that the samurai never developed any code of male chivalry towards women.[8] Far from being seen as objects of romance and tender feelings, women were seen clinically by samurai as mere functional vehicles to produce offspring.[9] They were not even favoured as partners for sexual pleasure, for homosexuality among samurai was—in the view of one specialist scholar—'not merely common but *normative*'.[10]

Certainly homosexuality was very widespread in the samurai world, and this too, like the samurai's non-intellectualism, was in no small part a reflection of ideology rather than simply natural behaviour. In the religious beliefs of native Shintō women were anyway considered impure (*kegare*).[11] This was further strengthened by the imported Chinese *yin-yang* philosophy, which led many males to fear that too much involvement with the female (*yin* or *in*) would be detrimental to their maleness (*yang* or *yō*).[12] In practice, however, most samurai, and those who sought to emulate them such as wealthy merchants, were unable or unwilling to live up to the strict *kōha* ideal of avoidance of women other than for procreation. As a result, bisexuality rather than simple homosexuality appears to have been the typical pattern of samurai sexual behaviour.[13]

By contrast to the *kōha*, there has long been a range of male types loosely classifiable as *nanpa*, or 'soft school', though this is not clearly defined and is perhaps best seen simply as less than *kōha*. The range includes the 'wimpish', the meek, and the timid, who by *kōha* standards show a lack of manliness by their lack of resolution and fortitude. In this regard Japanese male perceptions of softness overlap with those of western males. However, the Japanese concept also includes the assertively ostentatious and hedonistic, who are felt to show a lack of manliness by their self-indulgence and boastfulness. And, inevitably, it includes men who are too dependent on women—though in practice male dependence on women is very widespread, including among many who outwardly pretend to be *kōha* types.

Curiously, by western standards, deliberately enhanced 'effeminate', flower-like, graceful beauty has rarely been considered the antithesis of manliness in Japan, either by women or men themselves. Among other things this is seen in homosexual relations, where the often effeminate passive partner has never really suffered the unflattering image typically associated with such a role in the west.[14] Terms such as 'pretty boy' or 'nancy boy' or 'queen' are still normally used in the English-speaking world as a slur on one's manhood (despite changing attitudes towards homosexuality), but this is by no means so in Japan. There, the concept of *bidanshi* or *bishōnen* ('beautiful young man') is in many ways a higher male ideal than the *kōha*.

It is exemplified in drama, legend, and literature by Yoshitsune, the military hero whose exploits helped establish the shōgunate of his half-brother Minamoto no Yoritomo in the late twelfth century. Yoshitsune is invariably depicted as triumphing—at least in spirit—over those warriors possessed of mere brute brawn. He is treated as a superior being, almost more god than human. Yoshitsune died young, forced to kill himself and his family. He is seen as a tragic hero, not only for the circumstances of his death but for the fact that, as a *bishōnen*, he represents an appealing ideal. A similar example is that of the *kamikaze* pilots of World War Two, who are also known in Japanese as the 'Cherry Blossom [*Ōka*] Squadron' since they fell to earth while still fresh and beautiful. They too are seen as quasi godlike, and in fact were said to become honoured gods upon their death. By contrast, it is not difficult to imagine the reaction if a typical western military hero, exemplified in film by 'he-men' figures such as John Wayne, was likened to a flower by a would-be flatterer.

The idea of dying while young and beautiful and by association pure, of an existence untainted by the ugliness of decrepitude, is an important aspect of Japanese aesthetics. Aesthetics in turn play an important part in the conceptualising of ideals, including gender ideals, and not just in the simple sense of physical attractiveness. The Japanese *bishōnen* should still display perceived manly and relatively mundane attributes common to the *kōha* such as decisiveness, fortitude, and a selfless devotion to whatever cause he is fighting for. However, it is his very elusiveness, his very distance from typical reality in his necessary qualities of purity and beauty and transient youth and almost supernatural presence, that make him an even higher ideal than the more realistically attainable and sustainable ideal of the *kōha* type samurai.

There is more to gender than biological differences, and the *bishōnen* is an example of how risky it is to apply the gender ideals of one culture to the interpretation of gender in others. He may appear to many westerners as the classic soft type, but this would be a serious misrepresentation of his perception by fellow Japanese.

By contrast, many old-school males in Japan have no hesitation in consigning the male of the postmodern era to the soft wimp category. However, this too is something of a misleading over-simplification. In the last two decades or so, with the onset of the postmodern age and its less demanding values, and with the achievement of many of Japan's economic goals, it has understandably become increasingly common to reserve a part of the male consciousness for *mai hōmu* (my home). This is particularly so after the bursting of the economic bubble in the early 1990s, causing redundancies and pay-cuts that have cast doubt on the rewards for total company loyalty. The 'hard school' ideal has undoubtedly softened, but this does not necessarily mean that males have become soft in the sense of weak and hopeless.[15]

The 'new age man' in Japan is still—relative to other countries—inclined to be hardworking, nationalistic, and generally loyal to his company, but not slavishly so, for he now devotes time and thought to himself and his family, and even helps around the home.[16] He also indulges himself a little in recreational sport and other leisure pursuits. In short, he is an 'all round' man, who can balance work and family commitments, professional and personal interests. He may not contribute as much to the economy or other national causes as his predecessors, and in that sense may be a less 'valuable' man, but he is probably a happier and more fulfilled one.

How do women in the current age view their men? Broadly generalised female expectations of the male can be gleaned to some extent thanks to the Japanese obsession with catchphrases. As with so many aspects of life in Japan, there is a current catchphrase to describe the ideal male 'catch'—a literal 'catch' phrase, one might say. According to this encapsulation of popular wisdom, the ideal male partner should fulfil the *sankō* or 'three takais' (*takai* meaning 'high'/'tall'): he should have a *takai* salary, be a graduate of a *takai* status university, and be physically *takai*.[17] Since there is a strong correlation in Japan between attending a *takai* university and obtaining a *takai* salary, this means that two out of the three attributes relate to his potential as a breadwinner, while the third is physical and beyond his control. By western standards at least, this is not a particularly 'enlightened' view of the male and his expected role, and neither does it seem to say much for the females who endorse it. On the other hand, it may simply reflect reality. It is a fact that Japanese men are paid much better than women and are therefore more effective breadwinners. It is also a fact that, at 171 cm, Japanese men at the end of the twentieth century may well have grown 10 cm over their predecessors at the start of it, but they are still well short of western males (178 cm or so), and are perhaps a source of embarrassment to their women in an increasingly internationalised world.[18]

A more detailed picture of female expectations of the ideal male—a picture that does not risk sacrificing accuracy for euphony—is revealed in a recent survey of some twenty nations carried out by the Harlequin publishing company.[19] The main findings are given in Table 1.1 (reduced to Japan and three other nations, including Turkey as a non-western example). However, the survey may be felt to raise as many questions as it answers.

Table 1.1 Female View of Ideal Male

	Japan	*USA*	*UK*	*Turkey*
His most important trait				
Generosity	31%*+	4%	3%	9%
Intelligence	20%*+	8%	6%	13%
Loving/caring nature	14%*−	38%	41%	17%*−
He would most value				
Balanced, rounded life	44%	30%	51%	33%
Home and family	35%	63%*+	40%	40%
Career/financial well-being	10%	3%	6%	18%*+
He would be				
Older than me	58%*+	40%	37%	37%
About same age	23%*−	52%	47%	52%
He would always				
Be my best friend	42%	64%	60%	28%*−
Spend time listening to me	32%*+	13%	19%	19%

In his free time, he would				
Pursue a hobby	33%*+	13%	23%	21%
Join gym/play sport	21%*+	8%	10%	10%
Spend time with children	25%*−	46%	33%	23%*−
What attracts me most to him				
He makes me feel good				
about myself	37%*+	31%	31%	15%*−
His positive attitude	32%	31%	19%	26%
His mind	13%	5%	6%	21%*+
Sexual/physical appeal	4%*−	6%*−	12%	13%
His response to another female's 'come on'				
Flirt back a little	76%*+	45%	38%	23%*−
Ignore/reject her	13%*−	26%*−	33%	61%
Introduce me	5%	27%	27%	9%
His ideal material gift to me				
Jewellery	45%*+	39%	28%	8%*−
Flowers	23%	18%	21%	35%*+
His ideal job would be				
Top business executive	44%*+	18%	13%	19%
Doctor/dentist	11%	15%	14%	12%
Professional sportsman	2%*−	4%	6%	9%

*+: significantly above the overall average for all twenty nations
*−: significantly below the overall average for all twenty nations

The findings suggest that the profile of an ideal male for Japanese women is generous, intelligent, positive-thinking, and 'rounded'. He is an older male who would be a good friend to them and would listen to them, as well as making them feel good about themselves. They are also concerned that he should not be a complete office creature but should get some physical exercise, as well as time to pursue a hobby. Interestingly, he need not spend much time with the children. Nor should he become so involved in sport as to make it his career, for he should give importance to financial well-being by being a top executive. He need not be loving or caring, nor be romantic and give flowers, and he need not be physically attractive either (a little inconsistent with the third *takai*), but if he does manage to attract other women, then a little flirting with them would be tolerated.

Ideals in theory represent something other than the commonplace, but in practice it is hard to judge from the raw data how much the profile is influenced by such genuine ideals and how much by a practical compromise with reality. For example, does the relatively low level of desire for men to spend time with the children indicate that Japanese women prefer this activity to stay in the female domain, or do they simply think that it is more important for their hardworking partners to spend their precious free time getting physical exercise? Does the lack of expectation of physical attraction and romance indicate a genuine lack of interest in such things, or a conditioning by tradition (especially arranged marriages, which still account for almost a fifth of all marriages) not to entertain such expectations? Does the strong preference for an older partner indicate an ideal of maturity (suggesting the actual immaturity of many males), or a practical realisation that this increases the chances of financial security? Do women really not want a loving and caring husband, or is it a reflection of their traditional accustomedness to the 'hard school' male?

To seek answers to these and similar questions, it is clearly not enough to consider the male alone. Gender cannot be meaningfully studied in isolation. Concepts of maleness and related expectations cannot be properly understood without contrast to concepts of femaleness and related expectations, and vice-versa. Interactions between male and female, in sexual and other types of relationship, also need to be examined. Moreover, historical, economic, political, and other factors in the constructing of gender need to be taken into account.

1.2   FROM REIGNING EMPRESS TO SILLY SERVANT: THE HISTORICAL DOWNGRADING OF THE FEMALE

Clearly, to judge from the views of the *kōha*/samurai, women have not generally been held in high regard by men for much of Japan's history. Their lack of status has reflected this. The status of women in very early times, however, does not seem to have been so lowly. Women in those days appear to have enjoyed considerable authority and power as shamans, chieftains, and empresses. They had respect in various fields such as politics, religion, society, the arts, and even matters military.

In ancient times there were a number of real and mythical female figures of prominence, at least as many as in the ancient and early history of most nations. The supreme Shintō deity in Japan's mythology, which was first written down in the late seventh century,[20] is Amaterasu the Sun Goddess. Japan is one of very few cultures to represent the sun by a female. (And theoretically she has never experienced a decline in status.) The most respected of all the rulers of the hundred or so chiefdoms that made up Japan in the third century was Himiko, the queen of Yamatai.[21] She had come to power through warfare, and was acknowledged by Chinese visitors of the day as over-lord of the entire nation. In legends of roughly the same period the female warrior-leader Jingū was given great respect for her courage and fighting prowess. In the seventh and eighth centuries there were several reigning empresses. Court literature of the late tenth and early eleventh centuries was exemplified by female writers such as Sei Shōnagon and Murasaki Shikibu, the world's earliest novelist.[22] Even in the early stages of the samurai era there were occasionally powerful women figures, such as Hōjō Masako (the Nun Shōgun) of the thirteenth century.[23]

Though in subsequent history Japan may represent a particularly clear example of the subordination of women, in general the historical decline of female status appears to have been a worldwide phenomenon. It is a matter that very much needs further research. Many scholars attribute the original source of this widespread decline to the development of agriculture, which had several effects.[24] In prehistory humans had existed as nomadic hunter-gatherers. Women as gatherers had almost certainly played a more consistent role in the provision of resources than men as hunters, and had been respected for this. Agriculture brought about settlement. Settled areas soon became specific territorial bases, with boundaries that needed defending and if possible increasing. This led in turn to the increasing importance of men over women due to their greater physical strength and greater fighting ability. Moreover, agriculture-based settlement meant that—in contrast to hunting and gathering across open territory—resources and the means of production (granaries, tools, and so on) could more easily be controlled by small numbers of people. Here again in practice the superior physical strength of the male prevailed.

Such general theories may or may not help shed light on the decline of women's status in Japan. Agricultural settlement occurred in Japan from around 400 BC, in the southwest, and by the first century AD had spread over most of the area that was to form the basis of the Japanese state. Yet the heyday of Himiko, and even more so the reigning empresses of the seventh and eighth centuries, was considerably later than this. Even if it is argued that the reigning empresses had nominal authority only,[25] it is still a recognition of female authority and high status.

A direct causal link between agriculture and the decline of female status may therefore be open to question. However, it is undeniable that increasing militarisation would have been detrimental to women. Despite the existence in Japan and elsewhere of certain outstanding female warriors and military commanders, when it came down to brute force women were on the whole less useful and therefore less important than men.[26]

Both Jingū and Himiko were also said to be shamans, and this religious element may provide one important clue to the downgrading of the female in Japan (and possibly elsewhere). Owing to their obvious association with fertility, women were accorded considerable status in many early religions, including primitive Shintō. They were seen as direct links to the gods, gods who provided the essence of life as symbolised by birth. However, despite Amaterasu's continuing supremacy, as religions became more sophisticated and more politicised the simple focus on fertility, and hence on women, generally weakened. Males seem to have dominated the priesthood increasingly as protocol and ritual became important, and as religion became an obvious means of achieving power and control for the initiated over the uninitiated.

The development of writing meant that religious protocol and other matters could become codified and extremely complicated. Writing was introduced to Japan from China in the fifth century, by Korean scholars. The ability to read and write depended on a formal education, and here women seem to have been disadvantaged from an early stage. In particular, women in early Japan were generally discouraged from learning Chinese,[27] which for many centuries was to be the written language of religion. Instead, they were constrained to Japanese (whose written form gradually evolved as a modification of Chinese script). This may well have allowed women to dominate Japanese-script literature, but it did not help them in the area of religious authority.

Another important religious factor was the introduction of Chinese-style Buddhism into the country in the sixth century, very shortly after the Chinese writing system. This imported religion was effectively to dominate Shintō for more than a thousand years. Not only did Buddhism demand of its priesthood a considerable knowledge of written Chinese, even more importantly it was basically male-oriented.[28] Regardless of experience and age, nuns were invariably considered junior to male monks.[29] Some Buddhist sects even considered women to be fundamentally evil and incapable of salvation.[30] Prince Genji, ironically the hero of a work written by a female, Murasaki Shikibu's *Tale of Genji* of c.1004, reflects this line of thought. Pondering the nature of women, he observes to himself that 'If they were not fundamentally evil they would not have been born women at all.'[31]

Also strongly male-oriented was Confucianism, which is not a religion as such (lacking a deity) but is certainly an influential belief system.[32] It was introduced from China around the same time as Buddhism, and similarly defined women's status as inferior. For example, the Taika Reform(s) of the seventh century, heavily inspired by Confucianist thinking, resulted in a land allotment to a female that was only two-thirds of the allotment to a male, and in addition barred women from becoming government officials.[33]

It also seems likely that native Shintō too was influenced by Buddhist and Confucian attitudes towards women. From an early stage it had anyway displayed a certain ambivalence towards women, both respecting them and fearing them. Though they enjoyed considerable respect and on occasion even reverence, paradoxically women were also considered potentially dangerous, an embodiment of the elemental forces of nature that men could not understand and felt threatened by. In some regards they were viewed in similar fashion to the tapu or taboo in Polynesian beliefs. This word is commonly misused in the west so as to have strictly negative connotations, but more accurately it represents something awesome and powerful that is both sacred yet feared and best left alone, its powers best not tampered with. Women were associated with ritual impurity, known as *kegare*, due in particular to their association with blood in menstruation and during childbirth.[34] Even the mere presence of women could be felt to defile a place. In fact, until as late as the end of World War Two women were banned from Mount Fuji, their presence being felt to defile its sacredness.[35]

However, Shintō ambivalence towards women seems to have become more inclined to negativity after the introduction of the continental beliefs. It is probably not mere coincidence that the chronicling of Japan's 'official' mythology, which commenced in the late seventh century not long after the introduction of Buddhism and Confucianism, on occasion clearly places women in an inferior position to males, despite its recognition of Amaterasu as the principal deity. This subordination is seen, for example, in the disastrous first attempt at procreation by the goddess Izanami and the god Izanagi, who came down from heaven to populate the land. Their first child was born hideously deformed (and was abandoned) because—as Izanagi curtly informs his partner—Izanami botched protocol by speaking first when that was supposed to be the male's prerogative.[36]

It seems, then, that these various factors of Buddhism, Confucianism, some aspects of Shintō, and militarism each played a significant part in the decline of women's status in Japan. Of these it was probably a combination of Buddhism and Confucianism that struck the most damaging blows. Though the foundation for the decline in female status seems to have been set in place by the introduction of these two imported belief systems in the sixth century, the actual process of decline was, however, not immediate or absolute. Obviously, it required time for new beliefs to take root. In fact, despite the clear male favouritism of the Taika Reform(s) of the following century, the heyday for women on the imperial throne took place at that very time and continued for another century or so afterwards, during the period when the law codes based on the Reform(s) were enacted. From the early seventh to the mid-eighth centuries there were six reigning empresses, whereas after 770 there were only two.[37]

Ironically, some of the early champions of Buddhism were women, such as the non-reigning empresses Kōmyō (consort of Emperor Shōmu, r.724–49) and Danrin (consort of Emperor Saga, r.809–23). This suggests that its male favouritism may not initially have been so pronounced, and that probably it was Confucianism that was the stronger factor in demoting and subordinating women.

The status of women for some centuries afterwards, particularly through the Heian period (794–1185), seems to have been rather ambivalent. On the one hand they retained various substantial rights, such as inheritance. They even seemed advantaged in some matters, such as in the matrilocal marriage pattern according to which a husband joined his wife's family after marriage rather than vice-versa.[38] However, on the other hand they were also increasingly subject to their husband's authority. For example, a husband could divorce his wife with great ease. A wife was powerless to stop this. Neither could she herself initiate divorce. And it was also the custom for aristocratic women to be hidden from the view of males other than those of their immediate family,[39] as though they were some sort of protected chattel. (This was one reason for the popularity of screens and closed sedan chairs.) Further evidence of ambivalence was that changes were much slower in the countryside, where the great majority of the population lived. Here women continued to enjoy a better status than did women in the capital.[40]

The onset of the samurai era is symbolised by the rise to power in the late twelfth century of Minamoto no Yoritomo, who rose from being a provincial warlord to become the nation's first permanent shōgun (military ruler). Though ironically Yoritomo's own wife, Masako, was one of the strongest women in Japanese history, the arrival of the samurai age was to add further to the decline in female status. Yoritomo decentralised the power structure, and as power shifted from the court to the provinces, at first some women were advantaged by the weakening of many court practices restrictive to women. However, they eventually lost more ground than they gained. Not only were women disadvantaged by their relative lack of fighting prowess, among other things the warrior era brought a change from the pattern of matrilocal marital residence (*mukoirikon*) to that of patrilocal (*yomeirikon*)—that is, with a wife now joining her husband's family. Such marriages were often made for strategic reasons, and in some cases women were in effect used as hostages. As the country degenerated into civil warfare and the consolidation of territory became increasingly important, they also gradually lost their inheritance rights over property.[41]

When national order was eventually restored at the end of the sixteenth century, male fighting prowess ceased to be quite so important. Samurai typically turned into bureaucrats and administrators. One might logically expect women's rights and status to have recovered somewhat in this new climate. However, this was not to be. Indeed, far from it; it could be argued that this sudden threat to male importance helped lead by way of compensation to an intensification of ethics favouring the male, for it was not women's status that was revived, but Confucianism, which had tended to lapse during the centuries of civil chaos. In actual fact Confucianism was promoted by the shōguns of the Tokugawa period (1600–1868) as a means of preserving general order and orthodoxy throughout the land, and was not specifically aimed at reinforcing the subordination of women. Nevertheless, it certainly had such an effect.

Perhaps the clearest illustration of this is the work *Onna Daigaku* (Great Learning for Women) of 1716, a 'classic' of gender construction. The work is of unknown authorship but is widely considered to be based posthumously on a manuscript by the neo-Confucianist scholar Kaibara Ekiken (1631–1714, also known as Ekken). It clearly reveals the expected role of women, particularly amongst the samurai class which topped the hierarchical social order and was in many respects expected to set standards. A wife is told that:

> She must look to her husband as her lord, and must serve him with all worship and reverence, not despising or thinking lightly of him. The great lifelong duty of a woman is obedience. In her dealings with her husband, both the expression of her countenance and style of her address should be courteous, humble, and conciliatory, never peevish and intractable, never rude and arrogant—that should be a woman's first and chiefest [sic] care.[42]

It is also important that women are aware of their inherent short-comings:

> The five worst infirmities that afflict the female are indocility, discontent, slander, jealousy, and silliness. Without any doubt, these five infirmities are found in seven or eight out of every ten women, and it is from these that arises the inferiority of women to men. A woman should cure them by self-inspection and self-reproach. The worst of them all and the parent of the other four is silliness…. Such is the stupidity of her character that it is incumbent on her, in every particular, to distrust herself and to obey her husband.[43]

A woman had to obey her father as a daughter, her father-in-law as well as her husband as a wife, and her sons as a widow. She could be summarily divorced for a variety of often trivial and arbitrary reasons, such as talkativeness. She was expected to be the first to rise and the last to retire each day, so as to attend properly to the affairs of the home, for 'in her capacity as wife, she must keep her husband's household in proper order'.[44] Given that she was apparently too stupid even to trust herself in any particular, presumably her keeping the house in order was subject to her husband's guidance, and she herself became little more than a servant carrying out his instructions.

Though men too suffered from the imposition of Confucianist codes and the imperatives of duty, unlike women they were at least allowed to retain a degree of pride and dignity and relative independence. They were, after all, assured of their superiority, while a woman was denied even any self-confidence. The only possible way for a woman to achieve any sense of worth, according to Confucian teachings, was in compliantly fulfilling the subordinate role assigned to her.

She was in a no-win situation. If she fulfilled her subordinate role well, then she proved that this was her 'natural' role. If she didn't, then she was a bad wife who proved, by her very inability to do what was expected of her, that she was unsuited to any position of responsibility.

Interestingly, despite their own religion taking a less than positive position towards women, some Shintō scholars spoke out against this extreme demeaning of the female. In an age of reviving nationalism, they saw this as a symbol of the imposition of foreign ideas. For example, Masuho Zankō (1665–1742) wrote:

> Men and women are on the same level with no distinction of high or low, superior or inferior. To think of women as men's slaves or to expect them to follow men in all matters is a delusion based on Chinese manners and is a deviation from our country's Way.[45]

Confucianism was particularly influential among the samurai class, who accounted for less than 10 per cent of the population—though they were sometimes as much as 40 per cent of the population in towns, where the great majority of them were based. In theory all classes were expected to follow the standards of the samurai, including the Confucian code of conduct. However, though Confucianism was undoubtedly widespread in its influence, in actual practice it was less severe among the other classes. In the rural communities especially, women continued to enjoy a better lot in life, and earned respect for their hard work.[46] And in some rural communities the Heian matrilocal marriage pattern even continued right through till the Meiji period (1868–1912), surviving both the warrior era of the twelfth to sixteenth centuries and the revival of Confucianism that followed in the Tokugawa period.[47]

Confucianism unquestionably exerted a negative influence on the status of women in Japan, one that has lingered to the present day. Nevertheless, in some regards Japanese women have still been better off—or perhaps more exactly less badly off—than women in certain other cultures. For example, Japanese women never experienced the footbinding that Chinese women suffered. Moreover, not a few western visitors to Japan in the mid-to-late nineteenth century remarked favourably on the situation of Japanese women relative to women in other parts of Asia. One wrote, for example, that 'The position of women in Japan is apparently unlike that of the sex in all other parts of the East, and approaches more nearly their European condition.'[48] Another remarked that:

The student of Asiatic life, on coming to Japan, is cheered and pleased on contrasting the position of women in Japan with that in other countries. He sees them treated with respect and consideration far above that observed in other quarters of the Orient.[49]

One can only say that everything must be considered in its context of time and place and circumstance.

Despite their seeming preference for homosexual relationships, in practice most samurai—and the merchants and others who sought to emulate them—were unable to abstain from a sexual association with women. Samurai and merchants were mostly based in the towns. Urban males also included labourers, such as sedan bearers and construction workers, and they too were influenced by the behaviour of samurai and merchants. Thus the urban male's view of women in the Tokugawa period did include, despite the *kōha* ideal, an association with sexual pleasures.[50] Among other things this is reflected in the erotic prints (*shunga*) of the period, and erotic literature such as some of the works by the well-known novelist Ihara Saikaku (1642–93). The prints, for example, show a wide range of sexual behaviour, often a *ménage à trois* and sometimes a simple male–female engagement, but they do certainly feature women.[51] Female prostitutes—along with male prostitutes—were very much in demand, and whole wards, such as Yoshiwara in Edo (present-day Tōkyō) and Ponto-chō in Kyōto,[52] became red-light districts. Their regular clients included samurai, merchants, artisans, labourers, and also lesbian women. Some high-class prostitutes, or courtesans, even achieved considerable wealth and fame.

Perhaps the best-known symbol of the pleasure quarters of the Tokugawa period town was the geisha.[53] The term 'geisha' literally means 'artistic person', and refers to the geisha's training in musical and dramatic arts in particular, as well as their general command of etiquette. Aside from their artistic talents, the distinction between a geisha and a courtesan has always been rather vague, particularly with regard to the lower ranking *onsen geisha* ('resort geisha'). Officially geisha have not been classed as prostitutes, and were not, for example, included in the official ban on prostitution of 1956, but in practice they have been known to provide sexual favours in addition to the entertainment covered by their fee.[54] Many of them in Tokugawa Japan (and later) had a number of regular patrons, who vied both for the honour of 'deflowering' them[55] and for the honour of redeeming them from the geisha house to which they were bonded.

Redeeming was possible in the first place because many young women became geisha out of necessity, being sold or indentured to a geisha house by country parents who usually—but not always—needed the cash. Daughters who were sold to respectable geisha houses were at least generally better off than those who were sold into outright prostitution, often as early as 7 years of age, or those who were simply killed as infants. The Tokugawa period scholar Satō Nobuhiro, writing in the early 1800s, provides clear evidence of these sorts of practices:

> The one place where infanticide seems to be extremely rare is Echigo [present-day Niigata Prefecture], but in its stead the practice prevails on a large scale of selling girls over seven or eight years of age to other provinces for prostitution.[56]

The practice of selling daughters into some form of prostitution or male service continued until World War Two. It was part of a broader trafficking in children that was little different from child slavery, a trade that included boys and girls being sold off to work in mines and, after industrialisation, in factories. The life of these youngsters, and particularly the girls in brothels (though not a few boys sold to brothels also suffered similarly), was not at all pleasant. Many of them were brutalised, and some even preferred death.[57]

The official justification for all this was again Confucianism. Daughters who sacrificed themselves for the sake of the family finances were seen as paragons of filial piety, rendering splendid service to their parents. In fact, according to some observers it was almost a case of society conditioning daughters to believe it was their duty to become prostitutes to aid their families.[58]

Prostitutes, of course, are found in every society, and it is not for nothing that prostitution is known as the 'world's oldest trade'.[59] However, the existence of the geisha in Japan, and particularly the fact that they flirt and entertain and do more than just serve as a means of physical sexual relief like simple prostitutes, provides something of a comment on male expectations of women in Japan, even today. In particular, it provides an indirect comment on attitudes to wives, by virtue of the fact that geisha are not wives. Their role is to flatter the male ego. This applies to all Japanese women in one form or another, but in their way of flattering geisha are expected to be flirtatious and witty and fun-loving, while Japanese wives are expected to be more serious and earnest and supportive. In most western marriages the role of the wife combines both serious and 'fun' aspects. However, it seems that in Japan, from the Tokugawa period on, the roles have become separated. The weighty dictates of Confucianism made the wife seek to act with great propriety in her task of keeping the house in order, attempting all the while to 'cure her infirmities by self-inspection and self-reproach'. The geisha, by contrast, was a creature of levity crafted to compensate for this dullness. The wife and the geisha are, in this sense, 'complementary'.[60]

Surveys of Japanese women's views of their ideal male partner reveal that they do not expect much romance, and continue to be remarkably tolerant of their male partner flirting with another woman. This seems to reflect such an understanding of the role of the wife. Wives provide their men with orderly houses and support in their task of breadwinning, while geisha (and in more modern times casual girlfriends) provide them with a bit of sexy fun, and an escape from the pressures of the real world.

Though the geisha has come to represent an important aspect of femaleness in Japan, few people realise that the first woman geisha did not appear on the scene till 1751. Until then geisha had all been male.[61] The new female performers were initially distinguished by gender-specific terms such as *onna geisha* ('female geisha') or *geiko* ('artistic girls'). However, within just thirty years women had established themselves as a majority in that occupation and were able to claim use of the unqualified term 'geisha'. From now on it was the rapidly dwindling male geisha who had to use the gender-specific term *otoko geisha* ('male geisha') to distinguish themselves from their female counterparts.[62] The rapidity with which women geisha established themselves so soon after the appearance of works such as *Onna Daigaku* suggests again that it was some form of reaction to the effect of Confucianist preachings on the role of the wife.

Though other factors in other periods have played their part, it is the values of the Tokugawa period, especially revived Confucianism, that seem to have been particularly influential on both male and female attitudes towards women and relationships between the sexes in subsequent history. This influence continues even to this day.

The following Meiji period, with its numerous western-inspired reforms, brought some improvement in the status of women. However, this improvement was not great, especially by today's standards.[63] A number of prominent men, such as Education Minister Mori Arinori and leading educator Fukuzawa Yukichi, did try to promote women's rights. Actual advances, though, even in these two men's own field of education, were limited. For example, after the completion of coeducational elementary school females almost inevitably went on a separate educational track from males, with a view to enabling them more properly to 'cultivate womanly virtues'.[64] With the exception of some Christian institutions, entry into tertiary education was very difficult for women. Even by as late as the start of World War Two there were only forty women in Imperial Universities (the most prestigious of the universities), as opposed to 29,600 men.[65]

Women were restricted in choice of profession too. Teaching in an elementary school was one popular option, and women teachers did enjoy a certain degree of respect. On the other hand, during the Meiji period not one single woman was appointed principal of an elementary school. In fact, it was not until 1931 that such an appointment was to be made.[66] Most paid employment for women in Meiji Japan meant work in the textile factories. At the turn of the century women made up 90 per cent of the workers in weaving sheds and silk filatures, and 80 per cent of the operators in the cotton mills. Moreover, half of them were under the age of 20.[67] Most were sold into service by their parents, and most suffered harsh conditions both in their dormitory and their workplace.

The Civil Code of 1898 brought limited legal improvements for women. A wife now had the right to initiate divorce, but this did not include her husband's infidelity as a cause. A woman now had certain rights to inherit and own property and to conduct business, but these were largely theoretical since they usually required her husband's consent, and/or her being placed last in priority after all males in her family. Most importantly, women were not given the right to vote. Basically, despite certain concessions, the Meiji Civil Code upheld the old Confucian ethic.[68]

The continuing influence of Confucianism in attitudes towards women is seen in textbooks of the late Meiji period. For example, one text on morals issued in 1900 seems little more than a rephrasing of *Onna Daigaku*, with passages such as:

> Loquacity and jealousy are defects common among women, so care must be taken to guard against these faults. When a girl marries she must serve her husband and his parents faithfully … rise early in the morning, go to bed late, and devote all her thoughts to household affairs.[69]

Women in Meiji Japan were to make little real headway in terms of rights and status. Nevertheless, by the end of the period, and largely under the influence of western models such as literary heroines, a 'new type' of strong and independent-minded woman had definitely started to appear, though very much as the exception and not the norm. This change is seen, for example, in fact-based novels such as those by Tayama Katai.

Katai's most famous work, *Futon* (The Quilt) of 1907, recounts his real-life infatuation with a 'new type' young woman student, Yoshiko. Yoshiko had been educated at a Christian institution and had later stayed at Katai's home. He saw her as a Japanese version of Anna Mahr from Gerhart Hauptmann's *Lonely People* (*Einsame Menschen*, 1891)—a famous example of one of the west's own 'new women', along with Nora from Ibsen's *Doll's House* (*Et Dukkehjem*, 1879). Throughout the novel Katai contrasts Yoshiko with his 'old-fashioned' wife. He feels discontent towards his wife and a mix of attraction and anxiety towards the modern-minded Yoshiko, who in the end proves just a little too modern for him to cope with. Though Katai's comments are exaggerated, his comparison between old and new is illuminating:

> To Tokio [Katai] nothing was more regrettable than his having contented himself with his wife, who had nothing more to offer than her old-fashioned rounded-chignon hairstyle, waddling walk, and chastity and submissiveness. When he compared the young, modern wife—beautiful and radiant as she strolled along the streets with her husband, talking readily and eloquently at his side when they visited friends—with his own wife, who not only didn't read the novels he took such pains to write but was completely pig-ignorant about her husband's torment and anguish, and was happy as long as she could raise the children satisfactorily, then he felt like screaming his loneliness out loud.[70]

In fact, he often did scream out loud, berating his wife with comments such as:

> 'You old-fashioned people will never understand what Yoshiko does. You only have to see a man and a woman walking together and you think there's something strange going on, but you only think that way because you're old-fashioned. Nowadays women too are aware of themselves, and do what they want to do!'[71]

Though Katai, no doubt in the heat of the argument, gives the impression that self-awareness and independence were the new norms for women, the 'new woman' was in fact still rare. Her rarity can be gauged by modes of dress. According to a survey taken in the centre of Tōkyō as late as 1925—by which stage 'second generation' new types such as the *mobo* and *moga* (from the Japanised pronunciation of 'modern boy' and 'modern girl') were starting to appear under the influence of the western 'flapper' era—only 1 per cent of women were dressed in western clothes.[72] The same survey, by contrast, revealed that 67 per cent of men wore western suits.[73]

And in literature, too, there were few real advances by women. Despite one or two strong-minded individual women writers such as the poetess Yosano Akiko, who even dared to criticise the emperor publicly for cowardice on the occasion of the Russo-Japanese War of 1904,[74] it was to be some decades yet until women's writing really re-emerged on any significant scale. In fact, in the almost 1,000 years between the latter stages of the Heian period and the postwar period, there were only a handful of women writers who achieved recognition. This was despite the fact that in the late Heian period women writers had achieved a prominence rare elsewhere in the world at the time.

The first major women's literary society with feminist aims, the *Seitōsha* (Blue Stocking Society), was founded in 1911 under the leadership of Hiratsuka Raichō. Significantly, however, it was formed at the suggestion of a *male* literary critic, Ikuta Chōkō. The first issue of its journal, *Seitō*, contained a poem by Yosano Akiko, *Sozorogoto* (Rambling Remarks), that is still to this day used as a symbol of the women's movement in Japan:[75]

> The day when the mountain will move is coming.
> When I say this, no one believes me.
> The mountains have been asleep only temporarily.
> In antiquity, mountains, all aflame, moved about.
> No one need believe this.
> But, all of you, believe this:
> All the women who had been asleep
> Have now awakened and are on the move.[76]

Seitō became increasingly radical and aroused considerable criticism, including over the scandalous behaviour of some of its writers. It was the subject of government intervention on a number of occasions, suffered internal problems too, and finally ceased publication in 1916. The journal had been short-lived, but had helped create a climate that saw the appearance of a number of women's general-interest magazines, such as *Fujin Kōron* (Women's Forum) in 1916.

A women's political society, the Association of New Women, was founded shortly afterwards in 1919. Its very foundation challenged Article Five of the 1885 Peace Preservation Law, which prohibited women from joining political organisations. It also had other wide-ranging goals related to equal rights for women, particularly in the area of labour unions. However, it disbanded a couple of years later after achieving very little.

It was not until the appearance of the new constitution drafted by the Occupation forces in 1946, in particular the matters relating to women drawn up by a 22-year-old Russian-American woman named Beate Sirota,[77] that Japanese women gained substantial rights, including the crucial right to vote. In fact, the constitution and subsequent amendments to the Civil Code were, on paper at least, to give women in Japan more rights than women in many countries even today. Ever since the constitution became effective in 1947 they have had full formal equality in suffrage, property, marriage, divorce, guardianship, education, and the conducting of business. As one leading female Japanese scholar has observed, the challenge for women in Japan nowadays is thus not one of formally gaining equal rights, as it is for many women around the world, but one of gaining actual equality in practice, particularly with respect to equal opportunity.[78]

This, of course, means challenging convention and custom, and this is no easy task. Much of the treatment of women in present-day Japan still reflects traditional views, views held widely not only by men but women themselves. To change these is not simply a question of legislation or wagging fingers at chauvinistic men. It also requires fundamental changes in women's own internalised view of themselves.

1.3 TRADITION MEETS THE MODERN WORLD: THE HESITANT EMERGENCE OF THE NEW WOMAN

Despite the formal provisions of the new constitution, and despite recent improvements, it is still often the case in practice that Japanese women do not receive equal treatment with men, or enjoy the same opportunities.

The workplace is a clear illustration of unequal treatment. Women make up 40 per cent of the workforce, two-thirds of them in full-time positions. To improve their actual conditions of employment an

Equal Employment Opportunity Law was passed in 1986, as Japan's acknowledgement of the International Decade of Women. Nevertheless, women's pay, even for full-time workers, is still not even two-thirds of what men receive.[79] Ostensibly, the same wage is paid for the same job regardless of gender, but a major problem for women is that they rarely go on to senior positions.

One of the main results of the EEO Law has been the emergence of a 'dual-track' job escalator. New recruits can choose either a career track (*sōgōshoku*), which leads to management positions, or a clerical track (*ippanshoku*), which effectively restricts employees to secretarial or non-career positions. Pressure is often put on new women employees not to join the career track, such as by asking them to sign a contract in which they pledge not to start a family.[80] According to a 1995 survey of some 6,000 companies with more than thirty employees, less than 5 per cent had actually recruited career track women.[81] A government white paper released in 1995 showed that 40 per cent of companies still have a policy of placing female workers in 'jobs for which the female character and sensitivity can best be used'.[82]

The protracted recession that started in 1990 has led to the effective collapse of Japan's much-vaunted (and much-exaggerated) 'lifetime employment' system. Since this system only ever applied to males, its collapse should help females. However, it may take some years for the effects to flow through. The overall employment profile of women is still described by an 'M' shape—large numbers of young women workers, few in child-bearing years, and many returning in later years. The more flexible employment patterns that will follow the collapse of lifetime employment should mean that women's absence in middle years will become less important a factor in job and promotion opportunities.

There are still very few women in managerial positions in Japan, especially senior positions. Figures in this area can be a little confusing, as a result of different definitions of 'managerial position', but the overall situation is clear. Where it is defined most narrowly, as executive of a major company, then fewer than one in 500 are women, according to a 1997 survey of 2,500 major listed companies.[83] Small as it is, this tiny percentage (0.18 per cent) is still double the figure from a similar survey in 1988, so at least the trend itself is in women's favour. In terms of actual numbers, only 82 out of 44,925 major executives in 1997 were female. Most of these were related to the founder of the company, and only 29 had actually been promoted from the rank-and-file. The same survey revealed that among these 2,500 major companies, only four had a female president. Moreover, in each case she was related to the founder of the company.

When 'managerial position' is defined as team leader, section chief, or department head, Japan's Labour Ministry refers to just 3.9 per cent of such positions being occupied by women in 1994, though this is up considerably from 1.8 per cent in 1976 and 2.5 per cent in 1985.[84] Broader Labour Ministry definitions that combine managerial and administrative roles give figures of just under 9 per cent for 1995, which contrasts with 45 per cent in the USA and 65 per cent in Sweden.[85]

One specific example of the dearth of women managers is the field of broadcasting, which might be felt to offer more than average opportunities to women. However, in this field only 1 per cent of senior managerial positions and less than 10 per cent of positions as reporters are occupied by women in Japan. This contrasts markedly with the figures of 23 per cent and 41 per cent respectively in the case of the broadcasting industry in Sweden.[86]

With the exception of teaching, there is a similar dearth of women in other professional positions. Despite a steady increase, in 1997 only 13 per cent of Japan's doctors were women. In 1994 women comprised only 7 per cent of its lawyers, and 5 per cent of its certified public accountants.[87] Japan's first woman jumbo jet pilot (Tomoko Otake) took to the air as late as September 1997.[88]

Even if a woman does succeed in obtaining a responsible position, she is still not immune from suffering demeaning expectations that are not placed on male employees, such as having to make the tea. However senior, she may still also suffer sexual harassment.[89] In Japan, despite its prevalence, this was not even formally recognised as a problem till the term *seku-hara* was coined from the English in 1989.[90] There is still no direct legislation against sexual harassment itself, though since 1992 compensation has been awarded in courts in cases where it has led to a loss of employment.

The EEO Law itself has been criticised as 'toothless' in that in most areas it simply urges companies to make equal opportunities, as opposed to compelling them, and consequently lacks any means of enforcement. There have been relatively few changes to discrimination against women following its enactment, as is clear from direct observation, from statistics, and from academic studies.[91] Even if the EEO Law had bite to it, the fact that women 'voluntarily' choose the non-career track makes it difficult for legal action to be brought.

One reason given by employers for the dearth of appointments of women to senior positions is their lack of qualifications.[92] As a generalisation, this argument does carry some weight. Although quantitively a greater percentage of matriculating female students (48 per cent) than male students (43 per cent) proceed to some form of tertiary education, qualitatively, most (52 per cent) still attend two-year colleges rather than regular four-year universities. By contrast a mere 5 per cent of tertiary male students attend such colleges.[93] These colleges are often of questionable academic standards. They are generally referred to pejoratively as being in the business of 'bride-training' (*hanayome shugyō*), producing women in the traditional 'good wife-wise mother' (*ryōsai-kenbo*) mould.[94] Graduation from such a college obviously affects a woman's future career prospects. Enrolment patterns are slowly changing, as seen from the fact that in 1970 63 per cent of all female tertiary students were in two-year colleges, but this trend is less than dramatic, and it is still a problem factor in the overall situation of women in Japan.

It might be argued that if there were more women in politics, where they are seriously under-represented, then they might be able to do something about their situation. Women have typically occupied less than 5 per cent of Diet seats—the lowest in the developed world and again in particularly marked contrast to the 30 per cent or so in many Scandinavian countries—and only one or two cabinet positions.[95] Cabinet appointments are made by the prime minister, invariably a man. However, the number of women elected to the Diet is a reflection not only of the preferences of male voters, but also of female. In fact, women are not only a majority of the voting population but also have a higher voting turn-out rate than men.[96]

It would be too simplistic to argue against this that there are not enough women candidates fielded. In the October 1996 Lower House elections, which resulted in women occupying 4.6 per cent of the seats, women comprised 10 per cent of all the candidates.[97] This percentage of candidates is obviously still well below the percentage of women in the general population, but nevertheless their failure rate clearly shows that proportionately far fewer women candidates were chosen than men, and by a predominantly female voting public. That is, women themselves choose not to return female candidates.

It is usually men who are seen as the obstacle to women's equality in Japan. They certainly play their part, but clearly so too do women, for both sexes are still influenced by traditional attitudes towards gender roles—roles undoubtedly formulated largely by men, but internalised by women too.

However, despite this seeming reluctance to actually behave contrary to tradition, there is nonetheless clear evidence of recent changes in attitude, among men as well as women. We have already seen the emergence of a 'new age' male who is prepared to spend more time with his family and help around the home.[98] Repeat surveys by the Prime Minister's Office in 1987 and 1995 show that male attitudes are also changing towards the traditional female role of looking after the home and family and not going out into the paid workforce.[99] Results of these surveys are given in Table 1.2.

Table 1.2 Simple Yes/No Attitudes Towards Traditional Female Role

	1987		1995	
	agree	*disagree*	*agree*	*disagree*
Male	52%	20%	33%	40%
Female	37%	32%	22%	54%

Clearly, though action itself may take longer, in the last ten years or so large numbers of both men and women have switched from endorsing traditional attitudes to disagreeing with them. Women lead the men in disagreeing, but the actual rate of change is similar in both sexes.

There is also clearly, in both sexes, a large percentage of people who have yet to make their minds up and commit themselves definitively one way or the other. This points to the need for caution in interpreting surveys. In fact, if the idea of agreeing or disagreeing *somewhat* is introduced, as opposed to a simple choice between agree or disagree (or undecided), then surveys show a significantly slower rate of change. For example, in 1979, 76 per cent of men and 70 per cent of women agreed with traditional roles *to some degree*. By 1992, these percentages had dropped only to 66 per cent and 56 per cent respectively.[100] Another survey in 1994 showed 51 per cent of women still in agreement.[101] That is, if one wishes to play gymnastics with words and figures, well into the 1990s a majority of both men and women could be said still to endorse traditional female roles. On the other hand, a critic could argue the opposite, and both would have 'evidence' to support their views.

Nevertheless, however suspiciously one treats survey results, the trend is unmistakable. Attitudes are changing steadily, among both sexes. Actual behaviour, however, is changing far more slowly.

Moreover, there are still significant numbers of people who are hesitant about changes—again in both sexes. These are not necessarily confined to the older age group, either.

In fact, one group of the population often overlooked in the matter of gender roles is that of children. A survey conducted in 1992 by Tōkyō Gakugei University, canvassing the views of 10-year-old boys and girls in Japan, the United States, China, and Sweden, found that a massive 61 per cent of Japanese children wanted their mother to stay at home and not go out to work. This contrasted starkly with the 22 per cent of American children, 8 per cent of Swedish, and 0 per cent of Chinese.[102]

A possible explanation for this high Japanese figure, according to the principal researcher, was that Japanese men helped so little around the home. Children saw how tired their mother was in trying to combine household work with holding down an outside job, and concluded it was better for her not to take on a job. If that is so, then Japanese children must be very selfish, because only 4 per cent of them said they themselves helped with the housework. This contrasts with 19 per cent in the United States, 18 per cent in China, and a surprisingly low 5 per cent in Sweden (where perhaps many husbands do help around the home and therefore do not reduce their wife to such an object of children's pity as the Japanese working mother).

Companies, too, have formed an impediment to change, for they have found it advantageous to endorse traditional roles.[103] By promoting such a clear distinction between the sexes, with men expected to work in a company and women expected to look after the home, companies can extract maximum value from their 'lifetime' male employees, for these company creatures will not be distracted by considerations of the home. The affairs of the home are the concern of women, whom the companies are not really interested in employing anyway for any serious position because of their habit of leaving to have children. That is, the corporate world sees women as unreliable workers, but useful unpaid support staff. This should change significantly with the collapse of the lifetime employment system.

Most importantly of all, however, despite the fact that women lead men in changing attitudes towards traditional roles, many women themselves still continue to form a barrier to more complete change. This suggests that tradition is a more powerful influence on attitudes than legislation or criticism from outside. Many even seem locked by a sense of traditional duty into committing themselves to a role they do not necessarily enjoy. A 1994 government survey, for example, found that only 23 per cent of Japanese mothers actually enjoy child-rearing, in great contrast to the 72 per cent of American mothers and 54 per cent of Korean mothers.[104] No doubt this is partly due to the relative lack of help and appreciation from their husbands and children, and partly to the pressures and expenses of child-rearing in present-day Japan. It also surely reflects the fact that they feel duty-bound to the role of child-rearing. When one is duty-bound to do something, it is understandable that it becomes viewed as something less than enjoyable.

At the same time, when one is locked by duty in a no-choice situation, it is also a common reaction to make the most of it and take a pride in doing that duty, even convincing oneself that one is really in control of the situation. Many Japanese women continue to fiercely defend the home as their territory, and do not necessarily welcome male intrusion. Nor do they always welcome intrusion by western feminists, however well-meaning these might be. Feminists in the past who have tried to wean Japanese women away from the home have often been sent away with a scolding to mind their own business—at times mixed with a feeling of pity that such western women have somehow got things wrong and are missing out on a natural life.[105]

New Zealand is one western country that has long played a leading part in promoting feminism, particularly since the 1970s. However, criticism of Japanese women by New Zealand feminists in the late 1970s brought a strong reaction from a number of Japanese women resident in the country. In 1980, one in particular, a middle-aged woman named Miiko Rayner, wrote a long article in the country's leading newspaper that very firmly told feminists to back off, because Japanese women were very happy and in control of their own lot in life.[106] Though her arguments lost some of their force by the fact that she was married to a foreigner and living outside Japan, she nevertheless appeared to speak for many Japanese women of the day. The opening sentences of her article clearly reveal its tone:

> Every time I read about Japanese women being submissive, help-less, and an oppressed sex, I smile to myself. Outwardly it might appear that we are enslaved, but we all know that we are on to a good thing. We hold the power yet we are sheltered from the real hardships of life.

She went on to assert that Japanese women did not want 'equality' if that meant taking on the same responsibilities as men. Women were quite happy playing a supporting role to the male, for everyone had their role to play in Japanese society, and that of the female was less onerous than that of the male so women should count their blessings. The male's role was determined by his company as well as by social convention, and his power was in reality not so great. It was mostly just a show, just like his casual relationships with other women, which were tolerated by wives who appreciated the stresses placed on their husbands and the need for relief from these. In fact, women sympathised greatly with the hard life of males, and this was a factor in their wish to support them. Women were happy being left in charge of the household, which they saw as their domain. Marriage was a contract between two people who had to carry out their respective roles—the male providing for the household, the female managing it—for this was what society expected, and society's norms must be respected. Love was not necessarily relevant. Young people tended to react against this but they eventually learned the value of conformity.

Naturally, her views would be less supported by Japanese women in the 1990s, when among other developments there are in Japan too a significant number of feminists and others interested in women's issues.[107] The apparent selfishness in her comments—we're all right, tough luck for the men—is also unfortunate and unhelpful for Japanese women's image. However, the repeat surveys have shown that even well into the 1990s one woman in four—or one in two if 'agree somewhat' is included—still endorses traditional roles. The recent collapse of lifetime employment for males should continue to prompt change in ideas about gender roles. On the other hand, to judge from research on women's attitudes overseas, it is possible that the trend of change may not go very much further in the particular matter of a woman focusing primarily on the home rather than the workplace.[108] Clearly, however, there is still much room for improvement in Japan's case in such regards as offering more and fairer opportunity to those women who choose not to centre their life on the home, and giving greater respect and status to those who do.

Rayner's point about men's lot in life being worse than women's still has considerable truth to it, and still colours many women's attitudes towards change in traditional gender roles. In the 1990s Iwao Sumiko, one of Japan's relatively few female professors and arguably the nation's leading scholar of Women's Studies, has made observations about Japanese women that are in some regards similar to Rayner's:

Japanese women by no means want to be like men, spending inordinate amounts of time at the office and leading culturally impoverished lives. They know that with their wide circle of friends and freedom to work, raise children, pursue a hobby, join a volunteer group, or simply have a good time, they are far better off than men.[109]

Surveys again support this. Despite their seemingly widespread lack of enjoyment of child-rearing, it is significant that in a 1994 survey by the Education Ministry 65 per cent of women said that they would still choose to be reborn as women, as opposed to only 29 per cent choosing a male life.[110] This is not so different from the situation ten years earlier, which led Jane Condon to remark that most Japanese women were satisfied with their lot in life[111]—even though the satisfaction may only be relative.

Unlike Rayner, however, the women in Iwao's observations—or perhaps more exactly the women of the 1990s—do not seem content to do nothing at all to change gender roles. But it is largely the male role they wish to change, rather than the female, and in this they go beyond the mere passive sympathy shown by Rayner:

> Many Japanese women believe that happiness for both men and women would be better assured by a model of equality in which men currently alienated from their families and deprived of culturally enriching pursuits are given the same freedom, rights, and options in the three main areas of life (work [sic], family, leisure) that women currently enjoy.[112]

A key consideration in the matter of gender equality is the very concept of equality. In the west this is often perceived as some sort of universal principle applicable in all contexts. In Japan, by contrast, it is seen in a broader perspective, in terms of overall balance. As Iwao comments:

> In Japan equality is not so much the governing principle of democratic society as a tool to be taken up where appropriate. Sometimes there is more freedom in this approach than in the strictly principled approach. Questions of fairness and equality are conceived in the long term, multidimensional perspective. Although the husband and wife in a household or the co-workers in an office may not seem to be treated equally at any particular point in time, those involved consider the question from a broader perspective.[113]

In other words, Iwao reminds us that not all cultures want the same things in the same way, but that perceptions and approaches vary. The situation of women—and men—in Japan cannot be considered in isolation from the cultural context. At the same time, of course, nor should it be totally separated from the universal condition of women and men.

Certainly, there could be no disagreement in Japan or elsewhere that the Confucian treatment of women as second-class cannot be allowed to continue. Nor can the Confucian assigning of women rigidly and exclusively to the home, nor the under-representation of women in positions of authority. There must be equal respect for both sexes, and there must be provision for flexibility and choice. However, it is clear that many Japanese women continue to support the basic idea that a woman should look after the home. Tradition undoubtedly continues to be influential here, but it is hard to see it in the modern age as simple brainwashing, for many informed and internationalised Japanese women still think along such lines. They are influenced by traditional culture, as most of us are, but even allowing for the internalisation of externally imposed values, they seem able to objectivise it and to be aware of that influence. (If nothing else, enough westerners have brought it to their attention.) Moreover, they have made it clear that they do not want westerners to interfere, and that they are not damsels in distress.

The whole question of how a man and woman can on the one hand raise a family without depriving their children of proper parental attention, and on the other hand both enjoy the freedom to engage in other pursuits, while all the time ensuring there is sufficient financial security for the family as whole, is of course a major question world-wide, for both policy-makers and individuals. It is possible that the family-oriented stance maintained by many Japanese women and articulated by Iwao may have an influence on world thinking in these regards—though one would have to wait and see the full effects of the current changes in the workplace. But other factors need to be taken into consideration too, such as whether a less wealthy country than Japan could afford to have so many of its women at home rather than in the paid workforce. In any event, Japanese women are able to make a significant contribution to international debate on gender roles. Like anyone, they will benefit from genuine support from outsiders where they feel it is needed. But they do not need advice based on assumptions that western women have all the answers.

1.4   BOYS AND MADONNAS, FATHER-FIGURES AND VIRGINS: RELATIONS BETWEEN THE SEXES

It is stating the obvious to observe that if men and women did not form relationships, humankind would be extinct. For all the celebration of homosexuality in the world of the samurai—or for that matter the postmodern western world—the simple fact remains that every homosexual owes their existence to a heterosexual relationship between their biological parents. Though societies may initially form as a means of surviving through the strength of the group, and not primarily to facilitate procreation, once formed, no society could survive without male–female relationships. In that sense, such relationships are the fundamentals of any society.

It is highly probable that the prime mover in bringing and keeping the sexes together in a relationship is biological, in the instinctive drive to procreate and then to safeguard offspring till they themselves can reproduce. As a number of Japanese writers (and others) have believed, even the much romanticised thing called love may ultimately prove to be a biological stratagem based on pheromones and hormones, a clinical stratagem intended to help the process of bonding.[114]

Nevertheless, the actual relationship between male and female is more than the product of mere biological determinism. It has a strong cultural element too, as seen in the diversity of patterns in relationships throughout the world and throughout history. Not only the finer points of wooing and courting, but even basic matters such as norms of parenting can vary considerably between cultures. In Japan's case, maternalism is one such basic matter that does not necessarily match the western norm.

In all societies, women are strongly associated with motherhood. This is especially so in cultures such as Japan's where a woman's domestic role is such a major consideration. Nevertheless, 'mothering' may mean something slightly different to Japanese women than to women in the Anglo cultural sphere. Both cultures obviously give priority to mothering offspring. Both cultures also extend mothering to 'pseudo-mothering' of the male partner. However, it is in the matter of degree in these two types of mothering that the norms and expectations differ. In Japan, the distinction between wife and mother becomes relatively blurred, for the wife tends to play mother to her partner far more than in the west. And more so than in the west, Japanese mothers also tend to show favouritism to sons over daughters, obviously not unconnected to the strong male orientation of Japanese society.

The idea of a woman giving support and sympathy to the male has been a key factor in relations between the sexes in Japan. Japanese men, more it would seem than their western counterparts, have traditionally expected women in general and their wives in particular to support them and to be understanding and uncritical of whatever they do. In fact, by western standards their expectations in these regards often seem closer to those that boys place upon their mothers than adult men upon their wives. And for their part, wives have seemed happy to play out this pseudo-maternal role.

The 'son-on-mother' type of male dependence on women in Japan seems in no small part derived from a general form of dependence known as *amae* ('dependence', 'presuming upon'). As described by the psychiatrist Doi Takeo, *amae* is basically a need to be loved and protected and to presume and depend upon others in the way that a young child presumes and depends upon its mother.[115] Contrary to Doi's claims this is not unique to Japan, but it is certainly a common and characteristic feature of Japanese interpersonal relationships. Theoretically *amae* is supposed to apply to Japanese people as a whole—that is, both men and women—but in practice it applies particularly to men.[116]

In effect, Japanese men seem to want to display *amae*—they want to be 'mothered'—far more than western men do. The role of mother, or more exactly pseudo-mother, does not always have to be carried out by a woman. However, it does seem that when a Japanese man has a relationship with a woman, he frequently does want to be mothered by that woman whatever else he expects from the relationship. As one commentator on Japan has observed, perhaps with some exaggeration but with clear conviction, 'It is often hard to avoid feeling that in male-female relations in Japan every woman is a mother and every man a son.'[117]

Naturally, the woman with whom the male is most often in an appropriate situation for mothering is usually his wife (though actually he probably sees more of women at the office). It is therefore the wife who is most expected to play the role of mother. As another seasoned commentator on Japan observes:

> As little boys men were babied and given preferential treatment from their mothers. In private, many husbands look to their wives for the same kind of treatment. After children have been born, the husband's role becomes that of a favorite eldest son.[118]

It is not only the wife, however, who is expected to mother. Mothering can be sought and received from girlfriends, for example. This is clear from the lyrics of one of Japan's biggest-ever modern hit songs, *Lullaby of the Madonnas* by the young female singer Iwasaki Hiromi. Though it does not show in the English translation, the specific word *amae* is even included ('snuggle' in the second stanza).[119]

> Go to sleep now,
> Lay down your tired body.
> Let me close your weary eyelids
> With a gentle kiss.
> Oh, if only I could be born again
> I would be your mother
> And protect you,
> Giving up my very life for you.
>
> This town is a battle-ground
> And the men are all battle-scarred warriors.
> Please
> Soothe the pain in your heart
> By going back to those days when you were a babe,
> Be a baby
> And snuggle against this warm breast of mine.
>
> From that day,
> The day you let me see your tears,
> I decided to live for you.
>
> Romantic love can someday fade,
> But there is a deeper kind of love.
> And even if you should someday reject me,
> I shall always be watching you from afar,
> Your madonna.

Of course, western lyrics also abound with references to one's lover as a 'baby', but the term in English is surely not intended quite so literally. Moreover, in song lyrics it is mostly used by men to women (which perhaps raises an interesting question about paternalism and possibly even frustrated maternalism in western males). In any event, it is unlikely that western women would identify much with a song urging their menfolk to play baby to mummy after a hard day at the office.

Mistresses and even prostitutes can also be expected to play mother.[120] Playing baby to a prostitute occurs around the world, but it is usually considered deviant. This is not necessarily the case in Japan. Nosaka Akiyuki's 1963 work *The Pornographers*, which is treated in literary history as pure literature and not pornography, describes a visit to a massage parlour:

> The woman isn't allowed to feel anything. In short, it's as if you're treated by your own mother.... When you climax, the woman must pretend to be shocked and then wipe you clean. At that moment she really is your mother. You wrap your arms around her. She won't mind what you do, just like a mother and child.[121]

The blurring of sexual partner and mother clearly adds a new dimension to western views based on the Oedipus Complex. In fact, some Japanese psychoanalysts feel that Japanese behaviour is better described by the Ajase Complex.[122] This basically entails the female being all-forgiving towards the male, just as in Nosaka's masseuse who doesn't mind whatever her male clients do, and just as in Iwasaki's all-comforting, all-understanding madonna—the ultimate holy mother.[123]

The overlap between mothering and sex also inevitably raises the question as to whether mothers have incestuous sex with their sons. Logically, one would expect a relatively high rate of occurrence of this in Japan, as an extension of the mother's duty to raise her sons to full adulthood. There is apparently no official published research on incest in Japan, but Iwao is of the view that whereas the typical case of incest in the United States involves a father and daughter, in Japan it is mother and son, with 'mothering instincts spilling over into sexuality'.[124] Japanese literature reveals both types.[125] Incest—at least between siblings—was quite common in early Japan too, and in fact the ancient term *se* could mean either a lover, husband, or brother.[126] In short, the Japanese would seem to have long held relatively liberal views on the matter of incest. They are far from being the only culture to do so.

Obviously, it takes two to play the roles of mother and son. It is self-evident that men could not continue to expect to be mothered beyond childhood if women were not prepared to mother them, and vice-versa. Which came first in Japan, the male desire to be mothered or the female desire to mother, is an interesting question. There is evidence of a certain degree of *amae* right back through Japan's history, but given the traditional male contempt for women, it is likely that women took the lead in promoting a particular male dependence on them. Mothering very probably became especially strong as a result of women being left by Confucianism with no measure of self-fulfilment—and no means of achieving any degree of respect or power—other than in being a good wife and wise mother.

Mothering is undoubtedly a strong female instinct, yet if Japanese women's strong maternalism was a result of instinct alone, then one might expect equal maternalism to be shown towards daughters and even other women. Even in a male-oriented society, it could still be expected to take a more general form, such as a 'mother hen' type of attitude. This does not seem to be the case. The strong male orientation of Japanese maternalism suggests that it is indeed a reflection of the Confucian prioritisation of the male, and the need for a woman to successfully bring up her sons rather than her daughters. It is perhaps a case of socially channelled instinct.

It should not be thought, however, that 'son-on-mother' style dependence on females among adult males is given totally unqualified approval in Japan. Doi himself has remarked that *amae* can produce pathological problems when carried to excess in the case of men simply too dependent on their mothers or surrogate mothers.[127] This syndrome is now widely recognised, and is known as *maza-kon* (from the abbreviated Japanese pronunciation of 'mother complex').[128]

And of course, nor is 'son-on-mother' the only type of relationship between the sexes in Japan. As a sort of opposite, for example, is the 'father and young daughter' type. This usually involves the idealised figures of the 'cute (*kawaii*) virgin' and the worldly-wise, paternalistic older man. Though this may not be so widespread as the 'son-on-mother' type, it is nevertheless very common, perhaps because it acts as a sort of counter-balancing relationship that helps restore male control. In fact, in public, as opposed to in private, it may in some respects—particularly the cuteness of women[129]—be more common than the 'son-on-mother' type, for it helps preserve male 'face'.

It is not just a question of 'face', however. Many Japanese males genuinely seem to delight at the prospect of a very young sexual partner. This is sometimes known as *Rori-kon*, meaning 'Lolita Complex'. The ultimate delight is the incredibly sexy young virgin who, in her innocence and cuteness, doesn't realise just how incredibly sexy she is, and has to be initiated by an older, father-like man.[130] And even if she is aware of her own sexuality, and the male too realises she is aware of it, it still enhances things if she pretends not to be, for role-playing is extremely important in Japanese society.

Like many things Japanese, male sex with young girls plays its part in the economy, for an industry has arisen around it. Child prostitution has a long history in Japan, and has involved children as young as 7. Recently, the nation has been criticised internationally for a lax attitude towards it.[131] This criticism is primarily aimed at the notorious Japanese male sex tours to overseas destinations, where child prostitutes are particularly sought. However, there is also a casual form of child prostitution in Japan itself, known euphemistically as *enjo kōsai* ('financially assisted relationship').[132] This involves schoolgirls—according to one survey, 4 per cent of all senior high-school girls and 3.8 per cent of all junior-high girls[133]—'making friends' with an adult male, who (if he is particularly good at role-playing) professes to take an interest in them and their schoolwork. To help them in their studies he pays them a bit of pocket-money for their time spent talking to him. Sometimes it goes no further than talk, but it is far from unknown for sex to be part of the chat session.

As often as not it is the girls themselves who make the first contact. They do so through word-of-mouth, or through the traditional prostitute's practice of giving certain signals in certain locations, or through special dating clubs that use telephones to put people in touch. The girls are often known by the hybrid term *kogyal* or *kogyaru* (from *ko* [child] plus 'gal', and with obvious sound associations with 'call-girl'). Most of the money they earn through *enjo kōsai* ends up spent on the latest fashion accessory rather than their studies.[134]

These differing male ideals of the female suggest an ambivalent attitude. On the one hand there is a widespread wish to be mothered, even in sexual relations, but at the same time a widespread wish to have sex with young girls and to be fatherly—sort of—towards them. Clearly the age of the female plays a part in the image-making, and obviously a young girl would not realistically be expected to play mother. Yet it seems hard to reconcile Nosaka's mother-figure masseuse, or the mother-figure prostitute, with the innocent young 'virgin' barely in her teens.

There is a common factor in these two ideals, however, and that is the avoidance of female criticism of the male. Neither the mother figure nor the young virgin is likely to reproach the male for inadequacy or some other failure to do the expected thing.[135] The mother figure will not criticise because she understands and forgives everything, while the innocent young virgin will not criticise because she does not understand at all and therefore is not a position to be critical.

Male fear of criticism by the female would seem to be a reflection of the stresses placed upon the male in a society where he is supposed—at least outwardly—to be in control. By western standards Japan may well be a male-chauvinist society, but it may also be that this means there is price for males to pay, in the form of anxiety and frustration.

Anxiety and frustration are closely related. The Japanese male is anxious in case he is exposed as something less than superior. And while Buddhism and Shintō and especially Confucianism tell him he is superior to the female, in practice it is frustratingly hard for him to feel superior to a mother figure. A mother should be understanding and forgiving, but these very qualities also help make her superior in many ways. A mother is psychologically in control of her son, not vice-versa. A boy needs his mother. He depends on her. The problem for the male is that real mothers are female.[136]

It is surprising that, in Japan, dependence on mother-like figures seems to have continued so strongly beyond childhood. One might logically have expected males there to have long since tried to reject dependence on women as soon as they reached adulthood. Yet, whatever face they might put on it outwardly, in practice they do not seem to. Since their dependence on females is so unhelpful to the male cause, this seems one further reason to suppose that it was women who took the lead in encouraging it. This is hardly likely to have been done deliberately, though it might seem poetically nice to think so—the female revenge. Far more likely, as suggested earlier, it is simply an inevitable consequence of women being so constricted into a domestic role of good wife and wise mother. Since it was men who were largely responsible for these roles, it is in a sense a form of poetic justice after all that they themselves should suffer frustration and anxiety as a result.

Yet it is not just the men who suffer. Women do too. Though lingering ideas of contempt no doubt also play their part, it is almost certainly as a result of male frustration and anxiety that there is so much violence and sadism perpetrated by males on women in Japan, both in reality and fantasy. As a source of such trouble to the male, the female becomes once again a potential threat, adding to the deeper spiritual threat she has traditionally posed in her role as the embodiment of the elemental forces of nature. One way to cope with a threat is to avoid it, but clearly, however much *kōha* types may have tried to scorn female company, males cannot avoid entirely the much-needed female. So, to reassure themselves, males have to try to conquer and subdue the female threat. In modern history the doll-like geisha has represented 'tamed womanhood', one form of subdued threat.[137] However, perhaps in particular in postwar history,[138] and perhaps exacerbated by the prospect of a new liberated type of woman, male violence towards women seems to have been another common mechanism of response to threat.

This is especially so in fantasy, but it also happens in reality. Wife-beating, for example, was until very recently publicly admitted and even seen as a macho, *kōha* thing to do. Former Prime Minister Satō Eisaku publicly spoke of having beaten his wife regularly,[139] while the daughter of another former prime minister, Tanaka Kakuei, has publicly stated that her father beat her and that he even urged her husband to do so too 'if it makes you feel more like a man'.[140] Unfortunately, despite the widespread awareness of wife-beating, and despite the fact that unofficial surveys show it still appears to continue on a widespread and frequently horrific scale (requiring hospital treatment for a third of all respondents), no official research has been done on the topic.[141] The law too seems to turn a blind eye to such matters, though it is also true that very few incidents are actually reported.

Male aggressiveness towards women very frequently takes the form of sexual assault in one form or another. Wandering male hands in crowded Japanese trains have now become internationally notorious. Female exchange students from overseas are routinely cautioned by their host Japanese institution to prepare themselves against flashers and gropers. Surveys repeatedly show that as many as 95 per cent of all women travellers on subway trains have been molested at some point, though only a tiny percentage of incidents are reported.[142] Reported rape cases, in population-adjusted terms, are typically no more than a fifth of western figures, but again the extremely low rate of reporting crime in Japan has to be considered. One informed estimate is that the real number of rape cases is twenty times the reported number.[143]

However, it is in the world of fantasy, especially the comics (*manga*), that women receive particularly demeaning treatment from sexually aggressive and sadistic males. Comics are extremely popular in Japan, among adults and children alike. In 1995 some 2.3 billion comics were published there, accounting for 40 per cent of the nation's total of 5.8 billion publications.[144] They are not fringe publications. And yet, as numerous commentators have remarked, comic content that in the west would be considered outright pornography is freely available in Japan.[145] Remarkably, not only do most Japanese women seem to tolerate such material (or at least have done until very recently), some even buy it.[146]

More than 70 per cent of all Japanese children read comics, as opposed to just 20 per cent in the United States.[147] They are exposed to sadistic violence towards women not only in the adult comics they can easily obtain, but even in their own children's comics. As one specialist on comics observed, 'Japanese children are reading stories that make adult visitors from other, more "liberal", cultures blanch.'[148]

The heyday for this was probably the 1980s. Very popular children's comics from that time, such as the ongoing *Koro Koro* series that is read by some 2 million children each month, contain, amidst themes such as sport and science-fiction and school life, sexual and violent material that would be unthinkable in children's reading matter in most countries.[149] There are innumerable depictions of clothes being ripped off busty young women. There are scenes of girls having their bikini-bottoms torn off in the swimming pool by their school principal, in front of the class, and of robot monsters literally drooling at the prospect of pulling the knickers off a captive woman. In one story a male student has wings, which he uses to buzz around the female teacher, licking her.

In another of the stories a glimmer of gallantry threatens to intrude into the relentlessly demeaning treatment of women when a (primary) schoolgirl, who is being sexually abused by her male school principal and his robot assistant, is rescued by a group of classmates who belong to the Kin-Poko ('Balls and Dicks') Club.[150] However, no sooner is the girl partially untied than she is pounced upon by one of her rescuers, who thrusts his head under her blouse with the comment 'Wow! Great tits!', reappearing briefly with a look of bliss before disappearing head-first into her knickers.

Interestingly, there is also at least one girl member of the Kin-Poko Club. The inclusion of females is unlikely to be for reasons of political correctness, for this has never carried any importance in Japan (other than as lip-service to the west). It may be intended as a device to increase readership by making the comic more appealing to girl readers, perhaps the idea being that the presence of a girl will send out signals to girl readers that the KP Club is not *really* hostile to them. Most likely, however, it simply reflects the idea of women doing things on men's terms—in this case, literally under the banner of male genitalia. In the scene described above where one of the rescuers disappears into the victim's underwear, the girl member makes a token but unsuccessful attempt to stop him, as though girls are best advised to let boys be boys, for that is how they can best support them.

Basically, the male members of the Kin-Poko Club reflect in themselves male ambivalence. They appreciate that the principal's tormenting of the girl is wrong, but proceed to do the same themselves, driven on by what seems to be pure male lust at the sight of a helpless female. No doubt she will not be too critical of them whatever they do, for she is a female. Depending on her level of maturity ether she will understand and forgive, or not understand but accept uncritically the ways of the male.

It is indeed hard to keep remembering that many of the bustier and more nubile female victims are supposed to be *primary* school students. (The Kin-Poko Club members too are primary school students.) One wonders if that is simply because *Koro Koro* comics are aimed largely at a primary school readership. Or is it also a case of what could be less threatening to a male than a primary school girl? Is the comic writer, an adult male, writing such material genuinely for the intended benefit of his readers, or is he working out his own fears and fantasies, or doing both at the same time?

On one occasion the Kin-Poko Club decide to punish the principal. The form of their vigilante justice is intriguing. They push his genitals back up into his body to make him into a 'woman', illustrated in close-up step-by-step instructional frames. Again one is led to wonder. Is this intended symbolically to be a form of castration, which many people around the world might consider suitable treatment for sex offenders? Is it just a pubescent exploration of the potential of genitalia? Or is it a distinctively Japanese case of rendering the object of their sadism into more acceptable 'female' form?

Of course, the great majority of comic stories, in the *Koro Koro* collections and others, do not contain sex and violence. This is especially so in very recent years when they have been toned down as a result of western criticism. However, even if there were no sex and violence at all in the 1990s, it is still important to appreciate that the young readers of the 1980s are the young adults of the 1990s. They are the decision-makers of the next millennium. Their attitudes formed during childhood still have a very great bearing on life in Japan in the present, and will continue to do so for at least the next fifty years.

As it happens, despite the recent toning down there are still, in the comics of the late 1990s, elements reminiscent of the 1980s. In the June 1997 issue of *Koro Koro*, for example, in the very popular story "*Gakkyō Yamazaki*" (Class-King Yamazaki), a female teacher is bowled over on the way to school by tough guy Yamazaki, knickers showing as she tumbles. She is too injured to take the class, so Yamazaki takes it for her, impersonating her. Somehow he acquires an enormous pair of breasts to help him in his female impersonation, and when he enters the classroom he greets the class by ripping open his blouse to reveal the literally overwhelming breasts, which almost physically displace the front row of students. As he does so he makes a 'Freudian' slip by saying *'Oppai yo'* (Look! Tits!) instead of *'Ohayō'* (Good morning).

On the matter of Freud, another element which is still present in comics of the late 1990s, and which seems to have been less toned down than the sex and violence, is the fascination with toilet functions.[151] Observers have long remarked on this fascination among the Japanese.[152] Clearly, the common factor is genitalia. The western reader of both adult and children's comics very much forms the impression of entering a world of adolescence, or more exactly pubescence, where genitalia and their functions are being explored. This pubescence is something else long remarked on by numerous western observers.[153] A similar obsession is seen in the west in certain comedians known for their vulgar humour, but in the matter of frequency and degree Japan stands out a long way.

Japan, as again many have observed, is a nation brimming with sexuality. It is a land of so-called 'love-hotels', signalled by mauve neon lighting and Disneyland architecture, where rooms are booked by the half-hour by astonishing numbers of enthusiastic couples.[154] It is a land where—so some surveys suggest— a majority of husbands have had adulterous sex in the previous year.[155] It is a land that gave the world the 'bottomless café', where 'bottomless' does not refer to free refills of the cups.[156] It is a land where schoolgirls' soiled knickers can be purchased from vending machines.[157] It is a land where those who criticise pornography and pubescent sexual mores are—ironically—the ones likely to be labelled immature.[158] It is not a land for prudes.

It would be misleading to study relations between the sexes in any country by dwelling on sex-crimes or pornography or the red-light districts. It is also misleading—though less so—to dwell too much on similar aspects of Japan. However, neither can these aspects be glossed over. Though in the modern world relations between the sexes take a wide range of forms in a wide range of contexts, the most fundamental type of relationship is based on sex. Related basic attitudes colour many other forms of relationship between the sexes, including in the home and often in the workplace and even the public sphere.

In Japan's case, relations between the sexes have been complicated by Confucianism in particular. Male anxieties found throughout the world have become exaggerated in Japan by paradoxes in gender roles, often with unfortunate results. The picture is a confused one, but it is a picture that westerners need to consider in some detail if they want to really understand Japanese society.

1.5   THE BLURRINGS OF GENDER: HOMOSEXUALITY, BISEXUALITY, AND ANDROGYNY

In recent years in the west there has been a greater understanding of the fact that gender is not a simple matter of two clear-cut categories of male and female, but rather one of relativities. There is in addition increased recognition of the fact that gender—at least in a societal context—is not solely biological, but is also a reflection of socio-economic and other influences on the roles ascribed to each gender. In other words, it is now appreciated that gender definitions can to some extent be changed and varied depending on time and place and circumstance. 'Gender blurring' has become more openly recognised.

In Japan, there has long been recognition and acceptance of gender blurring.[159] This may at first seem surprising, in view of the *kōha* samurai male and his hard-line attitude towards women, from whom he was very keen to distance himself. But we have seen how this very contempt for women led the typical *kōha* to extol homosexuality, and in practice to be bisexual. By western standards, homosexuality and bisexuality might widely be seen as tending to undermine the very masculinity a hard school male strives to embody. However, Japanese attitudes to sexual preferences and behaviour have long been tolerant and by western standards—especially Christian ones— quite amoral.

Interestingly, some of the fiercest and seemingly most masculine males in Japan's history were homosexual/bisexual.[160] These include warlords such as Minamoto no Yoritomo of the twelfth century, approximately half of all subsequent shōguns, and the three 'national unifiers' of the sixteenth century, Oda Nobunaga, Toyotomi Hideyoshi, and Tokugawa Ieyasu.

Male homosexuality has continued to be widely accepted in Japan through to the present, even at points in modern history when elsewhere in the world it was frowned upon or worse. One (American) commentator has termed it a 'haven for foreign homosexuals'.[161] The psychiatrist Takeo Doi also comments:

> The attraction that homosexuals from the West are said to feel for Japanese society is probably due partly to the absence from the outset in Japanese society of any restraints on homosexuality, and partly to its extreme tolerance of expressions of homosexual feelings.[162]

Doi feels that the prevalence of *amae*/dependence makes it easier for people in Japan than in the west to form relationships with members of the same sex, particularly of an emotional rather than merely physical nature.[163]

He cites, as a perfect example of this type of homosexuality, the (male) homosexuality portrayed by the writer Natsume Sōseki in his 1914 work *Kokoro* (The Heart/Feelings), one of Japan's most famous novels. The basically homosexual protagonist, having allowed himself to enter a relationship with a woman, becomes confused, and proceeds to immerse himself in a homosexual relationship in order to 'restore the spiritual stability that had been upset by his relations with the other sex'.[164] Though Doi does not specifically take up the point, this is a clear illustration of the *kōha* view of women as impure and corrupting, and a preference for a 'purer' love with a fellow male. Another major point not pursued by Doi is that the principal homosexual relationship in *Kokoro* is clearly hierarchical, a young man falling in love with a *sensei* (teacher or mentor). This is very much in line with the Confucian overtones of homosexual relationships from the seventeenth century.

Longstanding recognition of 'gender blurring' in Japan is less surprising still when one considers the role of aesthetics. These vary between cultures much more than biological elements do. In Japan's case, aesthetics—especially the aesthetic appeal of elusive and transient purity—helped shape the traditional higher male ideal of the young and flower-like *bidanshi* or *bishōnen*, who by western standards was extremely effeminate. In fact, while representing a male ideal, by western standards the *bishōnen* really came close to a form of androgyny, in the sense of mixed or indeterminate gender.

Another key aesthetic underlying gender conceptualisation in Japan is a respect for the artificial and unnatural. This stems from the widespread Japanese ambivalence towards 'raw' nature, which in turn appears to reflect the ever-present threat of natural disaster.[165]

Unlike westerners, the Japanese rarely extol unspoiled nature as an ideal, but feel happier with a nature that is tamed by human hand—even if it is then given back a 'natural' look (as in Japanese gardens).[166] Raw nature symbolises threat and primitiveness, while artificiality symbolises reassurance of the ability of humanity to keep natural forces in check (at least to a point). It can be argued, for example, that the 'earthy' type of natural woman is associated with the primal forces of nature, and in contrast to the 'tamed' geisha of recent centuries is a particularly threatening type to the Japanese male.[167]

The aesthetic ideal of the artificial is seen in the fact that some of the most widely acknowledged portrayals of the *bishōnen* male ideal are achieved by women impersonators, particularly in the famed performances by the Takarazuka female theatre troupe.[168] This mirrors the well-known and highly acclaimed embodiments of femininity by male kabuki actors known as *onnagata* ('female form').

Kabuki itself has a relatively short history. Moreover, male actors only took on female roles in kabuki after women were banned from the stage in the mid-seventeenth century on the grounds that they incited sexual frenzy among the audience and often acted as unlicensed prostitutes. Nevertheless, the idea of 'cross-dressing' and 'blurring genders' clearly struck a chord with the tradition of the *bishōnen*. A rationalisation of androgyny was soon articulated. It was to the effect that the essence of a gender can only be truly objectivised and understood by someone not belonging to that gender, for those who are born into it are guided by instinct and unable to understand how or why they behave as they do.

This is made clear in the comments of the Tokugawa period kabuki actor Yoshizawa Ayame:

> If an actress were to appear on stage she could not express ideal feminine beauty, for she could only rely on the exploitation of her physical characteristics, and therefore not express the synthetic ideal. *The ideal woman can only be expressed by a male actor.*[169]

In a similar but more practical vein one present-day *onnagata*, Bandō Tamasaburō, has remarked:

> We personify women in an age of elegance. Many of the manners and movements we have perfected are lost in today's society. Actually, many women come to Kabuki to study us so they can understand how they should act.[170]

In the reference to 'how they should act' we see too a clear illustration of the importance of behavioural form in the construction of gender.

This sort of gender blurring in kabuki was generally opposed by Confucian scholars and government officials in the Tokugawa period, who felt it produced too much of a state of flux and thereby threatened order and stability.[171] Moreover, attractive male actors caused just as much unruliness among the largely bisexual kabuki audience as the female actresses had, possibly even more so.[172] However, though the authorities issued warnings that male actors should restrain the sexual overtones of their performances, and dress more modestly, and though they also banned child actors (who were popular as prostitutes), they did little in practice to stop the development of the *onnagata*. This perhaps testifies to the strength of the androgynous ideal.

The ideal of androgyny—sexual ambivalence—continues strongly today. In clothing, for example, top Japanese fashion designers such as Yōji Yamamoto and Rei Kawakubo have spoken specifically of a 'blurring of gender categories, freeing the wearer from familiar gender conventions'.[173] And probably even more so than elsewhere in the modern world, Japan has many androgynous popstars, predating western figures such as Boy George and David Bowie and Michael Jackson. The best-known is perhaps Sawada Kenji, an idol of the 1970s and 1980s in particular but still popular in the 1990s even though he is losing the youthfulness of the ideal *bishōnen*. His appeal has always been to a broad cross-section of society, not just the young.

A key factor in Sawada's appeal to women seems to be his very difference from the *kōha* type, for by no means all women in Japan or elsewhere prefer a rugged macho man. A poll conducted in Japan in the early 1980s (probably the peak of Sawada's popularity) showed that the two males considered the 'sexiest' were Sawada Kenji and the *onnagata* actor Tamasaburō.[174] *Bishōnen* also feature prominently in young women's comics.[175] This all suggests that the androgynous male is a type women find attractive as a genuine ideal, though awareness of reality might lead them to choose the older, steadier type of male partner featured in the Harlequin survey (Table 1.1).

Female androgyny and female homosexuality are obviously also to be found in Japan. It is very clear that in the Tokugawa period there were considerable numbers of women, especially prostitutes, cross-dressing as males (though this may often have been to increase their appeal to male clients). Lesbian sex was frequently depicted in prints of the period. Female prostitutes catering to female clients were not uncommon, and literary works such as those by Ihara Saikaku contain open reference to lesbian relationships. In modern times the female version of the *bishōnen*, though not as common as the male *bishōnen*, can be observed at the theatre in Takarazuka. It can also be seen in young women's comics, as can instances of lesbianism. However, young women's comics have focused primarily on male homosexuality and male androgyny and not female.

As this suggests, female homosexuality has not always been as open as male. While it appears to have been accepted in the Tokugawa period, it is clear that in more modern times—at least until very recently—it has not been accepted as much as male homosexuality. This may well be due to criticism from the west when Japan reopened its doors to the world at the end of the Tokugawa period in the mid-nineteenth century. At the time Japan was desperately keen to modernise and be taken seriously by the western powers. It usually followed western advice, even if it was not to its liking. The same western criticism that led to a reduction in overt male homosexual behaviour in Japan from that point on was almost certainly even more strongly directed against female homosexuality.

In any event, female homosexuality has been far slower than male homosexuality to re-emerge in modern times. Japan's first lesbian magazine, *Phryné* (named after an ancient Greek courtesan), was not launched till May 1995. The first declaration of lesbianism in the mass media was not until 1992, by the activist Hiroko Kakefuda. Kakefuda was also instrumental in the first open declaration of homosexuality (in modern times) by a high-profile female star in the entertainment industry, the singer Michiru Sasano. Sasano's autobiography—entitled *Coming Out* and actually largely written by Kakefuda—appeared in August 1995, just three months after the appearance of *Phryné*. Sasano followed her autobiography with a song entitled *Girl Meets Girl*, and a whole album of songs on a lesbian theme. Following these developments, female homosexuality will no doubt become more publicly acknowledged. However, it would seem there is not exactly a rush for homosexual women to 'come out'.

As is so often the situation in Japan, it is a case of males first.

Part Two

On the Fringes of Society: Minorities and Other Marginals

2.1 IMPURE OUTCASTS: THE *BURAKUMIN*

Living in a particular country does not necessarily mean being accepted into its society. This is not just true of foreign residents or recent immigrants. It can also apply to those whose roots in their nation go back countless generations. The reasons why such people are never fully accepted by their native society, but are marginalised on its fringes, reveal much about the values of that society.

In some regards Japan is not exceptional in its marginalising. Like many societies, it does not exactly embrace those who do not contribute to its prosperity and need to be supported, such as the severely handicapped and chronically unemployed. And again like many societies, neither does it welcome those who for one reason or another do not readily fit in, such as ethnic minorities with different cultural backgrounds and values. But Japan is relatively unusual in its automatic marginalisation from birth of certain full-blooded ethnic Japanese, a group who are in effect ritual outcasts, social scapegoats symbolic of impurity.

That group is the *burakumin*. The word literally means 'hamlet people', referring to the fact that they traditionally dwelled in hamlets on the edge of towns rather than in the towns themselves—classic marginalisation in the physical as well as social sense. There are many other terms for them, ranging from the insulting to the euphemistic, but few if any terms appear in the typical dictionary. Japanese prefer foreigners to know as little as possible of their existence, and even amongst themselves will often not actually speak of them but will just hold down four fingers, indicating four-legged animals.

However, most foreigners nowadays who have spent time in Japan do know at least that *burakumin* exist. There are some 2 million outcasts in around 5,000 settlements, which is a scale simply too large to be concealed.[1] Moreover in recent years the *burakumin* themselves have also been deliberately adopting a higher profile. Discussion of the 'integration problem' (*dōwa mondai*) has even started to feature in the curriculum of some schools, especially in areas such as those around the Inland Sea where three-quarters of all *burakumin* reside.[2]

They are an unusual minority group in that they are not ethnically different from mainstream Japanese, despite widespread beliefs—or more exactly claimed beliefs—among the latter that they are.[3] Nor are they different in their basic culture, though segregation from the mainstream has inevitably led to certain different patterns of thought and behaviour, such as with regard to self-image, expectations, ideals, and social mobility. And neither do they hold abnormal religious views.

However, it is very probably religion that has been the main agent in their marginalisation. Shintō considers work with the dead or with some forms of physical dirt to be impure (*kegare*). Buddhism similarly considers work associated with killing animals to be unclean. Thus, from the establishment of these religions around 1,500 years ago, jobs such as grave-digging, execution, butchery, tanning, and leatherwork were considered impure. Moreover, this impurity was felt to be a contaminant to others, and hence threatening, leading to the physical and social shunning of people engaged in such activities.[4] Worst of all, this 'infectious impurity' was seen as hereditary. Once born into this particular outcast class, there was no legitimate escape.

There was also, in ancient times, another outcast class known as *hinin* ('non-person'). Unlike the *burakumin*, or *eta* ('great filth') as they were then known, the *hinin* could sometimes be redeemed from their outcast status. The origins of this class are rather obscure. They may even have initially played a ritual role as purifiers of *kegare*, later coming to be considered contaminated by it through association.[5] Early *hinin* also included certain types of miscreants dismissed by their masters (like the banished knight of medieval Europe), and with time came to include other deemed misfits and socially undesirable types such as beggars, vagrants, pedlars, prison guards, fugitives, and itinerant actors.

During the Tokugawa period the *eta* and *hinin* were theoretically separate classes in the social hierarchy, with the *hinin* taking precedence, but in practice the two ended up merged as *senmin* ('base people').[6] It may be that the outcasts performed the important role of underclass for a class-conscious society, allowing the merchants—who in theory were at the bottom of 'accepted' social classes—to feel that they were not actually the bottom of the heap.[7]

The Tokugawa period also saw the formalisation of discrimination against them. Their settlements were omitted from maps. They had to wear certain types of clothing and display identification marks. Marriage with 'ordinary people' was prohibited. They were also banned from using the same shrines or temples as ordinary people and had to have their own. Their worth relative to ordinary people was even quantified. In 1859 an *eta* was beaten to death while trying to enter a 'normal' Shintō shrine, and in the court hearing that followed it was ruled that the life of an *eta* was worth only one-seventh of that of an ordinary person.[8]

In the Meiji period, discrimination against the outcasts was theoretically banned by the Emancipation Edict of 1871. However, the edict was not enforced in practice. The merging of *hinin* and *eta* became formal, both now being redesignated *shinheimin* ('new commoners'), though the term *burakumin* has prevailed and seems to be preferred by the outcasts themselves. In effect, the once-redeemable *hinin* have now become absorbed into the *burakumin* and share the same hereditary, irredeemable attribute.

Discrimination still continues against *burakumin*. Many companies purchase 'black lists' to check that prospective employees are not *burakumin*. Private detectives are hired by some families to check the background of the intended bride or groom.[9] Despite legal restrictions on their access since 1976, in practice checks still rely heavily but not exclusively on *koseki*, or household registers, which can indicate the likelihood of a *burakumin* background by their mere location. Though increasingly rare in recent years, tragedies of traditional double-suicide still occasionally occur when lovers are denied parental approval for marriage due to the discovery of *burakumin* origins. In economic terms, discrimination against *burakumin* in employment, in combination with relatively low levels of educational achievement, has meant that they have a high unemployment rate. Those who do work are for the most part confined to their traditional jobs in butchery and leatherwork, or casual labour on construction sites or in factories.

Response to discrimination has been varied. Some have accepted their lot in life, and with a negative self-image have shunned relations with general society.[10] Others have tried to 'pass' (*tōru*) into general society by concealing their origins. This can, however, earn the disrespect of fellow *burakumin*. Recently 'passing' has been criticised by

Murakoshi Sueo, Director of the Buraku Liberation Research Institute, as very unhelpful to the *burakumin* cause:

> The brightest people leave the community, depriving the [liberation] movement of young leaders. By 'passing' they not only give in to discrimination but tacitly condone it. It's a defeat for all of us.[11]

One of the best-known and earliest depictions of passing is found in the 1906 novel *Hakai* (The Broken Commandment), by Shimazaki Tōson. Epoch-making by the standards of the day, the work was partly inspired by European novels that addressed social problems, and partly based on actual observations. It featured a *burakumin,* Segawa Ushimatsu (*ushi* means cow), who had successfully concealed his origins and won respect as a schoolteacher. He then witnesses discrimination against another *burakumin* and feels moved by guilt and other pressures to 'come out' in front of his class. In so doing he breaks an oath to his dying father not to reveal his *burakumin* origins. Despite pleas from his students, Segawa ends up leaving his job and indeed leaving Japan. Symbolically but melodramatically, he goes to Texas to become a cattle-rancher.

The work was artistically poor, but it received high praise from the critics for its courage and sold well for its controversial theme. However, though good sales were predictable, no publisher had dared to take up the manuscript, and Tōson had ended up having to publish it privately. Though there were a few follow-up works by other authors, similarly dealing with society's undesirables of one sort or another, such works never became a major genre or movement. Japanese society has basically preferred not to focus on such elements.

In more recent times *burakumin* themselves have written novels. The best-known *burakumin* writer is the Akutagawa Prize-winner Nakagami Kenji. His works vividly and powerfully describe what it means to be a *burakumin,* and at the same time provide commentary on mainstream society and its sometimes shaky and hypocritical values. Unfortunately his works are only recently starting to be translated into English, and even more unfortunately, Nakagami died in 1992 at the early age of 46.[12]

Another response to discrimination, more in line with Segawa's eventual affirmation of his origins than with his father's wish to deny them, has been the forming of various *burakumin* associations that have assertively fought for *burakumin* rights. The first significant association was the *Suiheisha* (Levellers' Association) of 1922, which was effectively re-formed in 1955 as the *Buraku Kaihō Dōmei* (Buraku[min] Liberation League).

One of the BLL's favoured methods is 'thorough denunciation' (*tetteiteki kyūdan*), which entails forceful extraction of an apology from those who have been seen as guilty of discrimination.[13] The method has been widely criticised in recent times for its excesses, which sometimes stray into physical or other forms of intimidation of key figures such as politicians, writers, and publishers. Karel van Wolferen, whose 1989 work *The Enigma of Japanese Power* displeased the BLL by his discussion of this very point, is one whose experiences in this regard are quite well-known, with the BLL attempting—unsuccessfully—to stop the Japanese translation of his work.[14] Unfortunately for the *burakumin* themselves, the violence sometimes involved in 'thorough denunciation' tends to fuel deeply ingrained fears among the general public about a *burakumin* propensity for violence, thereby further entrenching stereotypes.[15]

The recent reinforcement of stereotypes by 'thorough denunciation' bears some similarity to the situation in 1947–8. In the elections held under the Occupation a leading *burakumin*, Matsumoto Jiichirō, succeeded in being elected to parliament (as a socialist). He even became vice-president of the Upper House. As such, he became the first *burakumin* to have an audience with the emperor. However, on this historic occasion, he pointedly refused to bow, causing public outrage and again reinforcing stereotypes about *burakumin* unruliness and vulgarity.[16] He soon lost office.

The government has made various attempts to address the problem of discrimination against *burakumin*. From the mid-1960s, largely under BLL pressure, a number of laws have been passed and funds set aside to promote integration and reduce the number of *burakumin* communities. However, despite material improvements such as the quality of *buraku* housing, and despite displays of ostensible (and sometimes unhelpful) deference to *burakumin*,[17] to a large extent the problem of discrimination and prejudice still remains.

It is often argued by mainstream Japanese that ongoing discrimination is in no small part the fault of the *burakumin* themselves, who prevent their own integration by maintaining a distance from society, as well as alienating sympathisers by their violence.[18] However, it is likely that the roots of the problem lie much deeper. It would seem that the *burakumin*, along with a number of other marginals, continue to play for many people in Japanese society an important role of symbolic scapegoats, despised, feared, and shunned, yet needed.

This is not just in the sense of being needed to form the bottom of society's pecking order. At a deeper socio-spiritual level, *burakumin* have been given a sort of licence to enter a taboo world, to do 'dirty work' associated with ritual impurity. It is no longer the work itself which is any real problem (for this can easily be done by foreign workers), it is the abstracted association with impurity. The *burakumin* have always been associated with trouble. They deal with dark and threatening forces, and thus in one sense represent those forces. And so, if things go wrong, they are somehow held to blame. They are the convenient embodiment of the undesirable, the threatening, the impure. They are in a way like the Devil is to Christianity, except that they represent impurity rather than evil (which is a much weaker concept in Japan than in the west). All societies have their scapegoats, but Japan's deep-rooted fear of impurity may mean that the existence of *burakumin* has become a particularly entrenched part of its society—but at a safe distance from the centre.

Attitudes towards *burakumin* represent a deeply ingrained socio-spiritual mindset. This is not something that can be easily changed by mere legislation or the injection of funds. Nor will western sermonising have any great effect. One looks rather to the continuation of *dōwa kyōiku* (education about the 'integration problem'), in a contemporary context of slowly increasing acceptance and tolerance, as the most realistic path to a solution. This will, however, take time.

2.2 PRIMITIVES: THE *AINU*

The indigenous Ainu of Japan's far north represent a different type of undesirability from the ritually impure *burakumin*. This does not mean they have no associations with impurity, but it is a special form of racial impurity they represent, not ritual. As a distinct minority group, ethnically, physically, and culturally different from the Japanese norm, they form a contradiction—an obstacle—to Japan's claim to be racially homogeneous. Yet they cannot be dismissed as foreigners. Far from it, as the native inhabitants of Japan, they threaten the right of the vast majority of Japan's population—known in this context as Yamato Japanese[19]—to call themselves 'Japanese'. The Yamato Japanese response in modern times has been basically to accept them as Japanese, but as a primitive version of Japanese. That is, unlike most other marginals, the Ainu are marginalised not only by typical factors such as cultural or geographical separation from the mainstream, but also by a time factor.[20]

The Ainu became a great source of interest to western observers after Japan's reopening in the mid-nineteenth century.[21] Many saw them as some sort of ancient lost tribe of Caucasians in a Mongoloid nation, a mysterious vanishing people pushed back into the northern extremes of the country by the majority Yamato Japanese and drawing ever closer to extinction.

It is almost certainly true that Ainu were once widespread throughout much of the country, at least as far south as central Honshū.[22] From around the seventh century—probably along with other indigenous groups of the day[23]—they were gradually pushed back ever further north by an expanding Yamato state, finally being contained almost exclusively in Hokkaidō. It is also true that they have come very close to extinction. Though people of Ainu descent are enjoying something of a renaissance in recent years along with many indigenous peoples around the world, there are still only around 25,000 persons who identify themselves as Ainu. Extremely few of these are pure-blooded.[24]

What is not true is that they are a European-style Caucasian people. This once-popular belief was based superficially on their physical appearance, in particular their relative abundance of facial and bodily hair, and a generally more 'European' facial structure than most Japanese. This assumption has now been shown to be insupportable, particularly as a result of the work of physical anthropologists.[25] The Ainu are descended from the Jōmon people, who were the predominant inhabitants of Japan prior to the arrival of Yayoi immigrants—forerunners of the Yamato Japanese—from the Asian continent around 300 BC.[26] Genetically they appear to be a mixture of ancient stock from southeast Asia and various Siberian and northeast Asian peoples.[27]

Culturally, their traditional links are primarily with peoples of northeast Asia, as seen for example in their shamanism. Ainu shamans were almost always women, yet paradoxically, women were not allowed to actually pray to the gods, for this was a male-only affair.[28] The spirits of animals too are believed to be able to carry messages to and from the gods. The main Ainu festival, in which a bear is sacrificed, is for this purpose. Specifically, the sacrificed bear carries a message from the local community to the spirits of their ancestors. Specially shaved sticks (*inau*) are also a means of communicating with the gods, and thus have a supernatural power themselves.

Ainu gods, known as *kamui*, include a vast range of objects from natural forces to spirits (including of ancestors), to plants to animals to beings human-like in appearance and with human foibles. They can exist either in the actual human world or in their own parallel world, which is also very much like the human world. Typically, a god or spirit is humanoid in its own world, which is invisible to humans, but can manifest itself in the human world in a variety of forms. The bear, for example, exists in its own world in human form and lives in a house similar to that of the Ainu. To the Ainu of the human world, however, the bear's house appears as a den.[29]

Kamui pervade all areas of Ainu life, and are associated with each and every natural feature. They are one of two principal orders of being in the Ainu view of the universe: the other order is that of humans. The word for 'human' is one and the same as *Ainu*. *Ainu* and *kamui* form dual elements of a harmonious universe, for they are interdependent. In effect, it is a world-view based on balance and harmony between humans and nature, between the visible and invisible, the known and unknown.[30]

There are a number of similarities between Ainu gods and Yamato Japanese gods, such as basic anthropomorphism, ancestor worship, and a variety of particularised objects possessing godhood. In fact, the Ainu term *kamui* is widely assumed to be a borrowing of the Japanese term for gods, *kami*. This is a surprising and questionable assumption. Given the relative antiquities of the Ainu and Yamato Japanese, and the fundamental importance of *kamui* to the Ainu dual world-view and indeed their whole way of life, it seems far more likely to be a case of the Japanese term being borrowed from the Ainu.[31]

The term *ainu* can also mean 'male' as well as 'human'. This, and the fact that women were traditionally not allowed to pray directly to the gods, may suggest a strongly male-dominated society. Yet this is not necessarily the case. In some regards males and females seem to have had almost separate cultures, enjoying mutual respect. Ancestry, for example, is traced back through the male line for males and the female line for females, though it is true that male lineage takes precedence in determining leaders. Women traditionally kept their ancestry secret from men.[32] However, the feature perhaps most associated with an Ainu woman's appearance, a tattoo around the mouth, was one that was certainly not kept secret from men, for it announced her readiness for marriage.

Activities were divided on a gender basis among the Ainu of old.[33] Men engaged in fishing and hunting (mostly deer and bear), and fighting when the need arose. Women gathered edible flora, reared children, and engaged in domestic tasks such as sewing, though they also sometimes fished like the males, and when the occasion demanded fought alongside them. The main hunting and warfare weapon was the bow and arrow, the latter sometimes tipped with poison. However, it was taboo for a woman to use a bow and arrow.

Though mostly hunters and gatherers the traditional Ainu were not nomadic, and had permanent settlements (*kotan*), with hunting-huts being used as temporary bases at strategic distant points. There was some farming of millet and vegetables, and also farming of dogs, which were used not only for food and fur but also as hunting and draught animals.[34] Settlements were generally small, comprising around ten households, and were basically self-sufficient. They were mostly isolated in separate river valleys, on riverbanks and/or in a strategic position for hunting game. Contact between settlements, other than in times of war or similar crisis, was relatively rare, the main exception being the annual bear-sacrifice ceremony. Dwellings were simple, with pole frames, thatched walls and roof, and an earthen floor. They had an open fire in the centre of the single room, and a wooden raised area for sleeping. The nuclear family was the norm, and typically, upon marriage a son would build his own house near that of his parents. That is, the marriage system was patrilocal, with a wife moving to her husband's place of residence.

Clothing usually consisted of a coat-like garment, calf-length for men and ankle-length for women. It was made of woven bark-fibre, hide, or fur, and in later days sometimes of cotton. Garments were often decorated with a distinctive wavy pattern. Footwear was mostly moccasin-style and often made of fish skin, and snow shoes were used in winter.

These elements of traditional culture are now almost entirely confined to museums.

Though it is known that the Ainu are closely linked to the early Jōmon people of Japan, it is not known when exactly they arrived in the country, or what route they took. Their forebears may have entered Japan at least 15,000 years ago, before sea-levels rose and submerged land-bridges with the continent. Though at one time probably widespread, from an early stage they established themselves particularly in the northern part of the land—especially Hokkaidō, which the Ainu themselves have traditionally seen as their homeland.[35] In these northern climes, for a thousand years or so after the founding of the Yamato state they were of relatively little concern to the Japanese further south, other than as barbarians to be kept as far away as possible or as occasional trading partners. (The Ainu sought Japanese lacquerware and metal goods while the Japanese sought Ainu bear-furs and dried fish.)

However, from around the fifteenth century, when Japanese traders started to make deeper and more frequent inroads into Hokkaidō, friction mounted. Trade continued with increased caution on the part of the Ainu,[36] but was interspersed with literally dozens of wars against the Japanese. Matters came to a head with a major war in 1668–72. Led by Samkusaynu (Shakushain), the Ainu revolted against the forced imposition of unequal trade agreements. They were decisively defeated. The whole of Hokkaidō (then known as Ezo) came under the control of the Matsumae clan, who had formerly had a precarious foothold in the southwesternmost tip of the island. The process of attempted Ainu assimilation then began. From the outset this was, however, only a limited form of assimilation, for the Ainu were not seen as proper human beings, and were assimilated only in an underclass or slave capacity.[37] Moreover, the nation 'Japan' still essentially saw the Ainu and their land as 'foreign'.[38]

Central government interest in Hokkaidō increased during the latter stages of the Tokugawa period, when Russian vessels started to pose a threat that led the government to strengthen its control over this new territory. In 1789 the Ainu rose up again against the Japanese, in the Kunashir-Menash Revolt, but were easily suppressed.[39] It was their last uprising.

At the start of the Meiji period the Ainu were, like the *burakumin*, theoretically given equal legal status with other Japanese. This was in line with a broader government policy to develop Hokkaidō as a *bona fide* part of Japan. This policy also included the encouragement of settlement by Japanese farmers and entrepreneurs. The Ainu were unable to continue their traditional main pursuits of hunting and gathering, but on the other hand found it difficult to make a sudden switch to farming. Many could not compete with the settler-farmers from the south and ended up renting out then selling their land to these settlers, often becoming labourers on land they had once owned.

The Former Aborigines Protection Act (*Hokkaidō Kyūdojin Hogo Hō*) of 1899 guaranteed each Ainu farming family a 5 hectare parcel of land, but also made this land subject to confiscation if not developed within fifteen years. (About a quarter of all such granted land was eventually confiscated.) In an attempt to stop them losing their land to settlers, it also forbade Ainu from selling land without the permission of the island's governor. Though the Act was theoretically intended to help the Ainu, in practice it can also be said to have disadvantaged them. First of all it dismissed the consideration that all the land in Hokkaidō might be theirs to start with. Then in the second place it denied them proper control over the small amount of land that was guaranteed them. In broader terms, it also denied them dignity. Despite numerous protests, the Act was not to be repealed till 1997.

Though the Ainu were treated nominally as Japanese from early Meiji on, they were in practice treated differently from mainstream Yamato Japanese. Discrimination soon came to be justified not on the grounds that the Ainu were alien barbarians but on the grounds that they were primitives.[40] The concept of 'primitive' was applied in a pejorative sense to separate them from the more technologically advanced and therefore superior Yamato Japanese. This line of thought was to continue in essence among many people into the present day. Indeed, ironically it was reinforced in people's minds by recent archaeological confirmation of the ancient existence of the Ainu, leading them to be treated as 'fossilised remnants of the Japanese past'.[41]

Like many indigenous peoples overwhelmed by powerful later arrivals, the Ainu of the late nineteenth century came to feel demoralised, demeaned, and culturally deracinated by their 'assimilation'. Among other things the policy of assimilation made no provision for the maintenance of their language. And while on the one hand it claimed to treat them as equal and fully integrated Japanese citizens, on the other hand it segregated them by, for example, enforcing separate public education for them (education aimed, moreover, at vocational rather than intellectual development).[42] Ainu self-esteem was further weakened by the obvious contempt with they were viewed not only by Japanese but also by westerners.[43] Their situation was still further aggravated by alcohol and disease. They became, in the words of one modern scholar, 'a pitiful, doomed people living in the most abject conditions of poverty, disease, and degradation'.[44]

However, though their situation did continue to deteriorate through much of the twentieth century and they did come close to doom, they were not to prove completely doomed. In particular, over the last decade or so the Ainu have participated in the world-wide revival of indigenous peoples, and their present mood is one of self-assertion rather than the prewar submission to assimilation. Since the

1980s the *Hokkaidō Utari Kyōkai* (also known as the Ainu Association of Hokkaidō), with some 16,000 members, has represented Ainu concerns, among other things lobbying for the repeal of the 1899 Former Aborigines Protection Act. The Association also took a high profile in protesting against a public statement in 1986 by then Prime Minister Nakasone Yasuhiro that Japan was comprised of a single ethnic group. One result was that the minister of justice eventually admitted that discrimination continued against the Ainu,[45] though the government as a whole was less prepared to admit this officially.[46]

August 1994 saw a major achievement for Ainu when Kayano Shigeru, a noted Ainu writer and founder of an Ainu museum, took up an Upper House seat as a member of the Social Democratic Party of Japan. (He had in fact come second in the July election, but gained the seat after the sudden death of the winner.) Although the Upper House has less political clout than the Lower, nevertheless Kayano's success has greatly strengthened Ainu lobbying power.

In the same year of 1994 Kayano's work *Our Land Was a Forest: an Ainu Memoir* (Japanese original 1980) appeared in English translation, thereby heightening international awareness of the Ainu situation. Though the work is not particularly polemical it does comprise a poignant statement of the Ainu cause. It reveals how Kayano himself had in his youth been virtually resigned to abandoning his Ainu heritage, and how he hated the indignity of 'being on show' for tourists and scholars. It also describes how his father, an alcoholic, was shamed by being jailed for 'poaching' salmon, and how his grandfather, as a small boy of 11 in 1858, was taken away by Japanese samurai for slave labour. Desperately unhappy, his grandfather cut off his own finger in the belief he would be considered unfit for work and be sent home, but his disability was ignored by the Japanese as trivial. He finally did manage to get sent home, however, after rubbing himself with the bile of a poisonous blowfish (*fugu*). This made his skin turn grayish yellow, convincing his Japanese taskmaster that he had contracted some terrible disease.[47]

The book also reveals Kayano's view of the Former Aborigines Protection Act, encapsulating the substance of Ainu grievance:

We are no 'former aborigines'. We were a nation who lived in Hokkaidō, on the national land called Ainu Mosir, which means 'a peaceful land for humans'. The 'Japanese people' who belonged to the 'nation of Japan' invaded our national land. Ainu Mosir beyond doubt was a territory indigenous to the Ainu people. Not only are the high mountains and big rivers graced with Ainu names, but so, too, is every creek and marsh, no matter how small.

Mainland Japanese crossed the strait to our national land hundreds of years earlier, but it was in the Meiji era that they began a concerted, all-out invasion. Laws like the Former Hokkaidō Aborigine Protection Act restricted our freedom first by ignoring our basic rights, as a hunting people, to hunt bear and deer or catch salmon and trout freely, anywhere and at any time, and then by compelling us to farm on the inferior land the Japanese 'provided'. In 'providing' land, the Japanese also legitimated their plunder of the region. The mountains around Nibutani, among others, became the Japanese nation's 'national forests' before we realized it and later were sold off to a big financial combine.

This makes for an unqualified invasion…. There is no denying that the people belonging to the 'Japanese nation' ignored the rights of the Ainu, the prior inhabitants….[48]

No doubt partly as a result of Kayano's activities and high profile, since the mid-1990s there have been major gains by the Ainu. Shortly after he joined the Diet a government advisory panel was formed to consider the situation of the Ainu. The panel presented its report to the cabinet in 1996. It acknowledged invasion of Ainu land and discrimination against Ainu, and recommended the enactment of a new law safeguarding Ainu rights.

In the 1995 *White Paper on the Environment,* the Ainu were cited as a model for preserving natural ecology—a reference described by one veteran observer of Japan as an 'unprecedented paean of praise for Ainu ecological wisdom by the Japanese government'.[49] In March 1997 a recent seizure of Ainu land was deemed illegal, in a ruling that constituted the first legal recognition of the Ainu as an indigenous minority.[50] The following month saw approval, in line with the recommendations of the advisory panel, of a new law aimed at preserving Ainu culture and recognising Ainu rights. The law itself does not specifically acknowledge Ainu as an *indigenous* minority, but a resolution accompanying it does. Moreover, at around the same time, Prime Minister Ryūtarō Hashimoto, in a very different statement from that of his predecessor Nakasone a decade or so earlier, also publicly acknowledged the Ainu as an indigenous Japanese minority. Finally, in May 1997, the Former Aborigines Protection Act was repealed, to be replaced by the new law, formally known as the Law to Promote Ainu Culture and Disseminate Knowledge of Ainu Traditions.

Thus the Ainu are now in a promising situation with regard to formal recognition. But their battle is not over. As has been the case with women's rights, the challenge now is to bring change to public attitudes.

2.3   NOT QUITE US: KOREANS IN JAPAN

Historically and culturally Japan is much indebted to Korea. Though their exact origins are unclear, the ancestors of the present majority of the Japanese people, the Yayoi people, appear to have entered Japan some 2,000 years ago mainly through the Korean Peninsula. Some 500 years later, it was similarly via Korea that writing and Buddhism were introduced. Many of Japan's early artisans and administrators were Korean, and many noble Japanese families had a Korean lineage. In a genealogical register compiled in Japan in 815 more than a third of the 1,182 aristocratic families claimed descent from Korean families, or from Chinese families resident in Chinese colonies in Korea.[51]

And yet, despite this one-time Japanese pride in a link with Korea and obvious respect for Koreans, in modern Japan Koreans have generally been treated with contempt and seriously discriminated against. The precise causes are hard to pin down, but among other things Koreans suffer from the fact that they look Japanese, but are not Japanese, and are in that sense a threat to the purity and uniqueness of the Japanese identity.[52] Unlike other foreigners, their foreignness is not immediately obvious, and this makes them all the more threatening. In some regards, as a look-alike 'Other', they are treated like *burakumin*, and tend to be seen as embodying that which the Japanese find undesirable. They are seen as a 'beggarly, inferior people' who are 'lazy' and 'generally unruly'.[53] In the lawless aftermath of the Great Tōkyō Earthquake of 1923, by which stage Japan had annexed Korea and Japanese attitudes towards Koreans were particularly hostile and contemptuous, thousands were even slaughtered simply for being Korean.[54]

Some of this attitudinal change may possibly be traced back to a deterioration in the relationship between Japan and Korea from around the thirteenth century, over the actions of Japanese pirates in Korean territory. However, this was largely a cause for negative Korean feelings towards Japan, not vice-versa. The same is true of warlord Toyotomi Hideyoshi's failed attempts in the late sixteenth century to invade Korea as part of his pan-Asia campaign.[55] It seems rather to be a case of Japan gradually developing over time an attitude of superiority towards Korea. This became particularly clear in the Meiji period, when Japan saw Korea as fair game in its plans for colonial expansion.[56] Japan's interference in Korea's political affairs grew steadily throughout the period. It culminated in the annexation of 1910, which was to last till 1945. From the Japanese perspective, Japan's dramatic modernisation made a stark contrast with what was seen as Korean backwardness and stagnation, leading to the strengthening of negative stereotypes.[57]

From the Korean perspective, Japanese brutality and arrogance during this period of annexation created an enduring legacy of bitterness towards Japan—a bitterness still revealed in surveys today.[58] As one Korean describes the situation, 'Koreans abhor things symbolic of Japan, such as the Japanese flag, kimono, and *geta* footwear. They refuse to adopt words of Japanese origin into their language.'[59] Japanese music and films are officially banned, though in practice they do enjoy considerable popularity, especially among the young.

After the annexation some Koreans did move voluntarily to Japan to seek greater prosperity, but many, especially as the war grew closer, were sent to Japan as forced labourers. When the war started, many were compulsorily drafted into the Japanese forces. Before 1910 there had been fewer than 1,000 Koreans in Japan, most of them students. By 1923 there were over 100,000, by 1940 over 1 million, and by the end of the war more than 2 million.[60] Probably as many again were part of the Japanese war effort overseas, including many Korean women forced into sexual service for Japanese troops—the so-called 'comfort women' whose grievances have still not been fully resolved.[61] At the end of the war about two-thirds of all Koreans in Japan returned to Korea, leaving around 650,000 who preferred not to return to their war-torn homeland. This is very close to the number of Koreans officially resident in Japan today, around 680,000. According to unofficial estimates in 1992 given by the Korean community in Japan, there are in addition as many as 300,000 illegal Korean residents, many of whom have taken advantage of Korea's removal in 1990 of restrictions on overseas travel for its nationals.[62]

With the annexation of 1910 Koreans became Japanese nationals, which guaranteed them certain legal rights though it did not prevent social discrimination. However, this nationality was lost shortly after the war as a result of deliberate government policy. After a period of rather vague status under the Occupation, from its end in 1952 Koreans in Japan found themselves formally categorised as foreigners.

The original draft of the Constitution, drawn up in 1946 by American Occupation officials, had made specific provision for the prevention of discrimination on the basis of nationality. However, in one of the few significant changes able to be made to the draft by the Japanese themselves, this was removed from the final document.[63] Moreover, birth in Japan was no longer a factor in determining Japanese citizenship. Since then Koreans, along with other foreigners, have theoretically been able to apply for naturalisation, but the strict rules for eligibility are such that relatively few Koreans qualify.[64] Despite these difficulties, in very recent years numbers obtaining naturalisation have increased, and in 1995 alone more than 10,000 Koreans became naturalised Japanese.[65]

Nevertheless, most Koreans in Japan today are permanent residents, not citizens, even though they may be third or even fourth generation born in Japan, and have Japanese as a mother tongue. Around 600,000 of the 680,000 or so Koreans officially in Japan—that is, about 90 per cent—fall into this category, and they also account for a similar percentage of all foreign permanent residents in Japan.[66]

The situation of Koreans in Japan has been further complicated by the postwar political situation in Korea. Following the splitting of the country in 1948, Koreans in Japan of North and South affiliation have each claimed to represent the Korean community. The rivalry between these two groups has not necessarily been helpful to the cause of Koreans as a whole in Japan.[67]

As permanent residents rather than citizens, Koreans have been denied Japanese government support in such form as social welfare and pension programmes. This includes those who fought for Japan in the war. Till recently they were also required, along with other foreign permanent residents, to have their fingerprints recorded. Following protests, especially criticism from overseas, these fingerprinting requirements were abolished in 1993 for all permanent residents (of any nationality). Social welfare restrictions have also been eased, though not entirely removed, in recent years. One celebrated milestone was the case of Kim Hyonjo. Kim was refused a pension in 1975 despite having paid premiums for many years. After a protracted legal battle, in 1983 he finally won the right to receive his pension—a right then extended to a number of others in a similar situation.[68] Japan's ratification of various international treaties, such as the International Agreement on Human Rights in 1979 and the

International Treaty on Refugees in 1982, also drew attention to discriminatory policies that were subsequently amended.

Although legal discrimination against Koreans in Japan has been reduced, actual discrimination still continues in many areas of life, not unlike the case with the *burakumin*. In employment, for example, not only are job opportunities for Korean (and other non-Japanese) residents limited anyway because many government jobs are open only to Japanese nationals, in addition there is significant informal discrimination. This is despite a number of successful landmark legal cases, such as that of Pak (Park) Chonsok against Hitachi. Pak, using a Japanese alias like many of his fellow Koreans, was offered a position by this major company in 1970 but, when it found out shortly afterwards that the would-be recruit was Korean, Hitachi withdrew the offer. Pak sued and eventually won the case, received compensation and had his offer of employment confirmed, and as of 1995 was still working for the company.[69]

The typical form of employment for Koreans legally in Japan is in the entertainment or service industries, or small-scale manufacturing. For illegal residents, it is casual labouring. Some have become involved in organised crime, rather ironically in view of the strong nationalism often associated with these criminal organisations. As with *burakumin*, many Korean applicants for white-collar jobs are unsuccessful as a result of careful screening of personal background by major companies—a screening that is also adopted for some prospective marriage partners.

It is true that there are a number of highly successful Koreans in business in Japan, especially in recent years, but they are generally self-made successes. Perhaps the best-known example is Masayoshi Son, president and chief executive officer of Softbank Corporation—a man described in 1996 by one well-known journal as 'Japan's star entrepreneur'.[70]

In recent years younger Japan-born Koreans have become more positive about their Korean origins. Not content to hide their background and pretend to be Japanese, as so many of their elders have done, they are proudly displaying their own ethnicity, yet without asserting it aggressively. At the same time, they are not necessarily keen to be thought of simply as Korean either, and in many cases wish to be identified as 'Koreans living in Japan'.[71] They prefer an 'integrative identity', one that is 'not locked into any sort of rigid patterns of denial or aggressive assertion of their Koreanness'.[72]

The younger generation of Japan-born Koreans do not always

enjoy the most harmonious of relationships with the older Korean generations, or with newcomers from Korea. Nevertheless, along with individual successes such as Masayoshi Son, they are slowly helping to bring about a change in the profile of Koreans in Japan, and increased positive recognition by Japanese people. This includes recognition of discrimination against Koreans, recognition seen for example by the formation in 1988, by *Japanese* lawyers, of the Association for Human Rights of Koreans in Japan. This association continues to meet regularly to draw attention to cases of discrimination.

The growing strength and world profile of the (South) Korean economy during the early 1990s, especially set against Japan's own economic difficulties, has also helped bring about a general increase in Japanese respect for Koreans. For all their negative feelings towards Japan many Koreans have acknowledged Japan's leadership in matters economic. This has risked a Japanese reaction of superiority, but in most cases the Japanese have responded positively and gratefully towards the acknowledgement. Similarly, the Japanese have not sought to capitalise on Korea's economic difficulties in the late 1990s (though it could be argued they are in no position to do so, with enough economic problems of their own).

Unfortunately, at the same time, Korea–Japan relations in recent years have not been helped—certainly in terms of Korean attitudes towards Japan—by the resurfacing of the unresolved issue of the wartime 'comfort women'. And some Japanese are still far from accepting of Koreans in their midst. Extreme anti-Korean feeling was seen, for example, early in 1997 when a planned book-signing by Japanese-born Korean writer Yu Miri, who had just won the prestigious Akutagawa Prize for literature, had to be cancelled after a bomb threat by a nationalist who claimed Yu was insulting Japanese.[73]

There are encouraging signs that life for ethnic Koreans in Japan is improving, but the picture is not yet a really happy one. They are still not really accepted as a proper and legitimate part of Japanese society.

2.4 HEROIC VILLAINS: THE *YAKUZA*

The *yakuza*, synonymous with organised crime in Japan, represent an unusual and paradoxical type of marginal group. While shunned by the vast majority of society, they often have strong links with society's elite. Moreover, in some respects they embody some of Japan's most traditional ideals. They are in that sense both heroes and villains, though it is the villainous side that prevails in their image, especially in recent years.

According to National Police Agency figures for 1996 there are some 80,000 *yakuza* in Japan.[74] This is a decrease of more than 10 per cent relative to the 90,000 in 1990,[75] partly reflecting reaction to a recent toughening of the law and hardening of attitudes towards them. Some have left the ranks of the *yakuza*, while others have gone 'invisible' behind a legitimate front. Technically the number comprises literally thousands of different gangs (*bōryokudan,* or *kumi* or *kai*), but in practice most small gangs are affiliated to larger ones. There are three main groups, accounting for more than half of all *yakuza*: the Kōbe-based Yamaguchi-gumi, and the Tōkyō-based Inagawa-kai and Sumiyoshi-kai. The largest is the Yamaguchi-gumi, with some 20,000 direct members and another 15,000 affiliates.

The origins of the *yakuza* go back at least to the early days of the Tokugawa period, to confrontations between gangs of displaced samurai known as *hatamoto-yakko* ('servants of the shōgun'), who terrorised towns and villages, and gangs of villagers and townspeople (*machi-yakko*, 'servants of the town'), who resisted them.[76] Interestingly, though they often claim to espouse samurai values, the *yakuza* themselves claim descent from the latter. These *machi-yakko* were predecessors of the eighteenth-century *tekiya* or *yashi*, who 'looked after' stalls at temple festivals, and the *bakuto*, who were involved in gambling. The terms *tekiya* and *bakuto* are still sometimes used today to describe specialist *yakuza*. The term *yakuza* itself derives from the three numbers *ya-ku-za*, or 8-9-3, which traditionally formed a useless combination in gambling. The name can therefore be interpreted as 'the useless ones' or 'the good-for-nothings', a depreciatory self-designation which appears to have been deliberately—even defiantly—adopted to show deviation from society's norms.[77]

And yet, despite this label of self-proclaimed social rebelliousness the *yakuza* have often been seen, by themselves as well as others, as embodying some of society's ideals. They have also long been accepted in certain contexts, and have even been readily employed by those in authority for certain types of 'work'.

Their embodiment of some of Japanese society's ideals is a reflection of their claimed *machi-yakko* origins. Despite their commoner status the *machi-yakko* tried to act according to the samurai code and had an image of 'chivalrous commoners'.[78] The *yakuza* as a whole have, at least until recent times, made very public the importance they place on supposed traditional samurai values such as loyalty, chivalry, courage, selflessness, and determination. The well-known practice of cutting off part of a finger, as a symbol of atonement to one's boss or of commitment to an agreement, is seen as the epitome of these values. Structurally, too, their gangs have represented traditional values such as hierarchy, respect for seniority, group identification, and person-alised family-like relationships, with vertical relationships within a gang expressed in familial terms such as *oya* (parent) and *ko* (child).

In short, they have represented many traditional ideals. As a result, despite the undoubted fear they arouse when members of the public actually encounter them, they have also had a certain positive, glamorised image of sorts. This is seen, for example, in the popularity of *yakuza* films in which they are portrayed as chivalrous outlaws in similar fashion to England's Robin Hood.[79] They have typically enjoyed—and indeed perpetuated—an ambivalent image, being seen as 'blood-thirsty gangsters' yet also as 'knights of old',[80] set apart from mainstream society, even defying it, yet also belonging to it and helping it maintain its values. Jacob Raz, who spent a year living with *yakuza* in the mid-1980s, comments:

> *Yakuza* declare themselves Japanese, very Japanese, while at the same time being both excluded from Japanese society, and exclud-ing that society.[81]

Their image is further ambivalent in that, while they represent some of society's most cherished ideals, their actual position on the fringes of society makes them escapist heroes of a sort.[82] Many Japanese would similarly like to flee from the constraints of mainstream society—or at least think they would like to flee—but lack the courage to do so. They can identify vicariously with the *yakuza*, and derive a certain thrill in doing so, but in the end they are also reas-sured that the *yakuza* suffer marginalisation for their defiance.

Yakuza have always asserted their conservative and nationalistic sentiments. In this they have had a particular bond of empathy with the similar-minded captains of Japan's government and industry. Many of these have not hesitated to make blatant use of *yakuza* in the claimed interests of the nation and/or their company. For example, *yakuza* have openly been used as strike-breakers, particularly in the early postwar period. Their use by a government-management alliance in the large-scale miners' strike at Miike in 1960, which led to a striker being fatally stabbed, is particularly notorious.[83]

A proliferation of scandals in the 1990s involving company pay-offs to *yakuza* has made the link between big business and the underworld common knowledge. In many cases the companies have had little option but to pay up or face trouble. In the case of larger companies 'trouble' often takes the form of awkward and disruptive questions being asked at Annual General Meetings by specialist *yakuza*— known as *sōkaiya* ('general meeting specialists')—who acquire shares and can legitimately attend such meetings. However, *yakuza* intimidation can also be a weapon for the companies to use. For years, many if not most major companies have paid *sōkaiya* to ensure that not only do the *sōkaiya* themselves not ask troublesome questions at AGMs, but that neither do other shareholders, with the result that the typical meeting lasts less than half an hour.[84]

In politics *yakuza* are often used as fund-raisers, bodyguards, and campaign workers.[85] But their influence goes much further. Through specialist powerful 'fixers' (*kuromaku*) they have been involved one way or another in the rise and fall of ministers, including even prime ministers.[86] Again, recent major scandals, such as the Sagawa Kyūbin Scandal of 1992,[87] have brought to international public scrutiny the massive extent of the interconnections between the underworld, the business world, and the political world—and for that matter also the bureaucratic world, which was once thought to be on a higher plane than the political world in terms of integrity.

Another reason why *yakuza* have been tolerated by the government is that they are seen as a means of safeguarding Japan against foreign crime organisations.[88] Though this may appear a slightly facetious case of nationalism being carried even into the extremes of the underworld, it also indicates a pragmatic realisation by the authorities that crime is always going to be present in society in one form or another, and that 'better the devil you know'. Logically, it does make sense to have one's criminal element operating according to known values, especially in a society that places great importance on the normal and predictable. *Yakuza* themselves have made this very point.

They have also claimed that they further serve society by acting as a surrogate family for society's unfortunates, keeping in check potentially disruptive and delinquent individuals.[89] These include members of less organised and more anti-social gangs, such as the *bōsōzoku* (bikie gangs). Again, this claim should be taken seriously, for it has proven over the years to be true. They have indeed taken into their fold a large number of former *bōsōzoku* members. As many as one third of all *yakuza* members are in this category. And the authorities' tolerance of organised crime by *yakuza* has indeed made for a more orderly life and society than would be the case with unorganised crime.

This is evidenced by Japan's internationally admired low rate of crimes perpetrated on random victims, such as mugging or opportunistic theft. Though increasing of late, this is still typically a fifth or less of the rate in most western countries. One factor in this is undoubtedly that *yakuza* keep their territories clean—partly because they prefer it that way, and partly to keep the police happy in line with a sort of unwritten deal. Kaplan and Dubro, in their special study of *yakuza*, write that 'Perhaps the most remarkable aspect of police-gangster relations is the *yakuza*'s function as a kind of alternative police force.'[90] Another specialist, a criminologist and long-time resident in Japan, has observed that *yakuza* do play an important part in controlling street crime, and that 'Japanese police prefer the existence of organised crime to its [organised crime's] absence.'[91]

Such use of well-organised and major gangs by the authorities to control lesser and more potentially unruly gangs and other hoodlums is no modern phenomenon. It can be traced back at least to the Tokugawa period, when the shōgunal government used *tekiya* and *bakuto* to keep order in the underworld.[92] Remarkably, in an example of deviation from the supposedly rigid class-based distinctions of that period, some gang bosses were even granted the samurai privilege of wearing two swords and using a surname.[93] Thus, co-operation between the authorities and the *yakuza*, and tolerance of and indeed positive recognition of the *yakuza*'s role in society, is something of a Japanese tradition.

The relatively low social disruptiveness of organised crime is, of course, only true when the criminal organisation operates according to established values, and keeps within informally agreed operational parameters. In Japan's case these parameters have entailed the *yakuza* basically confining their activities to so-called 'victimless' crimes—gambling, prostitution, 'brokering' deals between companies for a fixed 'commission', and so forth—and not hurting innocent members of the public. When these parameters are exceeded, then organised criminal behaviour can obviously be a more serious threat to social order than can unorganised crime, and the authorities cannot simply turn a blind eye. This change has started to happen in recent years in Japan.

In the past, provided they did not actually fall victim themselves to an organised and 'socially orderly' *yakuza* operation, members of the public, rather like the police, showed considerable tolerance towards the *yakuza*. Such operations might include property-owners being harassed into selling their property at a give-away price to developers, who employed as their 'agents' specialist *yakuza* known as *jiageya* ('land-hike specialists'). Victims of these and similar operations were considered by the public at large to be luckless individuals who somehow got in the way of big business or government interests. There was still a widely held feeling of security that *yakuza* did not pick on 'random' or 'innocent' victims. Far from it, they were seen as protecting the public from opportunistic criminals who did. In that sense, in combination with their representation of traditional values, they were viewed quite positively, even romanticised.

However, from around the late 1970s a gradual but unmistakable hardening started to occur in *yakuza* attitudes and activities. The reasons for this are not clear (or have not been made clear), and may include inter-gang conflicts, changes in leadership, or simply the influence of pressure from foreign crime syndicates. Westerners in Japan were among the first to notice this trend, for whereas in the past *yakuza* had usually put on their best behaviour in any contact with them, this could no longer be assumed. Among other things, cases started to be reported of young western women being forced into prostitution by *yakuza* gangs. *Yakuza* activities expanded into new crime areas such as hard drugs. They expanded geographically too in the form of a greatly increased presence overseas in places such as Hawaii and Asia. Firearms were used ever more frequently, and less care was taken to avoid hurting innocent members of the public.

The public became alarmed at this trend, and so did the authorities. Between 1980 and 1992, public complaints regarding gangs increased ten-fold, to approximately 20,000 per year.[94] As it became clear that this change in *yakuza* activities was no mere passing trend, and as *yakuza* involvement in various high profile 'money and mob' political scandals in the late 1980s and early 1990s became especially blatant, the authorities had to intervene. The relatively peaceful coexistence between police and gangster of days gone by was to suffer a rude jolt.

One major step taken was the Anti-Gang Law of March 1992. For the first time this enabled police actually to designate as criminal any organisation of which more than a certain number of its members had criminal records. In addition, the Law enabled police to clamp down on previously 'grey' activities such as loan-sharking, protection, coercion, and intervention in civil disputes, and allowed for tougher action in matters such as gambling and blackmail.

Ten *yakuza* organisations, including the three largest and covering about three-quarters of all *yakuza* members, were presently designated criminal. Some responded—perhaps ironically—by challenging the legality of such designation through the law-courts, in drawn-out litigation. Whatever the legal niceties, life generally became tougher for the *yakuza*. As a result, some *yakuza* members have left the gangs, taking advantage of special official programmes to assist their (re-)integration into mainstream society.[95] There have been quite a few cases of tattoos being removed, and toes being amputated surgically to replace missing little fingers.[96] Others appear to have moved their activities offshore.[97]

However, many *yakuza* activities have simply become less visible, with legally clean managers being appointed to front *yakuza*-run companies. This process has been helped by the enormous profits made by *yakuza* organisations during the economic bubble years of the late 1980s, when the price of land, which was used as collateral for easily available low-interest loans, rose enormously and the country was awash with money. This wealth, even before the Law was enacted, enabled them to invest heavily in legitimate businesses, leading to the coining of a new term *keizai yakuza*, or 'economic gangsters'.[98] Some *yakuza* themselves are also undergoing gang-run training courses on how to act like normal 'salarymen', adding to the invisibility of *yakuza* activities.[99]

The reality is that, despite the enactment of the Anti-Gang Law, despite life being made tougher for *yakuza*, and despite an overall decline in *yakuza* numbers in recent years, *yakuza* activities are continuing at home and abroad. Gangsters continue to take their percentage from construction projects. Many illegal immigrants are brought into the country through *yakuza* schemes, such as those involving bogus language schools. Scandals continue to erupt revealing ties between gangsters and officials, especially in areas such as finance and construction. The *sōkaiya* continue to be a problem. In 1997, in what has become the conventional attempt to thwart *sōkaiya* involvement, 2,355 out of 2,608 major companies with AGMs scheduled for June held those meetings on the same day (27 June).[100] Some 2,100 of them also requested a police presence at the meeting, with the result that as many as 10,000 police were assigned to these duties (ironically providing increased opportunity for crime elsewhere).

More poignantly, violence against members of the public continues to be a worrying trend. Just a month after the Law went into effect, in April 1992, film-maker Itami Jūzō was knifed for his anti-*yakuza* stance in his film *Minbō no Onna* (Woman against the Mob), which featured a woman lawyer opposed to the *yakuza*. In March 1994 a senior executive at Fuji Film, Suzuki Juntarō, was murdered by a sword-wielding *sōkaiya* for refusing to enter into a deal. Similar incidents continue to occur into the late 1990s, including the killing of mere bystanders. In August 1997, for example, a bystander was killed when a gang boss was gunned down by rival gangsters in a Kōbe hotel coffee-shop.

As the *yakuza* have changed, expanding their traditional activities and moving away somewhat from traditional values, police and public attitudes towards them have also changed. In proportion to this shift, there has been a change in the *yakuza*'s unusual social position of being accepted in part yet marginalised in part. They are still used by society's elite, but the relationship has soured. Among the general public they are now less accepted. Thus the balance between acceptance and marginalisation has more clearly inclined towards the margins. In that sense they are now moving towards a position similar to that occupied by members of criminal organisations in most other countries.

2.5   OFF-CENTRE: OKINAWANS AND OTHER OUTER REGIONAL GROUPS

Those who live in the geographical outer regions of a nation often risk being pushed to the outer regions of its society as well, and being treated as marginals of sorts. It is frequently the case that those who live in or near the capital or other major metropolitan centres associate themselves with being at the centre of things. They automatically treat their 'country folk', especially from remote regions, as somehow inferior, often questioning their sophistication and intellect or ridiculing a local accent or custom. Not unlike the case of the Ainu, though usually to a much lesser degree, outer regionals are sometimes marginalised by a time factor, being felt to be behind the times and therefore backward. The recent spread of communication technology has weakened this view, but it is still not extinguished.

In Japan, the *inakamono* (country bumpkin) has long featured as a source of tragi-comedy in literature. Novels of the dynamic Meiji period in particular reveal how young people luckless enough to have been born in the provinces spent much of their youth in a state of neurosis, 'yearning for the capital' (*miyako e no akogare*) and suffering an inferiority complex.[101] The cities promised not only cultural sophistication and excitement, they generally provided better wages and better material standards. This all led to the phenomenon of *dekasegi* ('leaving home to work'), which saw periodic influxes of country people into urban areas and further contributed to the stigma of being a country person. The same basic phenomenon and underlying attitudes are still noticeable today, despite both governmental and public recognition of the problems of excessive urbanisation.

Regions with a generally negative image in Japan include southern Kyūshū, Shikoku, Hokkaidō, northern Honshū, and Ura Nihon (the 'Back of Japan', on the Japan Sea coast of Honshū)). Ura Nihon did improve its image and affluence considerably in the 1960s and 1970s, however, as a result of the power and material benevolence of its most famous son, 'kingmaker' and former prime minister Tanaka Kakuei.

Centre–periphery discrimination can occur even if those on the edge are ethnically and culturally identical to those at the centre. It becomes worse if there are identifiable differences. This can happen when national boundaries have been geographically expanded at some point in history to incorporate—usually by subjugation—ethnically distinct or otherwise different groups. This was a factor in the case of the Ainu, and it can also be seen in the case of a distinct people at the other geographical extreme of the country, the Ryūkyūans or Okinawans.

The Ryūkyūs are a chain of some seventy islands running southwest from Kyūshū almost to Taiwan. The population is in excess of 1 million. The main island, occupying more than half of all the land area, is the centrally located Okinawa, whose name is often used to refer to the islands as a whole. It is only in recent centuries that the islands have been considered a part of Japan.

Genetically, the Ryūkyūans have much in common with the Ainu, though they are a separate people. They too have close links to the Jōmon inhabitants of Japan and have had limited input from the later Yayoi arrivals of around 2,000 years ago (though more than the Ainu have).[102] They are an ancient people, with a history of at least 30,000 years.

Their ancient lifestyle continued till relatively recently, by the standards of history. Despite some contact with mainland Japan during the Yayoi period around 2,000 years ago, rice and iron were not introduced till much later, around the eighth century. A neolithic existence of primitive agriculture using stone tools, combined with fishing, continued to be widespread until around the eleventh century (or later in some parts).[103] The process of nation-forming in the Ryūkyūs started from about the twelfth century, when several rival would-be ruling lines scattered throughout the chain starting vying for supremacy. The line from Okinawa eventually prevailed and its head became king. Though the new nation was not well endowed with natural resources, from about the fourteenth century it developed as a fairly strong entrepôt trading base, for the exchange of southeast Asian products such as sappanwood and spices with Chinese silks and ceramics and Japanese copper and swords. At this stage, the island nation paid tribute to China, recognising the Ming emperor as suzerain in the late fourteenth century. In practice, however, it remained largely autonomous.

Early in the seventeenth century the Shimazu Clan from the Satsuma domain in southern Kyūshū invaded the islands and established hegemony, though they did not entirely remove Chinese influence. For a while the nation paid tribute to both Japan and China at the same time. It was an unusual situation, with for example the succession of a new ruler requiring Satsuma's approval but with Chinese officials actually carrying out the investiture.[104] Then, with the need to strengthen the geo-political identity of the Japanese nation at the beginning of the Meiji period, the islands were deemed to be part of Japan by the new central government in Tōkyō. Japan's claim was asserted over that of China by a punitive expedition to Taiwan in 1874, which punished the Taiwanese for the murder of some Ryūkyūans—now treated politically as 'Japanese'.[105] Presently, in 1879, the islands became a formal prefecture, Okinawa prefecture.

However, the Ryūkyūans/Okinawans have never been particularly happy as part of Japan—or Yamato, as they still often refer to the mainland. From the outset of their incorporation into the prefectural system they felt aggrieved that they had lost local political autonomy without any real compensating economic benefits.[106] They still feel the same today, pointing to facts such as that industrial development lags behind the mainland, and that the average wage is only around three-quarters of that on the mainland. A considerable part of this income is derived from business associated with American military bases, whose very presence—imposed by central government policy— is seen as a symbol of the lack of local political autonomy.

World War Two saw a marked intensification of negative feeling towards Japan. Okinawans suffered very heavy casualties during the Allied assault in April–June 1945—in the order of 150,000 civilians— and were particularly upset by their treatment at the hands of the

Japanese, who did not hesitate to sacrifice them when the situation so demanded.[107] Furthermore, after the surrender Okinawans suffered the indignity of being separated from their new 'mother nation' Japan, remaining under foreign (American) control till their formal return to Japan in 1972. Even after this formal return, Okinawa continued afterwards to be the major site of American military bases in Japan, with three-quarters of all American military personnel in Japan being stationed there. The Okinawans felt betrayed and mistreated by the Japanese, feeling they had been sacrificed once again. Many were openly hostile towards Japan, among other things staging periodic protests, snubbing the imperial family, and on at least one well-publicised occasion burning the Japanese flag.[108]

Tensions with both America and Japan never really subsided. They came to a head in 1995 with the rape of a schoolgirl by three American servicemen. This was the cue for a massive movement to remove American bases, and by extension to reassert the principle of Okinawan control of Okinawa. A legal standoff followed between the governor, Ota Masahide (who refused to renew leases), and the prime minister (first Murayama, then his successor Hashimoto). After a year or so the central government eventually prevailed, but the situation continues to be tense. Feelings are still high, and relations strained.

On the positive side, in recent years there has been a revival of Okinawan identity awareness, similar to that of the Ainu but with a distinct 'Pacific island' element. There has been a renewed pride in being Okinawan, even leading to calls for a separate form of government.[109] This promotion of Okinawa is not confined to the Okinawan people themselves, either. In fact, there has recently been something of an 'Okinawa boom' throughout Japan. As one prominent example, Okinawan music currently enjoys considerable popularity nationwide, and the Okinawan singer Amuro Namie is arguably Japan's 'hottest popstar' of the 1990s.

There are several other groups of outlying islands and regions whose relationship with the mainland is worthy of note. One of the most interesting of these is the Ogasawara Islands.[110] Also known as the Bonin Islands (from a corruption of *bunin* meaning 'uninhabited'), they lie near the Tropic of Cancer some 1,000 km south from Tōkyō. Despite this distance, administratively they are actually part of Tōkyō—perhaps the world's most extreme 'outer suburb'. They were first charted by a Spanish explorer in 1543, who does not appear to have actually landed there. The first recorded landing and exploration was fifty years later, in 1593, by Ogasawara Sadayori, a member of the Ogasawara *daimyō* family. The islands were officially surveyed by the Tokugawa shōgunate in 1675, and included in a map of *Dai Nippon* (Greater Japan) in 1785.[111] They were uninhabited when discovered, though subsequent archaeological excavations have revealed that at one stage they were temporarily inhabited by a neolithic people.

Despite being explored and claimed by the Japanese they remained uninhabited till rediscovered in the early nineteenth century by American and British seamen, some of whom settled there. The first to really set down roots in the islands was the sailor Nathaniel Savory. Looking for a remote place to establish a pioneer settlement, Savory arrived from Hawaii in 1830 together with a handful of Americans and some twenty-five native Hawaiians, who provided most of the female contingent. Over the coming years they were to survive attacks by pirates and drunken whalers in a classic swashbuckling life as adventurers on a remote tropical island.

On his historic voyage in 1853 to reopen Japan, US Commodore Matthew Perry called in on the islands and hoisted the American flag.[112] However, in 1862 the shōgunate reasserted its claim. Savory, who was the chief representative of the island community, was obliged to reassure the shōgunate that they were not an American colony and to sign an agreement recognising Japanese sovereignty. In 1876 the Meiji government formally annexed the islands. All inhabitants, including Savory's family and other westerners (he himself had died in 1874), became Japanese citizens. Presently, as settlers arrived from Japan (with encouragement from the government), the language of the islands became Japanese. In some cases this led to the unusual situation of Caucasians speaking Japanese effectively as a mother tongue.

The islands' economic value prior to World War Two was under-recognised, for they were actually a useful whaling base and were rich in marine and tropical products, and very comfortably self-sufficient. However, what was recognised was their considerable strategic value militarily. The well-known battle in March 1945 for Iwojima (Iōjima), administratively part of the Ogasawaras, was particularly important for this strategic reason. By this stage most of the 5,000 or so population of the Ogasawaras had been evacuated to Japan.

Following the war, in similar fashion to the Ryūkyūs the Ogasawaras stayed under American administration beyond the end of the Occupation. They were the site of an American naval base (much smaller than in Okinawa), and were finally returned to Japan in 1968. However, unlike the case of the Ryūkyūs, during this postwar period links with mainland Japan were effectively severed. Only former inhabitants of *non*-Japanese ethnicity were allowed to resettle, and any necessary supplies were brought in from Guam, not Japan. Most of the few hundred inhabitants were involved in work related to the American base, and life in general was dominated by the US Navy.

After 1968, when Japanese were allowed once again to settle there, the population gradually increased and is now around 3,000. Most are engaged in fishing and tourism. The agricultural potential of the islands has still to be realised, and the limited farming that is carried out is still for little more than self-sufficiency purposes. The islands are becoming increasingly popular as a tourist destination—20,000 tourists annually by the mid-1990s—with a particularly good reputation among game-fishing aficionados. The vast majority of tourists are Japanese.

However, poor links with the mainland remain a problem for development in tourism and other fields. There is still no air-link, and the boat trip to the mainland is a daunting thirty hours. The poor links, combined with the sheer distance, also affect the prices of commodities, which in some cases are up to ten times those of the mainland. Other problems include insufficient facilities: there is no high school, for example.

On the other hand, the Ogasawaras face the classic problem of many remote tourist destinations, in that development might destroy the very lifestyle and environment that draws the tourists. Many of the inhabitants are reluctant to draw any closer to Tōkyō's administrators, or indeed to have any more 'Japanisation'. They are intensely proud of their international flavour. As Takashi Savory—Nathaniel Savory's great-great-grandson—remarks: 'Long before "internationalisation" was a catch-phrase, we were living that idea. And if that's lost, it's gone forever.'[113]

Like many outlying regions, the Ogasawara Islands have generally been neglected by those in central government. In this particular case, the neglect may in some regards have worked to the advantage of the islands, enhancing their value as an unusual and exotic tourist destination. Yet clearly, the inhabitants should not be deprived of proper facilities. To achieve the delicate balance between development and destruction, involvement and interference, a positive and comprehensive government policy is needed. This will require basic changes in the attitude of central government to the 'periphery' of the nation.

2.6   THE DREADED OUTSIDE THREAT: FOREIGNERS AND 'FOREIGN-TAINTED' GROUPS

The Japanese have long believed themselves to be a pure race. This has extended to ideas of uniqueness and superiority. Certainly, it is indisputable that they are a highly homogeneous people, in the order of 99 per cent. Foreigners on Japan's soil present a threat to that homogeneity, that purity, that self-assumed superiority, that uniqueness. As one Japanese psychologist has observed, 'The Japanese identity is threatened when foreigners are to be accepted into our midst.'[114] Foreigners also threaten the cosy security of cultural norms that prevail among a homogeneous people. They represent, then, an interconnected mix of negatives—the outside, the unknown, the threatening, the disruptive, the impure. In short, they are generally best avoided.

However, total avoidance has not always been possible or even desirable. Among other things, it is helpful to the maintenance of national identity to have at least some degree of contact with other nations, for contrast is important. Moreover, in history, Japan has on more than one occasion responded to potential outside threat by a form of 'identification with the aggressor'.[115] The Japanese have learned—then matched and surpassed—the strengths of the potentially threatening power, safeguarding themselves against it before attempting to return to the cosiness of a life as free as possible from foreign involvement. They have generally been very successful at it. But while learning from foreigners is one thing, and so too is mixing to some extent with foreigners overseas, actually having foreigners in Japan is quite another matter.

This aversion towards a foreign presence in the land was not always the case. Korean immigrants appear to have once been welcome in ancient Japan, and so were early Chinese visitors. Indeed, Chinese ways were adopted with enthusiasm as a means of gaining recognition as a civilised nation. Missions were exchanged between Japan and China.

However, during the middle ages, when the Mongol Chinese twice tried to invade the nation, attitudes towards foreigners became more negative, though trade with China did later resume if only erratically. They hardened particularly during the so-called 'Christian century' between the mid-sixteenth and mid-seventeenth centuries. European traders and missionaries first arrived in the 1540s, bringing with them relatively sophisticated firearms. This desirable technology, along with a Japanese curiosity in general towards things western, initially meant their presence was tolerated. However, as time passed they increasingly alarmed the Japanese with their bickering, politicking, unruly behaviour, and especially their assertion of an exclusive authority—Deus—that transcended both emperor and shōgun.

Eventually, with the exception of a small Dutch colony permitted on an island near Nagasaki, Europeans were expelled on pain of death, and Japan effectively became a 'closed nation' for the next 200 years. Dealings with the Chinese were also still permitted, but in general there was a very strong reaction against the foreign outside. So strong was the reaction against 'foreignness' that even those Japanese who were overseas at the time were similarly banned on pain of death from returning. This interlude with westerners had also helped make the Japanese more aware of their own identity, the contrast being greater than with the Chinese.

When forced to reopen in the mid-nineteenth century by western 'gunboat diplomacy', Japan rapidly learned how to become a western-style power. On a practical level this was in large part in order to once again be taken seriously as a civilised nation and thereby avert the risk of being colonised, but it did also reflect a genuine wish to rank high among the nations of the world, and to be respected for it. At the same time, the nation retained—indeed promoted—a strong sense of national identity and culture. In general it continued to be less than welcoming towards foreigners, some of them even being cut down by the more fervent nationalists. Specialist foreigners were invited to spend some time in Japan in order to pass on their knowledge, but there were few who stayed long-term.

When it was defeated in World War Two Japan had no option but to endure a foreign presence during the Occupation. It also had to suffer foreign involvement in its politics, economy, and society. It was Americans who wrote Japan's postwar constitution, Americans who put in strange un-Japanese things like women's rights. After the Americans left in 1952, some of their reforms were undone in practice, and made more 'Japanese'. Education, for example, was recentralised and put under strict control. Nevertheless there is undoubtedly still much that is American about present-day Japan. It would be a serious mistake, however, to see this as an indication of Japan's wholehearted endorsement of internationalisation. The same is true of the fact that in recent years there have been increasing numbers of foreigners working and living in Japan (about 1.5 million), and increasing numbers of Japanese travelling abroad (about 15 million annually). Foreigners are still basically viewed as creatures best kept at a safe distance.

Japan's negativity towards the outside world drew international attention during the strong nationalist mood of the late 1980s, when the nation's economic power—and at times arrogance—was at its peak.[116] Since the recession of the 1990s overt expression of such sentiment has waned, along with much of the arrogance, but the basic negative feelings towards foreigners have not. For example, though one might expect an 'international' city such as Tōkyō to have a relatively tolerant attitude towards those from foreign shores, in a Tōkyō Metropolitan Government Survey in 1992 almost 60 per cent of respondents said they preferred not to meet foreigners. In a 1994 survey conducted by the same body 64 per cent of respondents said they did not want any more foreigners in their neighbourhood.[117] This second survey also revealed that almost half felt anxiety or fear in the presence of foreigners, and more than half admitted to feeling that they, as Japanese, were exclusivistic and discriminated against foreigners. Then in 1997, in the similarly 'international' city of Osaka, 70 per cent of Japanese people surveyed felt discrimination against foreigners in regard to accommodation was acceptable.

Life is slowly improving for foreign residents, but they still face numerous types of discrimination, sometimes legally endorsed. Though the requirement of alien fingerprinting was finally removed in 1993 for permanent residents, non-permanent residents still have to have their fingerprints recorded. Even permanent residents still cannot vote, even in local government elections, though there is increasing recognition among Japanese lawmakers that this right should eventually be granted at the local level. It is still very difficult for a foreigner to obtain a mortgage, or public housing,[118] let alone a seat in the Diet, or a top position in a state university. It is still difficult to obtain any type of government employment, though some openings have appeared of late in local government offices and have even received a degree of central government approval.[119] Foreign lawyers have also found it difficult to practise, though some gains have been made in the last few years.

There are some exceptions to this unwelcoming treatment, such as foreign sports stars who are put in a sort of special category and allowed certain privileges usually reserved only for Japanese.[120] Similar treatment is accorded to a number of very long-term residents who are deemed to be safe provided they have demonstrated a sympathetic understanding of Japanese culture. Very short-term foreign visitors are also usually deemed harmless, and may return home with somewhat misleading stories of how open and welcoming the Japanese are towards foreigners. However, in the great majority of cases, 'once a foreigner, always a foreigner'.

Not all foreigners in Japan suffer equal discrimination, and this is not just a reflection of the length of their stay. The Japanese rank races and nations just as they rank most things. Those who come near the bottom have a particularly difficult time. As one long-time foreign resident remarks, among foreigners whites are first, then Chinese, then other Asians, then Arabs, then finally blacks.[121] Stereotypes abound:

> Germans are industrious and disciplined, thus wholly admirable, rather like Japanese themselves; the British are gentlemen, but lazy, sloppy, and increasingly powerless; the French are cultured but arrogant, the Americans frank but crude, the Swiss peaceful, and so on. In Asia, the Indians and Chinese are pretty hopeless now but were great once; the Thais are graceful; the Malays lazy.[122]

The Germans come out as Japan's preferred people—a preference held since the Meiji period when the Japanese greatly respected Prussian militarism, authoritarianism, strength, and national pride.[123] It was a preference that caused considerable discomfort when Japan ended up allied against Germany in World War One. And there was a much greater and more poignant discomfort for the Japanese in World War Two, when this time Germany and Japan were allies, for Germany openly treated Japan very much as an inferior.[124] Such rejection by Germany—the one western nation the Japanese could really identify with—was not helpful to Japan's attitudes towards foreigners in general.

Wartime Germany is indelibly associated in world history with its persecution of the Jews. Jewish people have been the subject of basically negative stereotyping in Japan too, though to some extent this has been balanced by another stereotypical view that accords them a certain respect for their business acumen. Thus overall one might say there has been a guarded ambivalence towards them. They were at least treated better by the Japanese than by the Germans. During Japan's expansionist phase in the 1930s, which coincided with intensified persecution of Jews in Europe, there was a serious but ultimately abortive plan to bring them into Manchuria. The aim of this was not only to develop its economy but also to lessen some of the international opprobrium levelled against Japan for seizing the territory.[125] The plan was informally called the '*fugu* plan'. The *fugu* is a poisonous blowfish which the Japanese greatly relish but which is potentially fatal and needs very careful preparation and handling. The nomenclature was deliberately chosen for these associations, and clearly illustrates Japanese ambivalence towards Jews.[126]

During the war the Japanese did not follow the demands of their Nazi allies to imprison Jews. Indeed there were some cases—very rare in Japan's history of treatment of foreigners—where European Jews were actually given asylum in Japan.[127] There was also a popular Japanese-authored book in the early 1970s that likened the Japanese and the Jews (albeit in a very limited way).[128] However, a decade or so later they were portrayed once again, stereotypically, as being involved in a conspiracy to take over the world's economy. Blatantly anti-semitic literature appeared on the bookshelves, literature which in most other countries would have been immediately banned.[129]

This sort of ingenuousness, in openly expressing negative stereotypes about other races and nations, has been a characteristic of Japan's dealings with the rest of the world even well into an age when international values have condemned such behaviour. A classic illustration was Prime Minister Nakasone's notorious comments in 1986 about blacks and Hispanics lowering America's intellectual standards.[130] Japanese always seem surprised when the world reacts negatively, but they usually continue undaunted, as if reflecting an assumption of some sort of entitlement to receive special understanding and licence for their attitudes.

One authority on blacks in Japan has concluded that typical Japanese attitudes towards them are characterised not only by association with crime and sex but in broader terms by 'the 3Ks'—*kawaii* (cute), *kowai* (scary), and *kawaisō* (pitiful).[131] To some extent blacks have enjoyed a certain popularity in recent years among young people who see them as 'cool' and like to associate with them. It is questionable, however, how much such associations are sincere, and how much they are a means of indirectly expressing rebellion against mainstream norms, as well as getting personal thrills from associating with the dreaded Other.

An illustration of this is the writer Yamada Eimi, known as the 'bad girl' of the Japanese literary world and a self-styled 'sister' and interpreter of black culture. Married to a black, and with an apparent history of relationships with them, she nevertheless reinforces stereotypes. For example, in her 1987 novel *Beddotaimu Aizu* (Bedtime Eyes), she writes about a physical relationship with a black:

Putting force into my lips, I tug his chest hairs, savoring his body odor. I recall a similar smell. A sweet and rotten smell like cocoa butter. From his arm pits came a strange smell. A corrupt odor, but definitely not unpleasant. As if *by being assaulted by a dirty thing, I am made aware I am a pure thing.* That kind of smell. His smell gives me *a sense of superiority.* It makes me yearn like a bitch in heat driven by the smell of musk.[132] [my italics]

This is not just a particularly clear illustration of the defining of assumed positive values in the Self by contrast with assumed negative values in the Other. It also reveals an almost fatalistic fascination with the Other, or perhaps more exactly the Extreme Other. In proportion to its very taboo-ness, to the very threat to normalcy it poses, for many people Extreme Other-ness acquires a certain fascination, like a dare, or like the thrill of dabbling with dark and threatening forces. The black in Japan is like the *burakumin* but safer. Unlike *burakumin,* ultimately the black can be rejected, dismissed as a foreigner.

Of course, the Japanese are not the only ones to think and act along these lines. Nor are blacks the only 'fascinating yet threatening' foreign Other to them. Though usually to a lesser extent, many foreigners—especially non-Asians—are perceived in this way. As one long-time Japan resident has commented, 'The Japanese are fascinated by foreigners but repelled by their foreignness'.[133] The fascination is not just one of curiosity about material things they can learn about. At a deeper level, they can learn about themselves from this foreign Other.

But foreigners are still essentially a threat, a danger that needs controlling or subduing. Another commentator, a specialist in marketing, has observed that, rather like raw nature, foreigners have to be tamed. Companies that can do so, by using foreigners in their advertising, win respect from the public.[134] He further remarks how Japanese often get a vicarious thrill by having exciting, unusual, and potentially threatening foreigners thrust in this fashion into their humdrum and orthodox lives.[135]

Many Japanese are inveterate stereotypers—so much so that they would find little to criticise in a westerner stereotyping the Japanese themselves. (In fact, they are the first to talk in sweeping generalisations about 'we Japanese'.) They apply simplistic stereotypes not only to individual races and nations, but to broad categories of foreigners. The stereotypes then become normative, and foreigners' behaviour is expected to conform to them. If it does not, then they are seen as particularly unpredictable and threatening. East Asians, for example, are expected to have some basic familiarity with Japan's language and script, as well as its culture. Westerners are not. Westerners are supposed to struggle with the language, leading to what one linguist has termed the 'Law of Inverse Returns'[136]—the highest praise being reserved for those with the poorest (and hence safest) command of it. Though the situation is slowly changing in recent years as more and more westerners achieve proficiency in Japanese, traditionally a westerner fluent in the language—and especially one able to read and write it—has been seen as abnormal and dangerous. They threaten in particular the Japanese belief that their culture, which is strongly linked to language, is impenetrable to westerners. The more westerners start to penetrate it, the less mysterious and unique the Japanese become.[137]

Asians, including certain Middle Easterners, do not usually enjoy a high level of respect in Japan. Iranians, for example, are high on the list of current undesirables. Rightly or wrongly they are associated with illegal immigration and 'unofficial' labour, as well as petty crime. Moreover, they are seen as particularly menacing due to their tendency to gather in large groups in certain parks in Tōkyō. Young men from Thailand, the Philippines, and Korea, and to some extent China and Pakistan, have a similar reputation for involvement in illegal labour.[138] Young women from the Philippines, Thailand, and other parts of Asia, known as *Japayukisan* ('Japan-bound girls'), are widely associated with work in bars, massage parlours, and brothels (*mizu shōbai* or 'water business').

Indeed, it is illegal workers from the Philippines and elsewhere who make up a significant part of the day-labour or casual workforce in Japan. There are estimated to be well over a quarter of a million illegal immigrant workers nationwide.[139] Most of them engage in work considered too demeaning and poorly paid to be of interest to most Japanese. As with so much of life in Japan, it is known by a catchphrase, another set of '3Ks'—*kitsui* (tough), *kitanai* (dirty), and *kiken* (dangerous). And because such work has to be done, and done as cheaply as possible, the authorities usually turn a blind eye. As one illegal foreign (Korean) worker explains:

> We do the sort of work that no Japanese will do—like cleaning out blockages in sewage pipes, for instance…. But these days I mostly work at the docks. Like nearly all the Koreans here [in this particular area], I've overstayed my visa. The authorities turn a blind eye.

Why? Because without us, the entire port of Yokohama would be paralysed. Even at times of high unemployment, there are still some industries with a labour shortage. Dock work is so gruelling and badly paid that Japanese won't do it. The companies rely on us, and the authorities know it.[140]

The largest legal foreign presence in lowly paid work is that of the Brazilians, who now number more than 150,000 and form the third largest (legal) foreign group in Japan after Koreans (680,000) and Chinese (230,000). Apart from a few exceptions such as soccer stars lured to Japan's new league by enormous salaries, the Brazilians have been brought to Japan to fill manual jobs that are no longer desirable among the Japanese but are still of higher status than those carried out by illegal labourers. They are preferred where possible over other immigrant labourers because of their traditional links with Japan. A considerable number of Japanese migrated to Brazil in the Meiji period in search of opportunity, and most of the Brazilians brought into Japan are in fact ethnically Japanese, making them more acceptable even if only in a low-ranking category.

The lowest-ranking of all foreigners in Japan are refugees, who in Japan's case are almost entirely restricted to Indochinese. In this particular matter, despite its general respect for Germany, the fact that Germany has been amongst world leaders in accepting refugees has led Japan to state explicitly that it wishes to avoid a so-called 'German situation'.[141] Japan's rate of acceptance of refugees relative to its own population is barely 4 per cent of Germany's, and less than 1 per cent of first-placed Australia.[142] In fact, until 1982, when Japan adopted the United Nations Convention on Refugees, it simply refused to accept any at all (other than on purely temporary grounds). Its justification was that it should not be seen as an asylum country because it was too densely populated and too homogeneous.

According to Ministry of Justice figures there were over 9,000 refugees in Japan by the end of 1994. Very few—just a few hundred—are granted formal refugee status.[143] Little or no provision is made for them, and they are hardly made welcome. In fact, more than half of all refugees who initially arrived in Japan have since moved on to a different host country.[144] As one Japanese professor of international law has commented, 'The Japanese government is eager to spread the word that refugees aren't welcome.'[145] Not surprisingly, Japan does not receive very many applications from refugees, and is one of the few major countries that has not filled its stipulated quota of refugees.

It is not just foreigners themselves who represent the foreign threat. Those of mixed Japanese and foreign blood (*konketsuji*) are usually treated as un-Japanese, and suffer social rejection and discrimination.[146] Even pure-blooded Japanese who have had too much association with foreigners can be treated as *gaijin kusai* ('smelling like a foreigner', or 'foreign-tainted').[147]

It is difficult to obtain accurate figures for *konketsuji* in Japan. Many have been fathered by US servicemen stationed there. Though they do not apply to Japan specifically, estimates in the past have claimed that as many as one US serviceman in ten stationed in the Far East has fathered a child by a native mother.[148] Later estimates talk of around 20,000 *konketsuji* in Japan.[149] Many of those fathered by American servicemen have moved to America. However, most of those who have remained in Japan, along with others born of a foreign father—in other words the typical *konketsuji*—have suffered particular difficulties, for until recently Japanese citizenship was determined by paternal blood. This meant they were denied citizenship and hence many welfare benefits, government employment opportunities, and so forth. Some of them acquired the foreign citizenship of their father, and as a result enjoyed certain rights as permanent foreign residents. However, many—especially those born out of wedlock and of unknown paternity—typically had neither Japanese nor foreign citizenship, and were considered 'stateless' by the Japanese government.[150] A change to the law in 1984 meant that *konketsuji* could now claim Japanese citizenship on the grounds of maternal blood instead of paternal, and this and other changes have improved the situation legally, but it is still not an easy life for them.

Socially, quite apart from the adverse affects of coming from a broken home, as many *konketsuji* do, they are disadvantaged by the widespread belief in Japan that anyone of mixed blood is impure—here in the sense of spoiled by mixing and thus inferior. In fact this negativity applies to a whole range of mixed things, even mixed drinks. Water, itself a symbol of purity, is the only really acceptable 'mixer'. One commentator on Japan, himself a *konketsuji* but with a Japanese father, remarks:

> Living in a more or less racially homogeneous society, the Japanese have trouble with the concept of a mixed drink and invariably consider that whichever was the superior of the two items becomes downgraded. Extended to race, this has a very unpleasant side.[151]

Mixing of blood is the most extreme type of inter-racial mixing, followed by mixed marriages (which have become more common and to some extent less unacceptable in the 1990s). However, spending any substantial length of time in a foreign country, excessive association with a foreigner, or even having a foreigner nearby for too long, can result in a Japanese person running the risk of being considered foreign-tainted.

For example, though the situation is slowly improving, young people who have spent more than a year or so studying overseas—typically while accompanying a father stationed there on business—can still find problems on their return. Sometimes the problems faced by these *kikokushijo* (returnee children) are narrowly educational, relating to syllabus discrepancies, but more commonly they are less educational than social. In the classroom itself the *kikokushijo* are often felt by their teachers to have developed un-Japanese habits such as questioning the teacher,[152] meaning that they have not been successfully socialised into Japanese norms of acceptance and conformity and are therefore 'problem children'. And in general they can be teased, isolated, and bullied for being somehow different and vaguely foreign—not purely foreign, which would be relatively better, but vaguely so, something less than pure Japanese and yet also less even than pure foreign. They are seen, in the words of one returnee, as 'non-Japanese Japanese'.[153]

There is an unusual factor in the *kikokushijo* issue. Unlike most marginalised groups, by the very nature of their situation the children are usually from wealthy and influential families, who are effectively part of society's elite. (Indeed, if they are elite enough, such as the imperial family, they can avoid any stigma at all because they are deemed to be of unsulliable Japaneseness and put in a 'special exemption' category.) Such families are not prepared simply to put up with being discriminated against. As a result, Japanese schools have been established in recent years in most foreign cities with any significant Japanese presence. This is ostensibly so that students from Japan can avoid slipping behind the Japanese syllabus, but an equally if not more important aim is to ensure that they can remain as much as possible within a Japanese socialising environment. There are also in many cases special educational programmes in Japan for returnees. Moreover, as the number of returnees increases—now around 10,000 each year—they become less unusual. For these various reasons, in recent years the *kikokushijo* have not been isolated and teased quite so much, and now have an ambivalent rather than outright negative status. But the key point is that they are still not fully accepted as pure and proper Japanese.

Another factor is the length of time spent overseas, which is important in the degree of deemed acquisition of foreignness and loss of pure Japaneseness. This too is now slowly improving. Up to a year used to be the usual limit of acceptability of 'maintained Japaneseness', but in recent times it seems to have extended to two years or so. This is in fact the minimum for formal definition of eligibility for returnee programmes and so forth.[154] It is sufficient time to allow short-term participation in an exchange scheme—which is in fact quite acceptable of late, as a showpiece but still relatively controllable part of internationalisation—but is not enough to complete an entire degree. (Again, royals and top elites are given special licence to stay longer for this purpose.)

For those going abroad as professional adults there tends to be a greater timespan allowed than in the case of more impressionable youngsters. The problem itself, however, remains. For example, in a study of Japanese physicists in the late 1980s, one anthropologist found their patterns of research abroad to be greatly affected by a fear of loss of their 'Japanese soul', plus the more practical problem of being viewed with 'deep cultural suspicion' on their return home.[155] One male scientist even searched for a Japanese wife who had never been abroad and who could teach him 'how to be Japanese again'. Scientists were observed seriously discussing how long they could spend overseas before losing their Japaneseness and their ability to lead a research team 'Japanese-style'. The general opinion was that up to three or even five years was probably all right, but not seven or eight.

Though attitudes to foreigners and foreignness are slowly changing, especially among the young, it is clear that there is still, for many Japanese, a considerable gap between Japan and the rest of the world. The age of genuine internationalisation may eventually be coming, but it will be a while arriving.

2.7   FAILURES: DAY-LABOURERS AND VAGRANTS

The security enjoyed by Japan's 65 million or so workers has been exaggerated in popular perceptions around the world. Only major companies offer the much vaunted 'lifetime employment', and even then it is almost entirely restricted to males, especially white-collar. In practice it has never applied to the great majority of the workforce, though it is true that it is a widely held ideal. The low rate of official unemployment—typically around 3 per cent—is also unrepresentative of actuality. It excludes several categories of people who would be deemed unemployed by most nations' definitions, such as school leavers yet to find their first job. By western standards, Japan's actual unemployment rate is probably double the official rate.

On the other hand, even an unemployment rate of 6 per cent or more is better than many nations. Despite the exaggeration and distortion, and despite the current recession (which has exposed the limits of the lifetime employment system), it is still true to say that the Japanese are better off than many in terms of job security. Among other things this is a reflection not only of the underlying strength of the economy, but of the general preference of Japanese companies, in times of recession, to reduce labour costs by cutting back working hours and pay rather than dismissing individuals.

Nevertheless, Japan does have a group of people who cannot look forward to a regular wage (or even any wage at all), or to decent working conditions. This group includes the chronically unemployable, and those who work on a merely occasional and often unrecorded basis, particularly day-labourers. In a nation where the work ethic is high and normative pressures are strong, the social stigma applied to such people is severe. In more practical terms they also suffer from relatively limited social welfare facilities.

The day-labourer or chronically unemployed person represents a particular type of Japanese impurity, that of failing to live up to some of society's most basic expectations. He—for they are almost entirely male, and it is males who are expected to do paid work—has failed to get a steady job, or even worse, he has deliberately rejected the idea of it. Many also tend to be itinerant, which is another negative and potentially socially disruptive factor. Those who have in addition failed to obtain or have rejected even a proper roof over their head are viewed especially negatively. Some day-labourers do live in their own homes. Most live in flophouses or dormitories in certain recognised areas in big cities (often moving between these seasonally), but some—perhaps 10 per cent or so—end up more or less permanently on the streets, as homeless. Together with the chronically unemployed vagrant, they are known as *furōsha* (literally 'floaters'). They not only float or drift around geographically. By 'drifting from the normal order of things' they have in a way taken on a form of pollution, and incurred the contempt—and fear—of society.[156] As one sociologist has commented:

> Given the heightened sense of social uniformity in Japanese society, the public response to homelessness often expresses the strict bifurcation between order and disorder.... To even hear about, let alone encounter, the homeless evokes a sense of fear and loathing. Such people are often regarded as the dregs of the economic miracle, the defiled 'other' threatening to pollute the entire social system.[157]

Like foreigners they represent disruption to norms, and therefore a potential threat, but at least foreigners have an order of sorts in their own way. Foreigners may be unpredictable by Japanese standards, but at least they earn a certain recognition for living up to the expectations of their own culture. By contrast, the Japanese who fail to get a proper job, or a home or even a proper roof, represent a more sinister threat. They are an Other from within, an Other that does not do the expected thing. Even if their situation is the result of misfortune rather than defiance, they represent failure, which is still a form of Other to be viewed with aversion.

Many—but by no means all—of the hundreds of thousands in the casual workforce in Japan are in fact foreign, being illegal immigrants from places such as the Philippines or Korea. However, they almost all live under a roof, however basic, in their own communities. Naturally they do not feature in official employment statistics, and they enjoy very few rights. They are not eligible for social welfare, and though they are legally entitled to labour accident insurance benefits from the government and compensation from the employer where appropriate, in practice compensation is given (if at all) on the basis of wage standards in their home country, which are invariably a mere fraction of Japanese rates.[158]

In his 1992 book *Underground in Japan* the Filipino Ray Ventura describes, from his own experiences, life as a day-labourer in Yokohama's Kotobuki district.[159] He writes how he and his colleagues would assemble around 5 a.m. at recognised pick-up sites to be bused off by some labour boss to a building site (or the dockyards or a factory). Here they would often have to do dangerous work with minimal safety measures, such as working as a *tobi*, equivalent to the English 'scaffolding monkey'. Usually the whole business was controlled by the *yakuza*. Because the work needed to be done, and few Japanese were keen to do it, the Japanese authorities would turn a blind eye.

Not all Japanese refuse such work, of course, and it is the Japanese day-labourers who are seen as the more sinister Other. They are probably anyway in a different category from the immigrant worker to start with. Ventura points out that in general the foreign workers are of a higher socio-economic status than the Japanese engaged in such work, since they at least have sufficient funds—raised by one means or another, often by a family collection—to get themselves to Japan in the first place. He sees the foreign workers as opportunists. By contrast, the Japanese day-labourers tend rather to be down-and-outs, or those who claim to have deliberately rejected mainstream society for the supposed freedom of the day-labourer's life.

Indeed, many Japanese day-labourers seem to look down almost smugly on the supposedly unfree salaried employee, feeling they themselves are advantaged by only working on an occasional basis and being able to move from site to site.[160] It is a sad self-delusion. In practice, day-labourers are far from free. They are controlled by labour bosses, labour brokers, and local gang bosses, and they are often dependent on others for welfare or charity. In fact, on occasion they are physically imprisoned as virtual slaves by the more ruthless labour bosses, and assaulted if they try to escape. This is especially likely to happen to the more extreme cases, the homeless ones who live on the streets, under bridges, or in subways. For example, when a group of homeless were evicted from their cardboard city in Shinjuku station in 1996, they were promptly preyed upon. One construction company 'recruited' a hundred or so, setting them up in a dormitory with 24-hour guards posted around it.[161] As one of the homeless workers himself commented:

> They crammed over 10 people into a 15-mat room [about 30 sq m]. The arrangement was for 7,000 yen a day, but none of us saw that money. If we broke the rules or tried to escape, they would beat us. They even had men on the work-site to follow us to the bathroom.[162]

Day-labourers are officially known as *hi-yatoi rōdōsha* ('day employment labourers') but more commonly as *tachinbō*, meaning 'stand around guys', a reference to their waiting to be picked up and bused off to a work-site. The places where the pick-ups are made are known as *yoseba* ('gathering places'), and the general areas as *doya-gai* ('flophouse districts'). *Doya-gai* are found in any major city, but particularly large areas include Kamagasaki in Osaka (about 25,000 day-labourers, though figures are only rough estimates), Sanya in Tōkyō (about 10,000), Kotobuki in Yokohama (about 8,000), and Sasashima in

Nagoya (about 6,000).[163] Naturally, these are not places the Japanese government would like tourists or even ordinary Japanese to find their way to, and they rarely feature with any prominence (if at all) on maps. Tōkyō's Sanya, for example, which is located near Minami-Senju Station, was 'disestablished' as an administrative district in 1974, being broken up into three parts each attached to nearby administrative areas.[164]

Some day-labourers have families, though they tend to have left them for one reason or another, but the vast majority are single men in practice at least. In recent years a few women have appeared in the *doya-gai*,[165] but in general the absence of women and children in these areas distinguishes them from the typical slum.[166] The cramped quarters that many of them live in are known as *doya* (flophouse or doss-house, from a deliberate reversal of the syllables of *yado*, the normal word for 'inn') or *takobeya* ('octopus rooms', a reference to octopus pots, which trap the octopus in a space too small to allow it to move). There are some 200 of these in Sanya, as one example. Some *tachinbō* live in labourers' shacks on the actual work-site (*hanba*, literally 'rice/food place'). And of course, some live on the streets, epsecially if they have not found work—and actually been paid for it—or received a welfare payment.

Social welfare comes in two forms, social security (*seikatsu hogo*) and extra-legal assistance (*hōgai engo*). These are administered by separate authorities—ward in the case of the former, civic in the case of the latter. Social security provides about 80,000 yen per month plus basic accommodation, usually in the form of a flophouse room. It is available relatively easily to those who can provide medical documentation of some long-term disability or illness. However, for those who cannot it is essentially left to the discretion of welfare officials. With the exception of a few localities such as Yokohama, most such officials have no special training in social work, and often lack the ability to make informed decisions.[167] Moreover, they are often hostile both to their own assignment to such a low-status posting within the civil service, and to the applicants themselves. Those applicants who do not receive social security have to apply for extra-legal assistance, which provides one night's flophouse accommodation and a basic food ration. This assistance is intended to be temporary only and is not issued on a repeat basis. By contrast, the streets are free and always available.

The permanent homeless, the *furōsha*, are usually unable to find any paid work at all as a result of age (most commonly) and/or meths dependency or similar. They make a little money sometimes by collecting thrown away items for recycling, or similar activities. However, more often than not they are dependent on welfare and handouts from charity organisations, most of which are Christian.[168] Though *furōsha* is the common term used of them, they are known officially as *tojō-seikatsusha* ('those who dwell on the streets'). Officialdom, however, has long ignored them. For example, it was not until July 1995 that the Metropolitan Government of Tōkyō—where several thousand *furōsha* are estimated to live—first issued a report on their plight. By this stage their numbers had grown due to the recession, and they could no longer be overlooked.

In recent years their plight has also been highlighted by a number of widely publicised incidents. In October 1992, for example, the media featured an incident in which more than 700 *furōsha* in Osaka's Kamagasaki district rioted over a cut-back in emergency economic relief. Then in January 1996 the increasingly embarrassing numbers of homeless in the passageways of Shinjuku station—the world's busiest station, and one much used by foreign tourists—led the police to stage a mass eviction of the 300 or so encamped there. This was not the first such eviction from Shinjuku, and there have been others since, but on this occasion it was met with particularly spirited resistance, with some *furōsha* even chaining themselves to pillars in the station. As a result, considerable attention was focused on the event and the general plight of the *furōsha*, in overseas as well as domestic newspapers.[169] However, the affair eventually passed. Most of the *furōsha* were persuaded to move to somewhere less obvious (some of them to a temporary shelter), at least for a while, and little really changed.

Few formal records have been kept of *furōsha* life. One of the few such records, by the Sasashima Clinic in Nagoya, suggests that their average age of death is only 55. This is more than 20 years below the national average for males. At the same time, the typical *furōsha* is of late middle age. This clearly suggests that they do not survive for long after becoming *furōsha*.

The government has admitted that the *furōsha* suffer serious prejudicial treatment and that something needs to be done to improve their lot in life.[170] However, it is not just a government problem. Each time the government proposes a rehousing scheme, for example, there is opposition from residents in the areas where the accommodation is planned. Public attitudes are strongly negative. On more than one occasion *furōsha* have even been beaten to death 'for kicks' by groups of youths.[171] And the *furōsha* themselves still seem to cling to self-deluding notions of freedom, perhaps as some form of defence against society's contempt. For whatever reason, they have difficulties not only in being accepted by society, but accepting society themselves.

All countries have their drop-outs and failures, the downwardly mobile and no-hopers. Proper reintegration into society may never be feasible for many of them. It is a problem that clearly needs seriously addressing by all governments, with a view to at least assuring a basic quality of life. The life of such people is particularly harsh in a hierarchical society, and in a society such as Japan's, with the additional factors of strong normative pressures and associations with impurity, especially so.

2.8   UNWHOLESOME: THE DISEASED

Disease is viewed in Japan as a distinctly threatening impurity. Such a negative view is hardly surprising, for disease is hardly welcome in any culture. Most cultures also associate disease with outsiders, and again Japan is no exception. In fact, the Japanese make a very close three-way connection between the outside and impurity and disease.[172] There is some justification for this. As an island nation, historically Japan has been isolated from many continental diseases. Through lack of gradually built-up natural resistance, it suffered quite severely when such diseases did finally arrive. In the eighth century in particular it was ravaged by smallpox introduced from the Asian mainland.[173] This continued to hit in waves for some centuries to come, sometimes reducing the population by as much as a third, till the disease was finally endemicised and a natural mechanism of immunisation evolved (notably in the form of the childhood disease chickenpox).

A serious contagious disease is an obvious major threat in any society. Those who contract one are invariably removed from that society by quarantining, or in extreme cases extermination. Even if sufferers recover, they may well continue to suffer the stigma of permanent association with the disease, being shunned and marginalised. Japan is again no exception, and in fact shows a stronger tendency than most to marginalise anything connected with serious illness. The fact that this can occur even when an illness is known not to be contagious (or at least not easily spread) suggests that the fear of serious illness goes beyond an understandable practical regard for one's own physical well-being or survival. To the Japanese a serious illness is also a symbol of dreaded impurity (*kegare*). It is a contaminating agent of the dark forces of pollution, an indicator of a state of things 'not being as they should be'. It is also, of course, as anywhere else, often a herald of death. Death is viewed ambivalently in Japan in spiritual terms. At times, depending on circumstances, it can be viewed positively as an act of heroism, and even of purification, but usually—and certainly in the case of death through illness—it is a strong impurity.

Though smallpox has not been a major problem in Japan since the middle ages, and neither have diseases such as bubonic or pneumonic plague, the nation as a whole has continued into the twentieth century to have a great fear of diseases such as tuberculosis.[174] TB was, in many regards, the AIDS of the prewar period in particular. Infected persons and their families were invariably considered defiled creatures, almost always shunned, and even sometimes exterminated. However, perhaps even more obvious marginalisation has been seen in the case of sufferers from leprosy. Leprosy in fact carries a low risk both of infection and mortality, but it does result in severely disfiguring physical ugliness. This has been a source of abhorrence towards it in many cultures, but particularly in Japan where beauty and perfection are such strong aesthetic ideals. Kagata Hajime, himself a leper, has remarked how lepers fall foul to a 'long-standing Japanese taboo against people with unsightly diseases'.[175]

Like almost all other societies, Japan has traditionally isolated its lepers in colonies as far away from normal society as possible. It has also greatly demeaned and dehumanised their existence—though not to the extent of medieval Europe, where it was not uncommon for live lepers to be catapulted into besieged towns. Under the Leprosy Prevention Law of 1908, lepers in Japan were forced to reside in special colonies. Kagata recalls how 'they were housed in filthy huts, clothed in concentration-camp-style pyjamas, issued with special leper colony yen to make it harder for them to escape, and told to die quickly so as not to be a burden'.[176] Not only that, the same law made it compulsory for them to be sterilised upon marriage.

Moreover, discrimination against lepers extended to their families. To spare their relatives problems in marriage and employment, lepers entering colonies invariably assumed false names.[177] Thus they were isolated not only from society and their families, but in a way even from their own identity.

Unlike most nations, Japan still continued to isolate lepers despite the development during the 1940s and 1950s of drugs such as promin which effectively halt the disease, and despite postwar medical knowledge of its low infectiousness. In 1996 the country had some 6,000 sufferers in fifteen leprosaria (all but two of which were state-run), mostly in remote parts of the country such as tiny Nagashima Island in the Inland Sea. Thanks to medical advances there are few new sufferers, and the average age of the residents of Nagashima and other leprosaria in 1996 was 71. With about 300 coming to the end of their natural lives each year, the disease is expected to be non-existent in Japan in the next few decades.

The Leprosy Prevention Law was finally repealed in April 1996, in no small part due to the progressive stance of Health and Welfare Minister Kan Naoto. Kan also apologised to sufferers on behalf of the government for the delay in abolishing the restrictions on their life and liberty. They are now free to return to society at large. However, because of their age and the former policy of sterilisation, most have no family to support them. In addition, social prejudice against them is still strong. As a result, most continue to reside in their present leprosaria on a voluntary basis.

The current most dreaded disease in Japan is of course AIDS, a disease particularly associated with outsiders—again with some obvious justification, for AIDS patently did not originate in Japan. Its first diagnosed AIDS/HIV case, in 1985, was—true to Japanese perceptions of it—a foreigner, a bar hostess from the Philippines working in Nagano prefecture. The following year saw the first diagnosed Japanese sufferer, a woman in Kōbe. She was alleged to be a prostitute who caught the disease from a foreign sailor. The allegations in this case were untrue, but clearly reveal the Japanese eagerness to see the disease solely as a foreign thing. Soon there were even serious calls for all foreigners entering the country to be screened for the disease.[178] However, though AIDS has a foreign origin, Japan, like many other 'victim nations', has necessarily had to come to terms with its presence. Outwardly, it did so surprisingly well. In 1994 it became the first Asian nation to host the annual International Conference on AIDS, which obviously drew large numbers of AIDS sufferers and carriers from overseas. This was clearly was a symbol of a somewhat more tolerant Japanese attitude towards the disease—at least officially.

Fortunately for Japan, though the presence of AIDS is real and an obvious source of concern, it is not a strong presence. According to

Ministry of Health and Welfare figures for December 1997 there are just over 5,000 AIDS/HIV patients in Japan, an extremely low figure for such a highly populated nation (especially one with such tolerant sexual attitudes).[179] More than 10 per cent of these are foreign residents. Moreover, unlike the case with most nations, almost half of all patients contracted the disease through specific circumstances that are unlikely to be repeated. They are haemophiliacs—in fact around half of all haemophiliacs in Japan—who received transfusions in the mid-1980s of imported blood products that were contaminated and not heat-treated by the Japanese authorities. When this became known a few years later it became a major national scandal and led to massive law suits, compensation, and indictments of senior figures.[180]

As in other nations, there is considerable sympathy for those contracting the disease through transfusion, who are seen as particularly innocent victims.[181] In fact, by Japanese standards there have been some remarkable displays of acceptance of them. In October 1996 a declared transfusion-infected victim, Ienishi Satoru, took a seat in the House of Representatives (Lower House) on a Democratic Party ticket.[182] One of the higher-profile campaigners for victims' redress, a young university student named Sawada Ryūhei (himself a victim), has become a popular figure, being asked to give public talks and writing books about his situation. One of his books is even being used as a text by some schools.[183]

However, Sawada remarks that in general discrimination against AIDS/HIV sufferers is still strong in Japan. Among other things he notes that many smaller hospitals simply refuse to treat them at all. As another Japanese writer on AIDS concludes, although Japanese attitudes towards AIDS sufferers are slowly improving, they are still some considerable way behind other nations in terms of sympathy and understanding. She feels that, aggravated by a 'shaky concept of human rights', an 'almost medieval prejudice against and mistreatment of people with the disease still festers in Japan'.[184]

Even if it is not contagious, serious illness still has a major stigma attached to it in Japan. The Japanese simply prefer not to have anything to do with it, and if possible not even to know about it. They marginalise it even in their thoughts. As one result, it has long been the practice for doctors to mislead patients over a sinister diagnosis. Typically, when a patient is found to have a major illness such as cancer—for the last two decades the single biggest cause of death in Japan[185]—it is usually just the family who are told the truth, not the patient. In some cases, not even the family is told the real diagno-sis.[186] The rationale is well-intentioned, and at the same time a form of fatalistic resignation: if the patient is going to die anyway, why bother to tell them and cause them to worry? They cannot escape this awful impurity, but the less they know about it the easier it will be for them.

In recent years it has become more common to tell patients the truth, but there is still much obfuscation.[187] Such concealment of information is aided by the fact that, unlike most developed nations, Japan still does not have a Freedom of Information Act.

Once they realise their illness is terminal, especially where suffering is involved, most Japanese people would prefer to die quickly. In fact, many would like euthanasia. In a Ministry of Health and Welfare survey conducted in 1993, 75 per cent of respondents said they would prefer to have treatment discontinued for themselves or a family member if suffering was involved and death was inevitable, and 15 per cent would request direct euthanasia.[188] Not the least reason for this is that terminally ill patients do not wish to become a burden to others.

Japanese attitudes to illness are clearly a factor in the nation's provi-sion of medical facilities, which have long presented a rather unusual picture to western observers.[189] It has only 1.8 doctors per 1,000 people, virtually the lowest rate of any major nation and barely half that of most. By contrast, it has more hospital beds than any other nation—15.6 per 1,000, about double the rate in most countries. Also, the average length of hospital stay, at around 46 days, is far longer than in all other developed nations and four times the rate of most.

The lack of doctors may among other things reflect a reluctance to enter a career involved with sickness. The abundance of hospital beds and the long period of stay no doubt reflect in part the large number of elderly in Japan, with the elderly being particularly prone to have protracted illnesses. But, importantly, the pattern of hospitalisation also reflects a reluctance to have a seriously sick person in the house. This is not just a result of logistical difficulties in looking after a patient in a typical cramped Japanese home. A sick person is impure, and should be kept away from normal things. By using the hospital as a sort of 'home away from home' for the patient, the home proper is kept pure. This 'home away from home' approach meshes with the trad-itional system of nursing in many Japanese hospitals, which provide only basic care and expect the patient's family to undertake many of the nursing tasks performed in other countries by professionals.

As in other cultures, minor illnesses and ailments present no difficulties to the Japanese. In fact, they can often become a source of sympathy, evoking that Japanese style of self-indulgent dependence known as *amae*.[190] Being seriously ill, however, is another matter. The seriously ill in Japan by no means receive quite the same sympathy a patient would expect in the west. They continue to be viewed as beings who can perhaps best be described in English as 'unwholesome', with its connotations of unhealthy, less than pure, and rather repellent. The fact that this term exists in English indicates that a similar concept is not unknown in the west. However, as the seriously ill can testify, 'unwholesomeness' has a greater and more real significance in Japan.

2.9 IMPERFECT AND NEGLECTED: THE PHYSICALLY DISABLED

The first child ever born in Japan, according to its mythology, was abandoned because he was born deformed.[191] This was not an auspicious start for the new nation. Ever since, the disabled person in Japan has been considered not only imperfect, an embodiment of ugliness, but at a deeper socio-spiritual level—and especially if they are actually born disabled—a sort of curse. Certainly, the physically disabled are far from pure. More practically they have also been seen as a burden, non-contributors to society, and in that sense suffer a similar stigma to that of the *furōsha*. Those whose disability results from serious illness suffer in addition the stigma of the diseased. Even in the case of victims of an accident or similar misfortune (such as the children born malformed in the 1960s due to Japan's notorious industrial pollution at the time), their treatment by society at large has not been particularly sympathetic. Basically, if not always actively shunned, the handicapped have been ignored till very recent times. Their presence, like that of the diseased, is something society prefers not to think too much about. As one specialist has commented 'For many years, to be disabled in Japan meant to be forgotten.'[192]

Even accurate data have not always been obtainable. On the other hand, data can be problematic anyway, for the definition of 'disabled' varies from country to country. For example, in 1990 Japan's Ministry of Health and Welfare gave figures for disabled (including both mental and physical) in the order of 3 million, which represented less than 3 per cent of the population. By contrast, most countries acknowledge around 10 per cent of their population to be disabled, with Sweden acknowledging a massive 35 per cent—its definition of 'disabled' extending, for example, to any person who has any degree of difficulty using public transport.[193]

The total number of recognised disabled has now risen to almost 5 million, of whom almost two-thirds are categorised as physically disabled. Of these physically disabled, two-thirds again are over 60 years of age. The number of disabled—however strict the definition may be—increases inevitably as the proportion of elderly in the population increases. Moreover, new forms of disability, such as Operational Overuse Syndrome, are also appearing in Japan as elsewhere.

In similar fashion to the slow but undeniable change in official policies towards afflictions such as AIDS and leprosy, in recent years policies towards the physically disabled are also gradually starting to improve, though it is far from a dramatic change. For example, during the United Nations Decade of Disabled Persons, from 1983 to 1992, a number of changes were made to the law, culminating in 1993 in the enactment of the Basic Law for Persons with Disabilities. Attempting to reflect the proportion of disabled but functional members of society, it stipulates that at least 1.6 per cent of the workforce of a company of appropriate size (necessarily a minimum 63 employees) should be made up of disabled persons. However, on the negative side, the Law has a similar major weakness to the 1986 Equal Employment Opportunity Law aimed at improving the employment status of women, in that it makes no substantial provision for penalising those companies that ignore it. There is merely a token fine (equivalent to approximately US$500 per month) for each such unfilled position, which many large companies choose to pay regularly rather than actually hire disabled persons.[194] This is despite the fact that the government provides incentives for the employment of the disabled, such as covering the first six months' salary and paying for office renovation to allow for wheelchair access or similar modifications.

In 1995 the government formally adopted a Government Action Plan for Persons with Disabilities, a long-term policy—with a budget of around US$80 billion—aimed at ironing out difficulties in the normalisation and rehabilitation of the disabled. Among other broad goals it aims to improve the safety and quality of life for the disabled, improve their ability to achieve a self-sustained social life, permit them to live harmoniously in the community, and establish a so-called 'barrier-free' society.

As further positive moves, though they remain the exception some companies have instituted exemplary practices for the employment of the disabled. For example, the supermarket chain Itō Yōkadō has exceeded its legal quota of disabled employees, as well as adopting a 'buddy-system' and a monitoring system to enable problems to be promptly addressed. It also runs classes in sign-language for its general employees. There are in addition a number of specialist disabled-person companies, such as the Tōkyō-based Japan Abilities Inc., whose business is catering to the disabled and a third of whose own workforce is composed of disabled persons.

One major problem for the disabled person who can work is that of commuting. Improvements are starting to be made in terms of provision of facilities for the disabled, but here again progress is slow and not always smooth. For example, Japan has a total of some 7,000 railway stations. In 1982 only 82 of these had elevators, meaning that in the vast majority of cases persons in wheelchairs had to suffer the indignity of summoning help to mount the stairs. By 1994 this number had increased to 336, but this still represents less than 5 per cent of all stations. When the focus is narrowed to the nation's 500 or so subway stations, 125 (25 per cent) have elevators, and the situation is somewhat better, but it still clearly leaves the majority without facilities.

In 1994 a law was passed calling for the inclusion of facilities for the disabled in all future buildings intended for public use. The law also applies to existing buildings if and when they are to be remodelled. However, it is yet another law which merely encourages rather than obliges, providing no penalty for those who choose to ignore it. It is little wonder that results have not been as effective as hoped.

For those who cannot work, welfare payments are not particularly generous. Typically, those over the age of 20 are entitled to a monthly welfare payment of between 65,000 and 80,000 yen depending on their degree of disability. Those who require professional home-help are entitled to a further 25,000 yen per month.

For the younger disabled, receiving an education has traditionally been difficult, but the situation is improving in recent years. While special schools have long existed for the blind and deaf, schooling for other categories of disabled was not compulsory till 1979. In effect, this often meant they received none at all. After it became compulsory, the disabled were typically left to fend for themselves at regular schools, with no special provisions—a rather unusual case of an effective category of marginals being forced into the mainstream, albeit by default rather than invitation. As a result many fell behind and lost self-esteem. Some schools themselves gradually took the initiative and started offering special tuition facilities. Then in 1992 the situation was formally improved when the Ministry of Education established a system whereby disabled students receive regular education in conjunction with training at special institutions geared to their particular disability. Problems remain, however, in the post-compulsory area of education, with the flow-on rate of disabled students to senior high school being about 25 per cent below that of non-disabled students.

With regard to specific and commonly recognised forms of impairment such as blindness and deafness, there is again a similar pattern of slow but definite improvement on the one hand, yet lingering problems on the other.

There are some 130,000 blind people in Japan (as opposed to the many millions with some degree of sight impairment). Unlike the situation in the 1970s, they no longer require special permission to undertake a range of everyday tasks such as riding on trains. Ordinary kerbstones on some major roads are also gradually being replaced with specially stippled stones to assist those with a white stick, and most major pedestrian crossings now have auditory signals.

However, assistance for the blind is still limited. For example, there are only 800 guide-dogs in the nation, as opposed to 4,000 in Britain—a tenfold discrepancy after population adjustment. Guide-dog trainers, even with a university education, receive only half the average wage for the nation. Donations to guide-dog associations (like other non-profit organisations) are hampered by tax laws that impose a low ceiling on tax-exempt donations and bequests. The use of guide-dogs in general is hampered, relative to countries such as the United States or Britain, by a scarcity of places permitting animals, and by the lack of appropriate legal rights for guide-dog users. Although attitudes have been slowly improving as a result of the work of activists and various educational programmes, in the words of the blind Kon Takao 'Japan still has a long way to go to catch up with such countries.'[195]

There are around 400,000 people in Japan with seriously impaired hearing, of whom about 160,000 are totally deaf. In recent years awareness of the plight of deaf people has been increasing. One indication of this is that currently some 32,000 people with normal hearing are studying sign language.[196] Volunteer sign-language interpreters have also been trained, with government subsidies, since the 1970s. In addition, a certification programme was introduced in 1989 for interpreters, making it a professional occupation. In 1997 technology for automatic sign-language translation was jointly developed by Matsushita and Kōgakuin University. Using dual cameras and screens, signs are translated into spoken Japanese and vice-versa. The equipment is initially to be introduced into post-offices and similar facilities, with expectations of broadened use in the future.[197]

Further improvements for the situation of deaf people include the increasing number of television programmes with captions (either in sign or written word, and either displayed on the normal screen or delivered by cabled addition). In 1990 the state-run Japan Broadcasting Corporation (NHK) even started a thirty-minute weekly programme for a general audience on learning sign language.

However, while this is definite progress, telecaptioned broadcasts in Japan are still rare compared to those of many overseas nations. In 1992 the five private stations in the Tōkyō region offered a combined weekly total of just over five hours, whereas five otherwise comparable stations in America offered a combined weekly total of 215 hours—a forty-fold discrepancy.[198] (In the same year NHK offered just 10.5 hours per week.) Moreover, whereas almost all evening programmes in the United States were captioned, those captioned in Japan were confined to relatively trivial programmes such as samurai dramas and cartoons.

Clearly, progress is slowly but inexorably being made in life for the disabled. Not the least reason for this is that Japan is necessarily becoming—however much it might try to resist—a part of the international community, and is therefore subject to international expectations. Moreover, as the use of electronic means of communication increases, more disabled will be able to enter the paid workforce while working from home-based computers. Though in one sense this will keep them isolated from the community, in another sense it will mean they will become recognised as contributors to society and its prosperity. This is an important factor in social acceptance anywhere, but especially in Japan.

At the same time, it would be unrealistic to expect traditional attitudes to disappear overnight. For some years yet, the disabled will have to continue to contend not only with their disability, but also with the basically negative attitudes of society.

2.10   SELFISH AND UNGRATEFUL: THE MENTALLY IMPAIRED

Mental impairment is by its nature less obvious than physical impairment. It is also such a broad matter that it becomes vague, ranging from the severely mentally ill and insane to the mildly intellectually or cognitively challenged. Moreover, it is more culture-specific than physical impairment, particularly when it comes to mental illness. There are of course a number of internationally recognised mental illnesses, such as schizophrenia or manic depression, that are diagnosed by a patient's behaviour being judged against internationally accepted norms. However, mental well-being is also often judged by an individual's degree of adherence to behavioural norms and values that are in large part culturally determined.[199] Yet on the other hand deviancy in itself is not necessarily a sign of a mental problem, even in a highly normative society such as Japan's.[200]

In addition, mental illness is often just a question of degree. It is usually associated with such behavioural traits as erraticism, irrationality, and in particular loss of self-control, but obviously such behaviour occurs with some frequency in everyday situations without being considered pathological or even particularly abnormal. Most people have on occasion had a fit of temper, or contradicted themselves, or said something totally silly, or acted on impulse. Such acts only really become a problem if they threaten danger or are maintained over any length of time. No society can easily accommodate a person who is chronically irrational, unstable, or dangerous, and Japan is no exception. The mentally impaired in general are seen, rather like the physically disabled, as unable to contribute to society, but in addition the mentally ill and unstable represent a danger to the normalcy and safety of society.

The distinction between criminality and mental illness provides particular scope for flexibility and cultural influence. For example, should a paedophile be treated as a criminal, or mentally ill, or for that matter both, or neither? Acts that in the west would be considered criminal are often seen in Japan rather as an indication of a mental problem. It has more than 300,000 people in its thousand or so mental institutions, more than the number of those in prison. The picture is reversed in the case of the United States, which has far more people in prison than in mental institutions.[201]

Three-quarters of those in Japan's mental institutions have been compulsorily committed. It is undoubtedly the case that they include a number of convenience committals, such as dumped elderly and troublesome *furōsha*.[202] It can be argued that life in a mental institution in Japan is often little better than prison, with many inmates being held behind bars.[203] Nevertheless, the nation's preference for seeing socially unacceptable behaviour as a mental rather than criminal matter is clear.

The interpretation of a 'mental' problem is in itself open to question and cultural influence. Does a person with such a problem have merely an attitudinal problem, or is something physiologically wrong with the workings of their brain? The west has tended to have mixed views on the matter, but in its treatment of mental patients Japan has clearly shown a preference for the former interpretation. Such patients are often deemed to be suffering from an excess of selfishness and a lack of awareness of the debt they owe to others in society. The responsibility for recovery is given largely to the patient (or their family). It is a case of know thy failings, heal thyself, and come back to society with the proper attitude, or else end up in an institution.

Two well-known forms of treatment illustrate this approach. The first is *naikan* ('inward looking') therapy, which is 'considered an exclusive product of Japanese culture'.[204] It aims to replace a patient's feelings of hostility towards others with feelings of guilt and indebtedness. The other is Morita therapy, developed by the Japanese psychotherapist Morita Shōma at the turn of the century. It aims to remove self-obsession and excessive introversion so as to permit proper social relations with others.[205] Both have the overall aim of social reintegration of those who have some perceived attitudinal problem that has prevented them taking a proper responsible role in society.

Some have argued that both these popular therapies are merely tools for social control of the non-conformist, independent-minded individual. One commentator, for example, has referred to Morita therapy as 'punishment for being out of key with the rest of society'.[206] There is no doubt some truth in this criticism. Non-conformism and independent-mindedness are usually frowned on in Japan and pressure applied to conform. By western ethics it is questionable whether mentally ill patients who show such traits should be expected simply to 'shape up'. Nevertheless, however misguided such treatment may or may not prove to be, the aim of integration should not be overlooked. It says much about marginalisation in Japan. In particular it suggests that, though the terms of social acceptance may be tough and unappealing to many westerners, those Japanese who initially reject the 'system'—provided they are not *burakumin* or members of a similar eternally marginalised group—are at least given a chance to redeem themselves. The problem is that if they are genuinely mentally ill, they cannot be expected to appreciate this.

The philosophy of reintegration underlying treatment received in *naikan* and Morita therapies is very similar to the philosophy applied to those found guilty of one-off criminal acts. More so than in many societies, such offenders are given a second chance—depending of course on the severity of the offence. If they sign a statement expressing contrition (a *hanseisho*), offenders of all but the most serious crimes stand a very good chance of getting off very lightly indeed by western standards. Japan's rate of (formal) imprisonment relative to conviction is less than 5 per cent of that of the United States.[207] By contrast, if they re-offend, they will be treated extremely harshly.

Those who are finally deemed to be mentally ill suffer a similar stigma to a diseased person. So too do their families.[208] Here again the diagnosis is often deliberately obscured. At times this concealment of reality can amount to irresponsibility on the part of the health specialist and can create serious problems. For example, it is well-known that the crash of a Japan Airlines plane offshore from Tōkyō's Haneda Airport in 1982, which killed twenty-four people and injured 147 others, was attributed to erratic behaviour by the pilot. However, it is not so well-known that he had been diagnosed as suffering from a relatively trivial psychosomatic disorder when in fact he was schizophrenic. A deliberate false diagnosis is suspected.[209]

The mentally ill and unstable represent one end of the spectrum of mental impairment. At the other end are the mentally slow, who in many cases, such as those with certain types of specific learning difficulties, might be more appropriately termed 'cognitively handicapped'. However, officially they are usually termed 'mentally handicapped' or 'mentally disabled'.

All medically corroborated mentally handicapped persons unable to work are entitled to the same welfare payments as the physically disabled, that is around 80,000 yen per month with an additional 25,000 yen in the case of professional home-help being required. Nursing is often expected to be the responsibility of the family.

Those who clearly suffer from a mental handicap that does not involve instability or danger to the public have in recent years been treated in similar fashion, educationally and socially, to the physically impaired. They are covered by the same recent laws, and are allowed and indeed encouraged to participate in normal life to the extent that their disability permits. There is, rather like the differentiation among AIDS sufferers, relative sympathy and support for those mentally afflicted as a result of a clearly identifiable trauma such as brain-damage from an accident or stroke. They are more readily accepted than those brain-damaged by disease or congenitally.

However, society is still far from fully welcoming. Not a few of the mentally handicapped who have found work as result of recent legislation have been both physically abused and financially cheated by their employers. Punishment has at least been harsh for these offenders. In 1997 a factory owner in Ibaraki prefecture was sentenced to three years' imprisonment for such acts. It is a 'good news, bad news' situation. It is good news that officialdom has treated such abuse so harshly, but bad news that lawyers believe the Ibaraki case is just 'the tip of the iceberg'.[210]

Attention has long been drawn to the plight of the mentally disabled and their families by the Nobel Prize-winning writer Oe Kenzaburō. Since the 1960s Oe has frequently written—in both (thinly disguised) fiction and non-fiction forms—about his son Hikari, who was born seriously mentally disabled. He and his family have also featured in television documentaries on the subject. Oe's own view is realistic, in that he does not conceal the difficulties of raising a mentally handicapped child, but he argues that it can and does strengthen the family. He feels society should be a 'family writ large' and make a greater attempt to help the disabled, rather than shutting them away. However, his writings have not, it would seem, greatly altered traditional views, and he has been criticised for focusing too much on the topic. It has also been claimed by some that the achievements made by his son, who has had some success as a composer, are due solely to the fame of his father. It is impossible to judge the accuracy of such comments, but the fact that they are made at all illustrates a still less than positive attitude towards the mentally handicapped.

Part Three

The Mainstream of Society: Being a Normal Japanese

3.1 BEING YOUNG: SOCIALISATION, EDUCATION, AND MUTED REBELLION

There is a widespread perception among western visitors to Japan that Japanese children are spoiled and ill-disciplined, especially the boys. Unchecked by their parents, children point and giggle at the funny foreigners. They butt into adult conversations. They queue-jump blatantly at bus-stops. Once on the bus they remain seated while infirm elderly people stand swaying precariously next to them. They are five times less inclined to help around the home than American children. They go to bed late, with young junior high students of 13 or so commonly staying up beyond midnight and even preschoolers often staying up beyond 10 p.m.[1] And they have every latest gadget and toy, with cost seemingly no object.

There are, inevitably, various academic explanations for this parental approach of seemingly letting the children do as they please—of making them the centre of the family, as opposed to the parents occupying that central role as is typical in the United States.[2] Spoiling (*amayakashi*), for example, is simply the assertive aspect of *amae*, the dependence syndrome so much a part of interpersonal relations in Japan. In terms of discipline, many Japanese parents sincerely believe that this should take the form of letting their children behave badly then subsequently making them feel guilty, as opposed to giving them an on-the-spot lesson.[3] Non-intervention is felt to be most effective in encouraging children to establish their own behavioural controls.[4] And obviously, the children are the future. If you don't prioritise them, you risk that future.

However, Japan is not quite such a child-worshipping, child-indulging society as it might seem on the outside. Among other things it has a long tradition of birth control, in which abortion has featured prominently—and continues to do so, since the contraceptive pill is still not easily obtained.[5] Unlike the limit of first trimester in most countries, a foetus can be aborted in Japan as late as 22 weeks—right up until the moment of viability. Before abortion became surgically safe, infanticide was common. This occurred not just in times of famine, but even in times of relative prosperity, with 'additional children traded off for goods and services' so as to improve living standards or status.[6] In recent years, despite the difficulty in obtaining the pill the birth rate in Japan has fallen to the point of national alarm. It is now just 1.4 live births per woman, well below the 4.7 of the 1930s and, most significantly, below the 2.1 needed to maintain population levels. Only 15 per cent of Japan's population is under the age of 15, as opposed to 22 per cent in the United States and 36 per cent in Indonesia.

Factors in this decline include the later age of first marriage for women (now 26.3 years, some three years later than in the 1930s), the increased number of women in the paid workforce (now around 40 per cent of that workforce), and the sheer costs and pressures of raising and especially educating a child. In the Tōkyō metropolitan region, where costs are highest and pressures greatest, the birth rate is a mere 1.1. It is rather ironic that in a country where so many women still endorse the traditional role of a woman as housewife and mother, motherhood is so limited, and actual enjoyment of child-rearing so low.[7]

Even when children have managed to get past the hurdles of abortion and infanticide, they have sometimes met with indifferent or callous treatment, even from their own parents. In history it was very common for senior military-political figures to surrender their children as 'goodwill hostages' to cement precarious alliances. In military clashes the children—even infant children—of defeated leaders were often executed along with their parents.[8] Among poorer families not a few children, even into relatively modern times, were sold into prostitution or similar.[9] Many, of all socio-economic levels, were adopted out—sometimes for the sake of the children, it is true, but often for reasons of economic expediency on the part of the parents, or (in the case of boys) so that some other childless family could acquire an heir to continue its lineage.[10] Further evidence of a less than devoted attitude towards children is seen today in the treatment of orphans in general, and the frequency of parental violence perpetrated on children.[11]

Though children may well seem indulged in Japan, and though the nation as a whole may well respect youth and childishness as aesthetic ideals, life for a Japanese child is certainly not all fun and games. Of course, the vast majority of children nowadays are not killed off in early infancy, nor sold into prostitution or other forms of child-labour, nor used as pawns or adopted out. They do have parents who love them and treat them as more than mere economic or political considerations. However, one major component of their childhood is education. The education process gives them skills and knowledge in an academic sense and in a broader sense also helps socialise them, enabling them to interact with others and learn society's values and expectations. It is also a clear illustration of the reality that life for children in Japan can be extremely demanding and constraining.

Education in Japan, as in most countries, is one way of improving social and material status. It has often been said that Japan is an educational meritocracy. This is an over-statement, for in fact educational attainment has less bearing on eventual socioeconomic levels in Japan than it has in Britain or the United States.[12] Nevertheless, it is important to gain a good education in order to improve one's chances of finding a relatively secure and prestigious position in one of Japan's major corporations or government institutions.

A 'good education' in Japan is one that gives the student an edge over others. Japan has long respected the importance of education, and as one result 96 per cent of all Japanese students progress to senior high school (that is, beyond compulsory levels) and 45 per cent proceed to tertiary levels, making them among the most highly educated young people in the world. High levels of educational attainment are virtually taken for granted. Thus a good education that gives that vital edge is not so much a question of degree of intellectual development or similar, but the more practical one of getting into an educational institution with prestige and the right connections. Connections mean a lot. The situation might even be termed an 'education chain', for elite companies and government offices generally have distinct recruitment preferences for graduates from certain universities, which in turn have links with certain high schools and so on right down to the level of elementary school and even, in some cases, kindergarten. The competition for places in elite institutions, including 'feeder institutions', is intense.

This is not necessarily a healthy state of affairs. Among other things it is very open to abuse and corruption. Many institutions strengthen their links with the next institution up in the chain by highly questionable or even downright illegal methods, such as tailoring their tuition to suit the entrance examination of that institution on the basis of actual specific knowledge of the examination. One way or another they acquire a reputation for successful placement in the next link, a reputation not unhelpful when it comes to setting fees. Money means a lot too. For those seeking to get into such successful institutions, bribes, in the form of donations or gifts, often work when ability fails, while paying for substitutes to sit entrance examinations is another useful ploy.[13]

As far as the family is concerned, life tends to become dominated by the need for children to succeed—success being determined primarily by progress through the chain. For families without the safety margin of 'discretional' money to spend, there is that much more pressure for their children to perform well in examinations. Mothers in particular have in many cases become completely obsessed with the educational progress of their children, especially their sons, becoming known as *kyōiku mama* (education moms). And enormous costs, which can be up to around the equivalent of US$30,000 per year at tertiary level even without the discretional use of money, also seriously affect the home and family.

The children themselves are required in some cases to take entrance 'examinations' even for kindergarten.[14] Beyond kindergarten, they are typically obliged to study far harder than their western counterparts. This is not only at school, which at 243 days per school year is some 30 per cent longer than in most western nations, and still includes most Saturdays despite recent trialling of a once-a-month five-day week system. They also have to study after regular school hours. For something like nine hours over three nights each week many of them—in fact the great majority of them at junior high school level—attend cram schools known as *juku*.[15] At home, they are often still up studying after midnight—or being spoiled by being allowed to stay up late, depending on your point of view. The pace gets even hotter. There is a well-known saying among high school students that '4 pass, 5 fail': the numbers refer to hours of sleep per night. In vacations, too, students receive more schoolwork than in the west.[16] Some Japanese educators themselves describe the situation as 'sweat-shop education'.

In many cases students are under pressure to succeed not only from their parents and teachers but also, as the result of internalisation, from within themselves. Among other things, this leads students to feel a high degree of dissatisfaction with their own ability and performance and a nagging sense of letting their parents and teachers down.[17] In short, school is not a happy and positive place for them.[18]

A key factor in all this is the emphasis on examinations, which dominate school life. Various terms such as 'examination hell' (*shiken jigoku* or *nyūshi jigoku*) or 'exam war' (*juken sensō*) reveal students' feelings about them. Ironically, though now an integral part of the education process in Japan, examinations are not a traditional part of that process. Historically, when Japan was enthusiastically adopting and adapting Chinese practices in the seventh and eighth centuries, it specifically did not adopt the Chinese practice of using examinations to determine bureaucratic appointments. It preferred instead the less potentially disruptive method of appointing bureaucrats on the basis of birth into the right family. Though examinations did start to appear for appointment to high office in the late Tokugawa period, it was only really in the Meiji period that they became systematically implemented into the education process. Moreover, even then this was in no small part due to the advice of an American educationist, David Murray.[19]

It may seem surprising that a nation like Japan, that greatly values order and stability and prefers to channel achievement into approved forms, could give such weight to examinations. These clearly have the potential to cause disruption if an otherwise unsuitable candidate manages to score highly. However, there are a number of safeguards. One is that successful progression through the chain, especially from junior high school to senior high school, is dependent not only on examinations but also on a confidential report from the teachers, known as a *naishinsho* ('personal report').[20] The *naishinsho* report covers character and behaviour as well as academic matters, and despite its importance it is not normally available to either the student or parents. A student with good marks but a poor report will not find doors being opened readily, and it thus becomes a very effective hidden means of control—an 'invisible whip',[21] in the words of one Japanese professor of education.

Another major safeguard is that the very nature of examinations in Japan, along with the nature of tuition, reinforces orthodoxy and discourages originality. The examinations are wherever possible multiple choice, leaving no room for critical analysis or nuances of interpretation on the part of the examinee.[22] Success in an examination is thus within controlled parameters.

Though there are some exceptions,[23] tuition accordingly emphasises rote learning of data, and does not encourage independent, creative, or analytical thinking. Thus, although it is widely known that by international standards Japanese students excel in certain fields, such as mathematics, many western commentators have serious reservations about the nature of education there. One has remarked:

> Exam-oriented Japanese students become virtual information junkies, drinking in as many facts as possible. They have to listen well and to think quickly, but not to express their ideas. Neither speaking nor writing is encouraged. Speculation, controversy, and interpretive relativism do not enter the classroom. Thought is weighted in favor of memory and objective problem solving with little official curricular interest in creativity.[24]

Moreover, the material taught is under strong central control by the Ministry of Education, which vets textbooks and permits only a small number, duly approved, to be used. Authors have little or no chance to comment on decisions or changes imposed by the Ministry's reviewers. The Ministry also exerts strong control over the rate of progress through the texts, meaning that on any given day throughout the nation school students at a given level will generally be learning more or less the same data from the same texts.

This strong central control has caused considerable controversy, particularly in the matter of modern history texts where Japanese acts of wartime aggression have been toned down or even entirely omitted.[25] Though some curbs have recently been placed on government censorship, young Japanese in general still have a very poor understanding of this crucial phase of their nation's history. Remarkably, there are even some tertiary students who do not know that the Pacific War ever took place, let alone that Japan lost it.[26]

Though such extreme ignorance is exceptional, it does suggest that the spirit of academic enquiry does not necessarily improve at tertiary level. Indeed, the generally poor quality of university teaching in Japan—with the exception of certain areas such as engineering and professional training—is another object of widespread criticism by westerners, and even in some cases by the students themselves.[27] For a start, roughly half of Japan's 1,100 or so tertiary institutions are junior colleges (*tanki daigaku*, or 'short-term universities') offering just two-year programmes, as opposed to the four-year programmes of regular universities. The overwhelming majority of students in these junior colleges are women, and the academic standards are generally questionable. Even at regular universities, programmes are hardly challenging, with an overall graduation rate of 95 per cent. Some courses do not even require a single book to be read.[28] In short, a student's time at university is seen as a sort of moratorium, an interval or 'playtime' of relative freedom and ease between the intense pressure of getting into the right institution and the drudgery of taking one's place in the workforce.

Only 5 per cent of students go on to postgraduate work in an educational institution, meaning that most research at this level is done 'in house' at companies. The ramifications of this for the advancement of knowledge are quite serious, for companies obviously pay more attention to applied knowledge than to pure knowledge. This is one reason why, for example, Japan has proportionately more 'reverse engineers' than most nations.[29] But Japanese companies—at least until very recently—have generally seemed to prefer it that way, for they are able to guide the knowledge and development of recruits to best suit the company, rather than taking on people with already fixed and advanced ideas of their own.[30] Companies clearly benefit from having recruits who combine a relatively untapped intellectual potential with a demonstrated ability to uncritically digest and regurgitate selected data.

The same recruits also usually possess a conformist and obedient personality, for this is another consequence of the education system. In addition to the conformity that necessarily follows from learning the same material from the same books at the same rate, Japanese school children are expected to conform in all manner of ways. Except in *juku*, there is a general lack of streaming, all students having to adjust as best they can to the level of the group. Beyond primary, they must wear uniforms, in some cases even when out of school on activities such as fishing trips. Moreover, they are subject to numerous rules and regulations often of a very pedantic nature, almost 'army-style' in that they sometimes seem to be just rules for the sake of rules. For example, there are regular inspections, at junior high school level in particular, to ensure that hair is of an appropriate length and style, that trousers are properly creased, and that skirts are of the right length and with the right number of pleats. Some schools even have a set procedure for asking questions, with arms having to be raised to a set angle in a set direction, and set phraseology used.[31]

Particularly effective in enforcing conformity is the fact that obedience to these school rules is not always directly monitored by the teachers themselves, but often by a so-called 'lifestyle committee' made up of students themselves. These committee members wait at the school gates each morning to check on arrivals, and any irregularity is duly reported and recorded in a diary carried by each student.[32] Such peer pressure is a powerful force, and is also used in teaching. For example, in elementary school, the teacher will not allow activities to commence until all students are properly attentive and ready. This also happens in the west. However, unlike the case in the west, the teacher in Japan will not necessarily directly rebuke any recalcitrant individual, but will often simply wait until the other students become irritated at the delay and chastise the 'problem student' themselves.[33]

The student is encouraged to be part of the group and do as the group does rather than stand out as an individual. This is further enforced at home in matters such as disciplining children either by making them feel guilty for letting others down (usually the mother), or by threatening them with not being let into the house. This is the opposite of the general western practice of threatening children with not being let *out*.[34] It also reflects the general approach to child-rearing in Japan. Whereas western children are generally encouraged to become assertive, exploratory, and independent, Japanese children are encouraged to become passive, quiescent, mindful of others, and dependent, or more exactly interdependent.[35]

One extreme form of peer enforcement of conformity is bullying (*ijime*). Bullying, along with the broad issue of intimidation and violence in the classroom, has been quite widely publicised in recent years, though it has always been present and is still less of a problem than in the United States.[36] However, patterns of bullying differ between the two nations. In the United States it usually involves confrontations between gangs, or one individual bully picking on a weaker individual. This is often for material gain, but can also involve frustration and jealousy, particularly against the class 'nerd', teacher's pet who is all brains and no muscle. In Japan, by contrast, there is little or no inter-gang fighting, or bullying for material gain, or picking on the smart kids. Bullying is centred rather on a group picking on some individual who, in some way other than high achievement, stands out from the rest, such as a returnee. Moreover, the teachers themselves will sometimes also join that group in picking on the unfortunate individual.[37]

Thus in one form or another youngsters in Japan are placed under a great deal of pressure to conform. Not unnaturally, some of them react against this—though not perhaps as many as westerners might expect. At the extreme end of the spectrum of reaction is suicide. Every year there are a dozen or so cases specifically attributable to the pressure of examinations or to bullying, usually with poignant notes left by the victim allowing no room for doubt. However, these receive disproportionate coverage in the media, giving the impression they are far more common than in reality. Similarly the overall frequency of child and youth suicides in the nation, though not especially low, has been exaggerated.[38]

Certain other forms of reaction, however, seem to be on the increase and are a cause of some concern to authorities. These include cutting school or even in some cases 'dropping out',[39] turning to drugs and alcohol,[40] violence,[41] and doing things 'for kicks' or for some trivial reason (including sex for pocket money).[42] But few youths actually end up with criminal records. Though the increase in drug abuse and violent crime are particular concerns, overall juvenile crime should be put in context. Juvenile crime rates have remained fairly stable in postwar times, and in fact have been coming down slightly in the last ten years or so. Only 12.2 out of every 1,000 juveniles were arrested in 1995, compared with the peak of 17.2 in 1983 and the low of 6.7 in 1955.[43]

Displays of deliberately outrageous non-conformist behaviour are also quite common. However, such behaviour is usually selectively outrageous, sufficient to send a protest message of defiance to teachers, parents, and other elders and figures of authority but not sufficient to incur peer disdain or serious and permanent marginalisation by mainstream society. Typically it involves such statements as orange-dyed hair, body-piercing, or 'way out' clothes. Paradoxically, some of this 'non-conformist' behaviour is patently conformist, but to a different set of norms. This is seen in the well-known groups of 'far out' teenagers who have traditionally gathered on Sundays at Tōkyō's Harajuku. Dressed in their uniform of dyed hair and ultra-fashionable clothes, they perform their state-of-the-art dances, supposedly expressive of their individuality but more often than not performed in a group, all carefully choreographed and co-ordinated by a whistle.[44]

In other words, in this and similar cases the youth who appears to eschew the 'system' is not a true free-wheeling rebel who has rejected all authority and constraints, but one who has simply—and almost always temporarily—chosen an alternative set of norms to follow. This is, of course, typical of many youths around the world, such as members of teen-sets or gangs who like to believe they are bucking the system when in fact they are simply replacing one code with another. But again, Japan is distinctive in the matter of degree. Few countries can present the sort of groupist expression of youthful individuality or conformist non-conformity seen at Harajuku. It is, at best, a muted rebellion against the norms of society. Japanese youngsters may well idolise James Dean, the tragic and youthful rebel without a cause, who is perhaps more popular in Japan than anywhere else in the world. However, at least nowadays,[45] they rarely become real rebels themselves—even though they may be felt to have more of a cause than James Dean did.

The weakness of really anti-social sentiment and behaviour is also seen in the virtual absence of vandalism. This is aided by the practice of socialising students into taking responsibility for cleaning their own schools, as well as becoming involved in the preparation of school meals and other acts that develop a bond between them and their school. Thus, they come to see the school as their own property and responsibility rather than as a symbol of the state and authority, and this attitude spreads to public buildings in general. To the Japanese, to damage public buildings is to damage their own property, for they realise that they themselves are the public. They prefer to make their protests in other, less socially destructive ways. And in the vast major- ity of cases, once the harmless protests are made, they eventually settle down to life as a normal conformist adult.

However, despite this general ultimate conformism, there are nevertheless concerns about deep-seated youth attitudes over the last few decades, attitudes which by traditional standards have not been helpful to society. They threaten to continue, albeit further muted, into adult life, where they would be even less helpful. As many western and Japanese observers alike have commented,[46] in recent years—essentially since Japan's achievement of economic super- power status around 1970—young people in Japan have shown a significant decrease in their commitment to serving society, indeed to anything serious. Instead they have shown a shallow form of egoism dominated by trivia, instant gratification, and materialism. In general, they have become characterised by a dissatisfaction towards the state and society as a whole, yet at the same time a reluctance to do anything about it. As a result they merely withdraw into themselves and end up apathetic, relatively complacent with their own personal lot in life. Apathy and self-centred trivial gratification seem to be key characteristics of present-day Japanese youth.

In a twelve-nation survey of 18–24-year-olds in 1988,[47] Japanese came bottom with regard to willingness to sacrifice personal interests for the sake of society (a mere 5 per cent, as opposed to a majority in Singapore, China, South Korea, and the United States). The Japanese came first with regard to 'getting rich' as their main goal in life (39 per cent, as opposed to a mere 5 per cent among young

Swedes). A domestic survey of 15–23-year-olds three years later found that less than 2 per cent of respondents were prepared to make major personal sacrifices to bring about a better society.[48]

To some extent this may perhaps be a reflection of worldwide postmodernism, though clearly it would not appear to have affected the youth of other nations to the same extent. Postmodernism has seen a general reaction against compulsion and a greater emphasis on choice and leisure, along with personal rights, a more accepting attitude towards consumerism and materialism, and a certain playfulness that looks negatively upon anything too serious. However, the trend seems especially noticeable among young Japanese. They have the highest rate of comic readership in the world, for example. Their trivial materialism is shown in novels such as the best-selling *Nantonaku Kurisutaru* (Sort of Crystal), written in 1981 by the young student Tanaka Yasuo and noted for its citing of some 400 desirable brand names.[49] Even during the post-bubble recession of the 1990s some youths have been prepared to pay a staggering price equivalent to US$4,000 [sic: four thousand US dollars] for the 'right' pair of jeans.[50] Trivial gratification reached a new extreme in the mid 1990s craze of *tamagotchi*, a key-ring computer game based on raising an infant pet to maturity.[51] The craze saw thousands of youths queuing overnight outside toy-stores. It even spread overseas—perhaps indeed a sign of the times—though it was soon banned in many countries as too distractive, and the youth in other countries anyway tired of it more quickly.

It might be argued that if the declining commitment of youth was an assertive form of selfishness then that would at least be something positive, something that might be able to be directed towards more desirable and constructive ends. However, it seems to be, to a large extent, a decline of any real drive at all. On the one hand young Japanese react against the 'system' but on the other hand they seem to lack any drive to do anything substantial to change it. One social psychologist has observed that they now have a 'passive reliance on the system', and that, in a projected form of *amae*-style dependence, they even view 'the system as mother'.[52]

Indeed, it is not just drive which is lacking, but in some cases even any obvious sense of real values. Among some young people there is even a discernible sense of emptiness bordering on nihilism. This is seen for example in the great popularity of the television (and film) cartoon series *Evangelion*, first aired in late 1995. The hero of this rather otherworldly cartoon is a 14-year-old boy called Ikari, who fights unspecified and mysterious enemies in a futuristic Tōkyō with the help of a humanoid robot called Eva. He is described as 'feeling a sense of emptiness', and 'repeatedly asks himself why he has to fight and what he is living for'.[53]

One Japanese sociologist has categorised the nation's youth into three main types: the 'street' group who enjoy fads and fashions; the increasingly withdrawn, 'stay-at-home' type equivalent to the western 'computer nerd' (known as *otaku*); and the 'goodies' who try to please their parents and do the expected thing.[54] The *otaku* and the 'goodies' are both attracted to *Evangelion*, even well into their twenties. The involvement of the goodies is particularly worrying to authorities, for they now seem to be starting to question why exactly they are trying to live up to their parents' values.

The increasing softness and 'wishy-washiness' of young people even seems to be reflected in their declining physical abilities, another source of concern. A recent Ministry of Education survey of 10–18-year-olds showed a significant decrease in physical strength, in the order of 5–10 per cent relative to ten years ago, across all ages within that range.[55] This physical decline has been masked somewhat by the increased success of Japanese in international sporting events, but these successful athletes appear to be the exceptions that prove the rule.

Some of the worrying attitudes among the nation's young people, such as a weakening work ethic, seem to be reflections of the times, and affect most countries for better or for worse. However, many of the problems among its youth are of Japan's own making. Enforcement of unthinking obedience and conformity may have helped the nation in earlier times, such as when it was rebuilding after the war, but it is not necessarily suited to the present age. In particular, unlike earlier generations Japan's young nowadays are inevitably exposed to international influences, and cannot avoid comparing their lot in life with that of youngsters in other countries. It is only natural that they should feel hard done by and constrained. Trivial self-gratification is understandable in a society which denies young individuals more substantial means of self-fulfilment. Following the herd when it comes to the latest fad is also understandable when there is so little scope for more meaningful self-expression. Passivity and apathy are understandable when young people are dissatisfied but not encouraged to think and act for themselves. Obsession with getting rich—even when materially already well-off—is understandable in a society so dominated by matters economic.

As early as 1984 there was official recognition of the problems in Japan's education system and of the need to produce young people more attuned to the present times. It became official policy that young people should be given opportunities to fulfil themselves as individuals, to exercise creativity and critical judgement, and to enjoy a better balance between study and leisure. A National Council on Educational Reform was set up as an advisory body to the prime minister (Nakasone), and promises of reform were made. It affirmed 'the value of individuality' and stated that 'a reformed educational system for the 21st century must uphold principles that place variety before uniformity and freedom before restriction'.[56] In particular, it repeatedly stressed a relaxation of the tight control exercised by the Ministry of Education. However, it produced no specific blueprint, and in practice little changed, at least not through government reform to the system itself (though there has been some limited trialling of a five-day school week as opposed to the traditional six).

Upon his election to the Prime Minister's office in 1996 Hashimoto Ryūtarō promised to treat educational reform as one of his top priorities. In line with this, in 1997 a new advisory panel to the Education Ministry made proposals for reform that it felt would lead to greater flexibility and greater scope for individuality.[57] Among other things the panel recommended scrapping the distinction between junior and senior high schools to make a merged six-year high school system, with the aim of lessening the pressure of examinations. It remains to be seen how the panel's recommendations will be acted upon and how effective they will be.

Regardless of government action or inaction, there are two factors of social change which should lead to real change in education. The first is the recent change in corporate culture. To a large extent this is a result of the bursting of Japan's economic bubble in the early 1990s, causing a recession which among other things has led to the dismissal of managers who once believed they were secure for life. The ideal of 'lifetime employment' has been seriously eroded, and there is now increasing flexibility in employment, in the attitudes and practices of both employers and employees. This will mean new options for young people to consider as careers, and there will inevitably be a flow-down effect on education. In fact, even before the bubble burst employers were anyway starting to seek a new type of 'creative and independent minded' employee, with graduates from top private universities such as Keiō and Waseda starting to become more in demand than those from traditional straitlaced public universities such as Tōkyō and Kyōto.[58]

The second factor is internationalisation, a worldwide trend in which Japan has, despite a seeming reluctance in some quarters, necessarily become involved. Over the last decade or so there have been increasing numbers of foreign students and other young people in Japan[59] as well as of Japanese young people studying or travelling overseas, as a result of university exchange agreements, working holiday visas, fathers working overseas, increased tourism, and so on. The fact that increasing numbers of foreigners are now teaching in Japanese educational institutions, and even of late occupying relatively senior positions in public universities (though the topmost positions are still usually denied them), suggests that in the not too distant future there may indeed be some degree of reform in the education system.

Thus, the youth of Japan present some concern for their elders and for the government. On the other hand, many a nation's leaders would wish they had Japan's problems. For all their shortcomings Japanese youngsters are in the main literate, numerate, obedient, polite, deferential to authority, and reasonably diligent and responsible. They do not regularly ambush police cars and set fire to them, as in Britain, or carry guns in their lunchboxes, as in the United States, or burn down their schools, as in New Zealand. And the youngsters themselves, despite obvious indications of unhappiness, still seem to enjoy youth more than adult life, as seen in numerous surveys indicating a widespread 'Peter Pan' wish not to grow up.[60] As one writer put it, 'The despair about growing up, and the hostility to the adult world, are remarkable for their intensity.'[61]

To better understand life from the perspective of Japanese youth, it is therefore also clearly important to consider what it is about adulthood that seems so unattractive to them.

3.2 BEING ADULT: SOCIAL RESPONSIBILITY, WORK, AND FAMILIES

Many countries seem to associate adulthood quite strongly with biological maturity and/or legal rights. These aspects are not ignored in Japan. The legal age of adulthood is 20, which is also seen as the peak of physical prowess.[62] However, for the Japanese, what matters most about adulthood is social maturity. A successful adult is obviously a product of a successful upbringing, and in Japan's case this means a person who has learned to be aware of their role in society and to relate in the socially prescribed way to others. Unlike the case in the west, where an adult is often measured by his or her independence, in Japan the reverse tends to be true. As one anthropologist has written, 'characteristics which make an American mature are precisely the same as those which are described as immature in Japan'.[63]

An adult who is too independent is likely to be considered *wagamama* (childishly selfish) and something of a social liability. Selfishness has strong connotations of immaturity, for a mature person is one who has learned to relate to others not only in the proper prescribed form but also with an underlying attitude of tolerance and 'give and take' (*yuzuriai*). *Yuzuriai* is a sort of reciprocal dependence, a flexible and practical 'back-up' lubricant in social relations for cases where, for whatever reason, the prescribed ideal form cannot be perfectly followed. Of course mature adults are at times going to feel hard done by, but they are expected at such times to show *gaman* (endurance), which is another measure of maturity and is in many regards the opposite of being *wagamama*.

The association between maturity and social responsibility is reflected in the term *shakaijin* ('social person'). It is used of a person who has taken their proper place in society and does the expected thing, especially one who contributes to society through being a productive worker. It is not necessarily the same as the legally defined adult, the *seijin* ('fully grown person'). For example, a postgraduate student in their late twenties may not be thought of as a *shakaijin*, even though they are a *seijin*, whereas an 18-year-old employee may be considered a *shakaijin* even though they are not yet a *seijin*.

The term *shakaijin* also reflects the male orientation of Japanese society. It is rarely used of women, though the same basic concept and definition of maturity—taking one's proper place in society and contributing to it through dutifully carrying out one's expected role—would apply to women too. As a result of this focus on the male, the work-contribution expected of a *shakaijin* has come to mean in particular paid work, moreover on a regular full-time career basis. In that sense, it could argued that the *shakaijin* is also a *keizaijin* ('economic person'). This is particularly true in postwar times, but even before the war, according to one economist of the day, 'the individual's worth consisted only in being an instrument of national growth'.[64]

The Japanese concept of the *shakaijin* contrasts markedly with the English-speaking world, which appears to have no equivalent term.

The word 'adult' is etymologically similar to *seijin* and simply means 'grown up' (in a clinical sense). Terms such as 'social stalwart' and 'bastion/pillar of society' are reserved for people who are exceptional in some way or other, and moreover they are by no means associated with employment. The term 'breadwinner', on the other hand, has connotations of mechanistic toil to support a family, and does not have quite the same sense of respected maturity among society at large. Perhaps the closest is the awkward phrase 'a full-fledged member of society' (the term given in Kenkyūsha's *New Japanese-English Dictionary*), though even this is not exact as an equivalent for it does not highlight the work element.

Although it might seem a product of Confucianism, the Japanese concept of *shakaijin* also contrasts with other Confucian countries. Neither China nor Korea uses the term, though they both use essentially the same character-script as in Japan and can understand it.[65] If anything, these two Asian nations seem to view adulthood more in western terms of freedoms and rights than in Japanese terms of social contribution. They also, as indeed like any nation, attach various obligations and duties to adulthood, and not just freedoms and rights, but Japan does seem to be quite distinct in its development of the concept of the socially mature and responsible, economically productive *shakaijin*.

Work and family are the two main elements in adult life in any society. In Japan's case, work seems to have been given particular weighting, certainly in modern times. Indeed, it has been claimed by some scholars that the work group is the basic unit of modern Japanese society, not the family.[66] Most societies also make a gender-based division between (income-generating) work and family, with the male primarily taking on the former responsibility and the female primarily the latter. This role division is particularly clear in Japan, at least since industry displaced agriculture as the main form of employment. Whereas in recent decades roles have tended to become rather blurred in many societies, this is not quite so obvious in Japan. Change is unquestionably occurring, but it is slow. As discussed earlier, Japanese women's participation in the paid workforce is still basically an 'M' pattern, with their middle years being devoted to family duties. Despite a number of recent developments, few women follow full-time careers, and few achieve senior work-related responsibilities. Basically, in Japan paid career work is still the male domain, the family is the female's.

It is likely that in the not-too-distant future work practices and role division will change more noticeably. The protracted recession of the

1990s has meant lay-offs and a loss of faith in the company for many employees. The effective collapse of lifetime employment for males has opened up new opportunities for women, as well as career changes for men. Internationalisation and postmodern values are also slowly but inexorably bringing changes, especially to the idea of sacrificing self-interest for the sake of one's work. Nevertheless, traditional attitudes should not be written off lightly. They will continue to influence matters for some years yet.

At the same time, 'tradition' needs putting into context. Traditional attitudes firmly linking the female and the family are very deep-rooted, going back to at least the Tokugawa period in particular. However, the roots of workplace attitudes do not run quite so deep. In fact, there have been a number of myths—or more exactly exaggerations—about traditional Japanese work practices and attitudes. They represent a mix on the one hand of superficial attempts to explain Japan's economic success, and on the other of ideals deliberately promoted by the captains of Japan's industry and politics.

One such exaggeration is that the Japanese are by nature dedicated workers—or in more negative terminology, 'workaholics', a term and image popularised by the same notorious European Communities Commission report of 1979 that labelled their homes 'rabbit hutches'.[67] Supposed evidence was seen in the fact that for much of the postwar period Japanese workers averaged some 300–400 more hours per year than typical western workers, and only took around half of their allowed paid holidays (which were anyway far less generous than in the west).[68] Moreover, there was almost no concept of a working week limited to five days.[69] Top Japanese businessmen such as Sony's president Morita Akio also promoted the idea that Japanese were somehow more comfortable with the idea of work than were westerners:

> Japanese attitudes towards work seem to be critically different from American attitudes. Japanese people tend to be much better adjusted to the notion of work, any kind of work, as honorable.[70]

In the 1990s working hours have decreased and vacation take-up rate has increased, partly as a result of cut-backs in business volume through the post-bubble recession, and partly as a result of a declining work ethic. However, the idea of Japanese being by nature workaholics has persisted thanks to the practice of so-called 'service overtime' (*saabisu zangyō*). 'Service' in Japanised English can also mean, as here, 'voluntary' or 'free'. Service overtime supposedly entails workers voluntarily staying behind at their workplace for a few hours each night, basically to help their company out through the difficult recession by working 'off the record' for no pay, but also because they just love to work. Anecdotal evidence suggests that up to three times more overtime is worked in the form of 'service' than overtime that is actually recorded and compensated.[71]

Of course, there are employees in Japan, as in any country, who genuinely do wish to help out their company, if only in some cases out of a pragmatic realisation that if the company goes under then so do the employees (a sense of 'shared fate' that does seem to be genuinely strong in Japan). There are also undoubtedly some genuine work-aholics, though in the west such people are usually viewed as suffering from some form of pathological condition such as obsessiveness or hyperactivity. It is also true, as many unemployed or incapacitated persons will confirm, that work is a significant measure of genuine self-esteem (as well as social esteem) and can often in itself be satis-fying. However, it would be naive in the extreme to assume that service overtime—or working on the weekend or declining a holiday—were purely manifestations of such internal drives on the part of the employee, and had nothing to do with external pressures placed upon them by the company.

The issue is a complex one because external pressures, if strong enough and long enough, can become internalised. If employees are constantly told that Japanese are dedicated workers and dedicated workers put in unpaid overtime, then they can end up feeling inade-quate and abnormal unless they comply. The distinction between external and internal pressure, between shame and guilt, becomes blurred.

In actual fact, many westerners who have worked in Japanese companies are of the view that the workload itself is not usually that great.[72] Rather, it is a question of simply being there, putting in the hours, working slowly but steadily as in a marathon not a sprint, and always being at the company's beck and call, even if it means a stint of a couple of years on special duties in the provinces, away from one's family.[73] 'Being on call' also involves what at first glance appears to be a leisure activity, spending the evening—either before or after the service overtime—eating and drinking with colleagues.[74] Just like the practice of starting each day by singing the company song, it all serves to strengthen the bond between company and employee, just as do other 'leisure' or 'recreational' activities (sports events, outings, and so forth) organised by the company.

In recent years, partly as a result of critical questions asked by westerners, Japanese workers themselves have started to question the extent to which they are expected to work—or more exactly to offer themselves as servants of the company. So long as the company provided security the Japanese workforce tended to be relatively accepting of company demands, though even during the 1980s the issue of *karōshi* ('death by overwork') was on every worker's mind. Since the lay-offs during the recession of the 1990s workers' attitudes have become more cynical. There is an increasingly prevailing view that they have been expected to work longer than they really want or consider reasonable.[75]

Moreover, they are by no means happy in their work, and for that matter were already less than happy even when security was on offer. In fact, comparative surveys suggest that the Japanese are barely half as happy as westerners in their work.[76] This suggests not only a negativity towards company demands beneath their outward acceptance, but also an attitude not readily compatible with workaholics or a people who are exceptionally well 'adjusted to the notion of any kind of work as honourable'.

Research on basic attitudes to work from other angles, such as the terminology associated with work and leisure, and examination of historical practices, also supports the view that the Japanese are not workaholics by nature. In early Japan work was seen as *ke* (mundane), which had negative connotations, rather than as *hare* (bright), which was associated with leisure and pleasure.[77] And in 604, when Japan's first constitution was drawn up, it was necessary to admonish officials for their tardiness by actually incorporating the need for punctuality into the constitution itself.[78] Japan's history reveals numerous other illustrations of a less than instinctively dedicated attitude towards work.

It seems most likely that the ideology of some sort of special Japanese diligence was fostered during the Meiji period, when Japan was attempting to modernise and industrialise.[79] This entailed making maximum use of its only major natural asset, its people, by developing and harnessing their energies.[80] Nationalistic sentiment was also mixed in, so that working hard became synonymous with making Japan a major world power. A shirker was disloyal not only to his employer but also to his nation, unworthy to be a Japanese. It was a process repeated after World War Two. In both cases it was unquestionably successful, though one has to ask at what cost. Certainly, even as early as the 1970s, by which stage Japan had achieved superpower status, some Japanese people were starting to question the cost. Some were already feeling that they had done enough, and the *mai-hōmu taipu* ('I value my home' type) started to appear alongside the once ubiquitous *mōretsu-gata* (fiercely determined type). The trend became even more pronounced in the 1980s and especially the 1990s, further evidence that the Japanese cannot simply be stereotyped as naturally dedicated workers.

However, this does not mean that the Japanese are a work-shy people. Indeed, despite historical examples and recent trends that show the limits of their dedication to work, they still display a work ethic and seriousness of commitment that would be the envy of many governments. Though the work ethic has undoubtedly declined somewhat relative to the immediate postwar period, hard work is still genuinely respected, and the shirker viewed with contempt. It is simply that the seeming enthusiasm with which the Japanese approach work has been over-simplified and exaggerated. They work hard, or perhaps more exactly long, and they take their work seriously, but they are not workaholics by nature. They like to see a task through, and will *ganbaru* ('stick at it') quite tenaciously till the job is done, but they do not leap for joy each morning at the prospect of a hard day's work ahead.

The idea of being a committed employee, a worker who loyally serves his company and nation in the expectation that he will receive lifelong security in return, leads on to another major exaggeration about Japanese work practices, that of the so-called 'lifetime employment system' (*shūshin koyō-sei*). A concomitant to this is the 'seniority system' (*nenkō-sei*), according to which promotion and pay increases are based primarily upon length of service (that is, loyalty), as opposed to specific ability. In an interesting blurring of work and family, the company is ideally portrayed as a happy caring family, the bosses its parents, the workers its children. The company family's care for its children subsumes their real families. It provides houses, assistance with education, various other social and domestic benefits, and even in some cases company graves.[81] A family is, after all, supposed to be a cradle-to-grave affair.

At the height of Japan's economic success in the 1970s and 1980s voluminous literature was produced extolling the benefits of this lifetime employment system and the key role it was seen as playing in Japan's postwar economic 'miracle'. Much of it was by Americans lamenting their own nation's economic performance and growing

social problems. Much was also produced by Japanese commentators—particularly academics who had little actual experience of life
as a company employee—seeking in self-congratulatory fashion to
explain exactly why Japan was so successful. These were mostly
writers in the genre of *Nihonjinron* ('theories about the Japanese').

A myth was soon generated that this lifelong familial care of
employer towards employee was a part of Japanese tradition from
time immemorial, and that all Japanese workers were treated in such
a spirit of benign if demanding paternalism. Seen among other things
as the key to harmonious industrial relations, the lifetime employment system became linked by *Nihonjinron* writers to claimed
Japanese instincts for harmony, consensus, self-sacrifice, familial
groupism, commitment, long-term orientation, and so forth, instincts
that supposedly made the Japanese unique in the world. Japanese
management practices, which were seen as largely deriving from the
lifetime employment system,[82] became models for the world to
emulate, although the more cautious advocates did draw attention to
the need to take cultural differences into account.[83]

Undoubtedly, for many Japanese employers and employees alike,
lifetime employment is a sincerely aspired-to ideal, and for a while it
was actually put into practice for a significant section of the workforce. Among other things, it has been an ideal underlying the
continuing Japanese preference to reduce pay and work hours in a
recession rather than number of personnel—which is one reason why
unemployment has been lower in Japan than in most countries. It is
also true that there does seem to be a genuine Japanese preference
for workers to perform as a 'family-style' group rather than as discrete
individuals, as a united community rather than a mere assemblage of
persons. And, while any employer anywhere in the world would naturally rather have harmony than conflict among the workforce, it may
well be true that the Japanese ability to work in groups is more effective, and the workplace less characterised by conflict, than in many
nations.

However, it is all a matter of degree rather than absolutes, and the
degree of exaggeration is considerable. Though to some extent historical precedents can be found, such as some of the merchant houses of
the Tokugawa period, lifetime employment as such is hardly a longstanding tradition. In substance, it is largely a modern creation, and
moreover shows some western influence. Security of tenure and
accompanying pseudo-familialism, together with the seniority system,
first appeared on any significant scale in the Meiji period. They were

means of attracting and retaining gangs of roving manual workers, and also young girls for work in textile factories. The policy was helped by a Meiji government survey of companies in the western world, which found that those who adopted such an approach had better employee retention and less labour conflict.[84] It later spread to white-collar workers in some companies. In particular after a series of major labour disputes in the postwar years up to 1960—the absence of conflict in the Japanese workplace being another exaggeration—it became enshrined as an ideal policy for employers to follow, along with the idea of in-house 'enterprise labour unions' as opposed to trade-based unions.[85]

In practice, however, lifetime employment since the war has only ever really applied to employees of major corporations,[86] and even then generally only to salaried males, especially white-collar. Women have almost always been excluded, as well as subcontractors and casual workers. Though precise figures have never been produced, informed estimates as to the percentage of the workforce actually receiving security of employment that might be termed 'lifetime'— even at the peak of Japan's economic success—are generally in the order of 15–20 per cent, with the most generous estimates going to 30 per cent. These employees are known as 'salarymen' (a Japanised English term), and are considered the elite of the workforce.

Those who do not make it to the elite level, such as those who failed to go on to tertiary education or for some other reason ended up in smaller less affluent companies, enjoy less income (sometimes barely half of the salaryman's wage), less security, and fewer privileges in general. To supplement their income they may well end up doing 'cottage work' at home in the evenings, perhaps acting as very low-level subcontractors for some major corporation and producing small parts for later assembly in a factory. Most commentators on Japan's labour issues—Japanese and western alike—tend to ignore such workers. When they do mention them, they seem to assume they are quite happily reconciled to their lot in life. One commentator has likened the situation to a sport in which lesser players just accept that they don't make it into the top team, and give their support to the players who do.[87] However, it is questionable whether their attitude is really so philosophical.

The limited reality of lifetime employment is further seen in the fact that it has generally been restricted to a working lifetime rather than an actual lifetime, though it is true that there are not a few cases where employers have, through pensions, 'golden handshakes', and post-retirement consultancies, given security of income and other benefits to key employees for a genuine lifetime. The definition of a working lifetime is in practice variable, and does not necessarily extend as far as the official retirement age of 60 (at which most state pensions commence). Some employees have found that their company expects them to end that working life as early as their late forties, depending on business conditions and the record of the particular employee.

Also, inevitably, promotions and wage increases have come less and less to be based on seniority. They were never based exclusively on it anyway, but even semi-automatic promotion on the grounds of length of service would mean that some people would end up overpaid in high positions for which they were not competent. That would be bad management and very cost-ineffective. Moreover, in a typical pyramid-shaped company structure, for even a majority—let alone all—of the members of a given cohort of recruits at the base to expect promotion to a given higher level after a given number of years would unrealistically require the pyramid to expand continuously and quite dramatically.[88]

In other words, the lifetime system (at least in conjunction with the seniority system) only works in a period of relatively high speed growth. Japan enjoyed such a period particularly in the 1950s and 1960s, at a growth rate of around 10 per cent per annum, but after the Oil Shock of 1973 this slowed to half that rate, and in the recession of the 1990s to much less than half that again. This has led to increased consideration of actual merit in the matter of promotions, and decreased consideration of seniority. Recent complex technology, especially computers, has also led to an increased need to recognise specific job skills and merit. Indeed, in some cases length of service could even be considered counter-productive.

The onset of the very serious post-bubble recession in the early 1990s brought about a marked increase in the practice of 'shoulder tapping' (*kata-tataki*), a reference to an employee being asked to come and see the boss to discuss the matter of early retirement. As the recession continued, outright dismissals (or substantial demotions) began to occur, even of upper managers with many years' loyal service behind them. In fact, a total of 60,000 managers nationwide were dismissed in the two-year period 1992–3 alone.[89] Among other things, this has led to a huge increase in the number of managers joining rapidly burgeoning independent unions, and in many cases resorting to legal action—Japanese aversion to litigation being yet another exaggeration.[90] Many feel betrayed and are now openly bitter and disillusioned. Though the survivors will outweigh the victims, and their conservative values will probably prevent any sudden revolutionary change, the image of the caring, familial corporation has nevertheless been dealt a major blow.

This does not mean that there have never been, or that there are no longer, any 'worker-friendly' companies. Some have genuinely tried to make their workers happy by introducing more vacations, flexitime, and 'casual dress days' when salarymen are allowed to forgo their business-suits and manual workers their 'team uniform'. Sony, for example, has long been popular among graduates for its 'worker-friendly' practices, though a recent survey showed Mitsubishi the highest-ranking in this regard.[91] However, it does mean that in many cases the degree of employee faith and trust in their company has been greatly diminished. As one corporate commentator recently remarked, 'People are realizing that they can't depend on their company.'[92]

Inevitably, the demise of the lifetime and seniority systems, together with international trends such as increasing specialisation, has also affected such areas as the labour market. At the height of the lifetime employment ideal it was assumed that a salaried employee would remain with the same company for all his working life. Accordingly, there were few opportunities or incentives for a mid-career change to another company. Indeed, anyone who tried to change company—and any companies who took them on—risked being blacklisted. That is now ceasing to be the case. Loyalty is obviously still preferred, but now there are even numerous 'head-hunting' agencies which specifically target mid-career specialists.[93] And whereas new recruits once used to be appointed *en bloc* at a given point in the year, thereby forming a clear cohort, they are now often taken on year-round, in similar fashion to the 'as and when needed' policy common in the west.[94] In other words, the labour market has become much more flexible and western in character.

Job-training has also been affected. Knowing that they could expect to retain their employees long-term, employers have until recently preferred to take on raw undeveloped (male) recruits and make them into company men.[95] Rather than being given specific training from the outset, for many years such recruits would be rotated through various departments and jobs within the company, becoming versatile and acquiring a good knowledge of company affairs in a range of sections before finally settling down in an area in which they particularly excelled. This generalised experience and broad knowledge of their company gave some justification to the seniority system. However, that too has all started to change. Employers cannot assume any more that their employees will stay with them long-term, and as a result they have had to minimise job-rotation. Though some degree of job-rotation is undoubtedly beneficial to both company and employee, the extremes of the traditional system were not suited to the production of specialists, so in an age of increasing specialisation it may be a change for the better.[96]

As the Japanese labour market becomes increasingly similar to the western market, where individuals market themselves on the strength of their special skills and take the best offer without committing themselves for life, it also seems highly likely that Japanese employees will be less and less prepared to allow the company to dominate their lives.[97] Company houses, company loans, marriages arranged by the company, and even graves arranged by the company, should increasingly become a thing of the past, and people should necessarily start taking greater control of their own lives. In other words, the 'company creature' will become much rarer, and concepts of a personal life and a family life will become stronger. Leisure, too, will play an increasingly significant role in people's lives. It seems unlikely that Japan will see again the likes of the employee who, in a vegetoid condition after a stroke attributed to overwork, was able to utter only one word—not his own name, nor that of his wife, but that of his company.[98] Or the employee who is prepared to spend as little as five waking hours per week with his family.[99] Or even eventually the employee who automatically introduces himself in non-work-related situations by first identifying his company (though group identity itself will probably still remain for some considerable time, for it is a deep-rooted tradition).

One does not have to be a Marxist to realise the degree of control and domination that companies have exercised—or at least had the potential to exercise—over individuals, for essentially economic ends. Some have termed it exploitation or dehumanisation or enforced submission.[100] One can clearly see that the 'enterprise union', for example, has effectively prevented workers in any one company from achieving solidarity with those in other companies in support of claims for improved working conditions. The bonus system, which involves about one-third of an employee's remuneration being given in the form of a vague bonus that can be adjusted for various reasons (the employee's performance and attitude as well as business conditions), is clearly able to function as a threat as well as a reward. Similarly the seemingly positive practice of rewarding employees who contribute useful suggestions can be a two-edged sword, for the 'suggestion-box system' also necessarily highlights those employees who do not contribute any suggestions. The job-rotation system, too, can be seen as actually disempowering workers, in that it renders them mere employees of such and such a company rather than capable workers in their own right.

Since corporate culture has been so dominant in modern Japanese society, changes in that culture will necessarily have significant ramifications for Japanese society in general. However, as indicated earlier, many aspects of corporate culture are not necessarily deeply rooted. It is not only the lifetime employment system that is essentially quite modern and even western-influenced. Other 'Japanese' practices adopted and adapted from the west in modern times include, for example, the suggestion-box system and quality control.[101] Japan has clearly been able to implement changes in the workplace in the past, and it can do so again. Indeed, it has already started to do so. As Japanese management practices have fallen from grace, increasing use is being made again of western managerial knowledge. In April 1996 an event occurred that would have been almost unthinkable ten years earlier, when a westerner—the Scot Henry Wallace—was appointed to the top position at the headquarters of one of Japan's major companies, Mazda.[102] And in its business practices in general Japan is now trying to follow western models again, particularly the Big Bang style of deregulation pursued by Britain.[103]

The key question is the extent to which these changes in corporate culture will affect deeper-rooted traditions, such as attitudes towards women and concepts of dependence and group-based identity. There will certainly be significantly more scope for personal freedom and the development of a more western-style independence and individualism, but only the Japanese themselves can decide how much they take up these opportunities. History suggests it will be a conservative and cautious change. The Japanese are pragmatists and can certainly change fast and quite dramatically when they absolutely have to, at certain levels, but at the same time the security of the established way of doing things has very great appeal to them.

Changes in working life will obviously have a great impact on family life. But they are not the only agents of change. Factors such as urbanisation and the aging of the population also play their part. And as with working life, over-simplifications and exaggerations have confused the picture of family life in Japan.

One major exaggeration has been the tradition of the *ie* ('house'), a form of extended family. Prior to the war the *ie* was a legal entity, transcending the concept of the legal individual (although the property of an *ie* was registered in the name of an individual, its head). It was also often an economic unit, as well as a welfare unit. That is, the head of the *ie* took legal, economic, and social responsibility for all its members. Typically it consisted of the retired head and his wife, current head and his wife, heir (usually the eldest son of the head) and his wife, and the heir's unmarried children and unmarried siblings. That is, it was three- or four-generational, but with only one couple from each of the married generations—a 'stem family' structure. Though the *ie* was organised on vertical generational lines, its head was not usually from the senior generation in terms of simple age, but from the senior working generation, typically in his forties or fifties.

Above all, it was continuity that mattered, and pragmatic means were adopted if necessary to ensure this. In particular, while blood lineage was obviously preferred it was not paramount. The headship normally passed to the eldest son, though if that son was in some way considered unsuitable it was not uncommon for a brother to replace him or for another male to be brought in as an adoptee (*yōshi*), usually through marriage to a daughter of the family. Also, to keep the *ie* at a manageable size, younger siblings of the new head were normally obliged to leave to set up their own *ie* (*bunke*, or branch house), which maintained links to the main house (*honke*) in a network known as *dōzoku* ('same family/clan').

The *ie* has even been used by some Japanese scholars as the basis for a grand theory of a unique Japanese form of civilisation.[104] However, with the exception of military houses and some merchant houses, the *ie* proper—at least as a legal entity—is actually relatively modern. For the population at large it only became formalised as an institution in the Meiji period. It was seen by the government of the day as an effective means of social organisation and control, in keeping with desirable Confucian ethics such as filial piety and with the idea of a family state under a benign father-figure emperor.[105]

Nevertheless, despite the modernity of the formal origins of the *ie* for the general population, it is true that the Japanese have long had a fairly widespread preference for the informal extended family. This is particularly so of rural families, and the fact that Japan maintained an essentially agrarian economy longer than most western nations adds to the relative depth of its extended family 'tradition'.

The *ie* was abolished as a formal legal entity just after the war by the Occupation forces, who saw it as detrimental to the rights of the individual. Of course, the informal pattern of extended families did not disappear overnight, and remained particularly in evidence in the countryside. However, as urbanisation gained pace, the extended family inevitably lost ground to the smaller nuclear or single-member family. More than three-quarters of Japanese people now live in urban areas, and few have space to accommodate their aged parents or siblings, even if they were so inclined.

In fact, even some decades before the war, waves of urbanisation had already effectively weakened the *ie* system. Although those moving to urban areas were still formally registered as members of an *ie*—either as members of a *honke* in their *furusato* ('old country village') or as heads of a new *bunke*—in practice the households started by very many of them were nuclear or single-member. The national census for 1920, for example, revealed that as many as 54 per cent of all households were nuclear.[106] This is not so different from the 59 per cent of families in 1995,[107] as shown in Table 3.1.

Table 3.1 Trends in Downsizing of the Family

	1920(%)	*1995(%)*	*Extent of change*
Nuclear	54	59	× 1.1
Single-member	6	23	× 3.8
Extended	40	18	÷ 2.2
Combined nuclear and single-member	60	82	× 1.4

Given these figures, it is confusing that some commentators state that 'in Japan today, the nuclear family ... is nearly universal'.[108] The confusion is one of definition. A 'nuclear' family is officially defined in Japan as a married couple only, or a married couple with their unmarried children, or a single parent with unmarried children. Technically, single-member households are not nuclear families, though clearly in practice it would seem they are often treated as such.

Although nuclearisation has been exaggerated, it is true that the extended family has declined, and that there is a pronounced trend of 'downsizing' of the family. However, a more significant factor in this downsizing than nuclearisation proper has been the growth of the single-member household. These accounted for just 6 per cent of all households in 1920, but 23 per cent in 1995.[109] That is, the combined percentage of nuclear and single-member families has risen from 60 per cent in 1920 to 82 per cent in 1995. (Again, see Table 3.1.)

As we shall see, reasons underlying the trend towards increased numbers of single-member households include a later average age of marriage, an increase in the number of people not marrying at all, an increase in the divorce rate, an decrease in the number of children (to keep a couple together), and an increase in the number of old people living alone. Though many of these may be small factors in themselves, the cumulative effect is significant. Overall, it is a cause of some concern since it clearly suggests a tendency towards fragmentation, which is very much the opposite of the 'one big happy family' image that Japan has tried to promote of itself.

Not only does the urban family in space-starved Japan find it difficult to accommodate aged parents, so busy has life become for the working generation that they are often unable even to visit those parents. The Obon religious festival in July has tended to become the standard occasion for visiting old parents in the *furusato*, and in that sense once-familial relations with the older generation have become almost ritualised. In some cases the breakdown of these intergenerational family ties has become so extreme that professional actors are hired to play out for aging and unvisited parents the roles of son/daughter, spouse, and grandchildren. One Tōkyō-based company in particular, with the rather strange name of Nihon Kōkasei Honbu (Japan Efficiency Headquarters), has made a reputation for itself in this rent-a-family business. Its fee for a three-hour 'family' visit in 1992 was equivalent to US$1,130 plus transport costs.[110]

Imminent changes in working life should mean in theory that such companies will have dwindling business in the future, since real children and grandchildren will have more time to visit. On the other hand, having the inclination to visit is another matter, and not all sons and daughters are dutiful when it comes to respecting their aged parents. Particularly with the pressures of modern working life Japan has become a society where convenience is paramount, whatever the cost, and that is not something easily dispensed with even if the pressures are eased. The fact that such a business could find clients at all also illustrates deeper-rooted Japanese preferences, such as a willingness to accept the artificial, and the importance given to role-play.

The old practice of arranged marriages (*miai kekkon*) has also declined markedly since the war. Whereas before the war more than two-thirds of marriages were arranged by parents, this proportion is now down to less than a fifth.[111] In their stead, 'love marriages' (*renai kekkon*), which were once considered quite outrageous in some circles and the stuff of romantic novels, have now become the norm.

Here too there is a need to be careful about terminology, and also to perceive things in relative terms. Even in prewar times the degree of 'arrangement' could vary, and few families other than those of the aristocracy would insist on forcing through a marriage for political or economic reasons in a case where the couple themselves were not in the least fond of each other. Similarly, a 'love' marriage could range from the rare one in which a besotted couple defied their parents' wishes and married by elopement, to the far more common one in which a local couple who had known each other as friends since childhood gradually deepened their relationship with careful encouragement from parents who approved the match. In other words, the boundary between 'love marriages' and 'arranged marriages' has always been blurred.

Even though the marriage itself may not be arranged very often nowadays, many couples still meet each other in the first instance through someone else's well-intentioned introduction, often in the workplace. There are still perhaps not quite the same opportunities for individuals in Japan to meet members of the other sex as in many western countries.

The marriage ceremony itself is another example of myth-making about Japanese tradition. Almost all westerners and Japanese alike think of a 'traditional' Japanese wedding as a Shintō ceremony. The traditional (and extremely expensive) *kimono* worn by the bride and the traditional *haori* and *hakama* (short coat and divided skirt) for the male enforce the idea of tradition and antiquity. So too do the Shintō rites of purification, making votive offerings to the gods, and exchanging *sake*. It is all visually impactive and very 'Japanese', and understandably glamorised.

However, the 'traditional Shintō wedding' is in fact quite modern. It is a creation of the late Meiji period, specifically beginning with the wedding of the Crown Prince (later Emperor Taishō) in 1900 and adopted by commoners for the first time in 1902.[112] Clearly, it was part of the nationalist myth-making that took place at this time, a process that involved in particular the promotion of the image of the emperor as a Shintō god and father of the nation. Even so, the majority of weddings prior to the war were not Shintō, but civil affairs. In postwar times, the popularity of Shintō weddings has tended to fluctuate in line with the strength of nationalist sentiment at any given time. The Shintō wedding is also popular for its photogenic nature. It now accounts for slightly more than half of all weddings.

A significant change is seen in recent times in the growing popularity of Christian ceremonies. Around 40 per cent of all couples now have an equally photogenic and even trendier chapel wedding, despite the fact that only around 1 per cent of the population identify themselves as Christian. This is a further example of the importance of situational role playing and external appearance in Japanese society, as well as providing a telling comment on Japanese attitudes towards religion. Some couples, perhaps wanting to 'hedge their bets', even have both a Shintō and Christian ceremony.

More and more Japanese couples are now marrying overseas, partly to save on the enormous expense of a wedding in Japan—averaging 6,570,000 yen (around US$60,000) in 1995[113]—and partly to start their married life with an unforgettable exotic element. Places like New Zealand and Australia seem particularly popular as marriage venues, along with the 'old faithful' Hawaii. This trend, which is expected to involve as many as 10 per cent of all Japanese couples within the next few years, may well have an adverse impact on the number of Shintō weddings.

A further change in marriage patterns is that people are marrying later. In 1950, the average age of first marriage for men was 25.9 years and for women 23.0: in 1995 this had risen to 28.5 years for men and 26.3 for women. In fact, Japanese women now marry later than women in any other nation except Sweden.[114] In 1995, nationwide 67 per cent of men between 25 and 29 years of age, and 48 per cent of women in the same age group, were single.[115] The figure was highest in Tōkyō (76 per cent and 59 per cent respectively), clearly suggesting a link with working careers. In 1950, just 1.5 per cent of both men and women in the 45–50 age group were single, but in 1994 this had risen to 6.7 per cent for men and 4.5 per cent for women.[116] Again, figures were higher still in Tōkyō.

Moreover, more marriages are ending in divorce than in the past. This is in part because since 1947 women have been able to initiate divorce, and in recent decades in particular have become more assertive of their rights, but it is also part of a worldwide trend. In 1970 there were only 0.93 divorces in Japan per 1,000 people, but by 1994 this had risen to 1.57.[117] However, this divorce rate is still far below the 4.6 of the United States, and significantly below the 2.0–3.0 range typical of European countries. Though the children may well be more prioritised in a Japanese marriage than is the case in the United States, and may well keep many more marriages together, their presence is not always a deterrent to separation, for almost two-thirds of divorcing couples in Japan are parents.[118]

Overall, marriage in Japan is still a firmer institution than in many countries—some 98 per cent of Japanese women still marry sooner or later, which is high by world standards[119]—but it is showing significant signs of weakening. The declining birth rate also means that children are less automatically associated with marriage. At the same time, focus on family life is strengthening in proportion to the decline of focus on working life. This trend can be expected to continue. Eventual consequences should include more balanced and flexible roles for husband and wife. There should also be a slight recovery in the birth rate (though not to prewar levels), since parents will have more time to focus on their children, and since women should not be quite so disadvantaged as in the past by taking time out from a career to have children.

On the other hand, a major remaining obstacle is that of the cost—and quality—of living, which among other things is clearly linked to the fact that large numbers of people are crammed into small spaces. Unless Japan decentralises, as many commentators have urged,[120] dense urban conglomerations will continue to adversely affect the quality of life in such matters as stress levels, environment, commuting time and so forth, and accommodation will remain extremely cramped and expensive.[121] This will obviously continue to have an effect on family size, and family life.

3.3   BEING OLD: CONFUCIAN IDEALS AND THE REALITY OF DECREPITUDE

The proportion of old people in today's Japan is a major problem for the government. Japanese society is the fastest 'greying' society on earth, as a result of a combination of the decreasing birth rate and increasing longevity. This is seen clearly in Table 3.2.[122]

The average life expectancy (at birth) has advanced steadily in recent decades. For females, it is now 83.0 years (up from 70.2 in 1960).[123] This is the highest in the world by a significant margin, topping France's 81.8 (up from 73.6 in 1960). For males, it is now 76.6

for males (up from 65.5 in 1960). This is beaten only by Iceland's 77.1 (up from 70.7 in 1960). If both sexes are combined, Japan's has the world's highest overall longevity. Elderly people, usually defined as 65 or older, now account for 16 per cent of the population, as opposed to the 5 per cent mark typical for much of its modern history. The figure is predicted to reach 27 per cent by the year 2025.[124] In the late 1990s the percentage of elderly overtook that of the young for the first time, giving a certain poignancy to the statistics about greying.

Table 3.2 Population Percentages of Young and Old

	% Young (–15)	% Old (65+)
1920	36	5
1930	37	5
1940	37	5
1950	35	5
1960	30	6
1970	24	7
1980	23	9
1990	18	12
1997	15	16
2025	?	27?

At the moment one or two countries, such as Sweden, do have a slightly higher percentage of elderly (around 17 per cent), but their rate of greying is slower than Japan's. Thus, by the year 2025, if predictions are accurate, Japan will have a higher percentage of elderly than any other nation (Sweden being predicted to have around 25 per cent, and most western nations around 20 per cent).

Moreover, within the 65+ elderly category itself, it is the higher age groups who in relative terms are increasing at the fastest rate. For example, currently the 75+ group occupy 40 per cent of the overall elderly range, but this is expected to rise to 57 per cent by 2025. The number of centenarians, though small in absolute terms at less than 10,000, is currently increasing by around 13 per cent each year, which is more than twice the current rate of increase for those in the 65–74 bracket.[125]

The ramifications of this greying are enormous. In cold and clinical economic terms, the ratio of productive workers to non-productive supportees will decrease markedly. In 1980 there were 12.3 working-age people per aged person: by 1995 this had declined to 5.1, and by 2025 it is expected to be only 2.4.[126]

Pensions will also be seriously affected. There are currently two forms of pension (excluding private investment schemes), which together provide universal coverage for all elderly Japanese. The Employees Pension, which is clearly intended for wage-earning employees, was established in embryonic form during the war years but did not really become operational till 1954. It currently provides on average around 200,000 yen per month, and is payable from age 60. The National Pension, set up in 1961 to cover self-employed and others not covered by the Employees Pension, pays only around a third of that amount, and is payable from age 65. Contributors to the Employees Pension Scheme, who have their contributions matched yen for yen by their employers, currently pay 16.5 per cent of their income. This is already a major increase from the mere 3 per cent in 1961, but according to Ministry of Health and Welfare predictions premiums could rise to around 30 per cent of income by 2025.[127]

In more human terms, the fact that it is the most senior age groups that are proportionately increasing the fastest will mean there will be increased percentages of physically and mentally infirm people requiring virtually constant attention and nursing, not merely financial support. Not only will welfare costs rise, there will need to be significant infrastructural changes to cope with this changed demographic profile.

What can the government, and/or employers, do about this situation? As one extreme policy they could, of course, simply abandon any concern for Japan's unproductive old folks. This is not quite so far-fetched as it might seem. In the mid-1980s Japan did in effect attempt to abandon some of its old people physically as well as socially, by exporting them. The idea was known as the Silver Columbia Plan ('silver' being a euphemistic reference to the elderly), and had the backing of the powerful Ministry of Trade and Industry.[128] It entailed packing the elderly off to retirement villages overseas, which the Japanese government undertook to build at its own expense. Targeted countries were those with relatively low populations, notably Australia, and to some extent the whole idea was modelled on German and Dutch retiree villages in Spain. Some in Australia were enthusiastic about the idea. One immigration official, for example, thought it would be good for Australia to tap the experience of retired Japanese employees from high-tech industries. It was also hoped that Japan could send retired doctors to work in the less popular northern parts of the country.

Eventually, however, when the plan became more widely known the Australian public voiced its overall disapproval, indeed outrage. So too did other members of the international community. The plan was dropped. It was replaced in 1989 by the Golden Plan of the Ministry of Health and Welfare, which was much more politically correct and promised to increase welfare facilities for the aged.

It was to be some time before the promises of the Golden Plan began to be implemented, but it is a fact that in very recent years there have been a number of changes—some quite major—carried out in its name. For example, there has been some adjustment of such mechanisms as pension provisions and the 'mandatory' retirement age. In 1994 a bill was passed requiring full pensions under the Employees Pension Scheme to commence at 65 rather than 60, to be phased in through one-year hikes every three years starting from 2001. It is expected that this will mean pension contributions around 2025 will only be in the order of 25 per cent rather than 30 per cent. Since most companies still follow a practice of requiring employees to retire at 60, provision was made for a partial pension to be paid in the years 60–65. Government pressure has also been put on companies to lift the retirement age to 65.

In addition, there are also plans for a public nursing care insurance scheme, and in May 1997 legislation was passed to allow for this.[129] The passage of this legislation was described by one professor of geriatrics as 'epoch-making' in the history of Japan's social welfare, for 'it showed that the ailing elderly should be taken care of by society and not just by individual households, as is traditional in Japan'.[130] Other specialists have echoed this view, welcoming the government's recognition that care for the elderly is a responsibility for the state and not just individual families. Though there are a number of logistical problems in the planned scheme in its current form, and some fine-tuning will be necessary,[131] in substance it is unquestionably indicative of a major change in social policy.

In recent years there has also been an increase in the number of nursing institutions and special hospitals for the aged. However, the 1996 *White Paper on National Life* pointed out that while there are 1.4 million elderly people in need of nursing, the combined capacity of special nursing homes for the aged can only handle about a fifth of that number. In practice, the great majority of elderly in need of nursing currently have to rely on family. More specifically, nursing in the family is carried out overwhelmingly (around 86 per cent of cases) by women—wives, daughters, or daughters-in-law.[132]

This lack of facilities will probably mean that, in the short-term at least, the new public nursing care scheme will usually take the form of nursing in the home, rather than in a specialist facility. There have already been encouraging developments with the appearance of mobile medical teams offering home care, which takes some pressure off the family itself.[133] Home care should be welcomed by most of the elderly, who do not like institutions, yet on the other hand very much hate the prospect of becoming a burden on their families.[134]

Relying on one's family for support, even if a burden to them, might seem a perfectly reasonable expectation in a supposedly Confucianist society such as Japan's, which in theory ought to follow ideals of filial piety and respect for the aged in general. The negative attitude of old people towards having their family look after them may therefore seem surprising. However, the fact is that such ideals are yet another example of exaggeration. In reality, old people in Japan have rarely been fully assured of respect, nor parents assured of piety from their offspring, to the extent that Confucian theory might suggest. The major exception to this would perhaps have been the late Meiji period and subsequent prewar decades, when the government was most earnestly trying to promote the idea of a family state headed by a father-figure emperor to whom filial piety was due, and when certain 'traditions' were exaggerated or even created. Indoctrination of duty was such that real personal feelings were often effectively lost. Early western observers may well have been misled by this.

It is true that more old people in Japan still live with their families than is the case in the west. In fact, a majority do. This is undoubtedly one indication of Confucian duty being carried out in the main. However, there are limits to this. It is possibly truer to say that, despite this widespread obedience to duty, the stronger tradition is not the existence of real respect for the elderly, but a lack of it. In this matter the deep-rooted reverence for the aesthetic ideal of youthful beauty and purity prevails. The elderly are far removed from this ideal, and are much closer to the impurities of decrepitude and death. The imposition of the duty of caring for elderly parents may well have added to the fundamental negativity with which they have been viewed.

There is evidence of strong negative feelings towards the elderly as early as the first heyday of Confucianism in Japan, in the seventh and eighth centuries when the nation was enthusiastically adopting Chinese practices. The leading socially aware poet of the day, Yamanoue Okura (c.660–733), described attitudes towards old people as not so much a case of mere lack of respect, but of downright disrespect:

> ....with staffs at their waists,
> They totter along the road,
> Laughed at here, and hated there.
> This is the way of the world...[135]

There are not a few places in Japan—the most famous being in Nagano Prefecture—with a hill named Obasuteyama, which means literally 'hill for abandoning granny'. Some scholars deny that this practice of *obasute* (abandoning granny) or *oyasute* (abandoning parents) actually happened, but others seem to accept that it did, though very probably not as a matter of course.[136] Obviously, it is unlikely to have happened to those still fit in mind and/or body, but for the more seriously incapacitated, especially in times of hardship, it would be naive to assume there was no such practice. Indeed, the literature of the medieval period makes much reference to the practice of *obasute/oyasute*, particularly in terms of the agony of making such a decision.[137]

It may be that lack of fundamental respect for the elderly has worsened somewhat in modern times, for a number of reasons. Their burgeoning numbers and the consequent greying of society have meant that they have a strong and negative association in people's minds with being the cause of a major social problem. The decline of the extended family and the increasingly cramped accommodation of the modern urban family have made care for the elderly more difficult, and made them seem even more of a burden. In Japan even more than elsewhere, the rapidity of change in technology and lifestyle has meant that the knowledge and wisdom of the elderly— once a major source of potential respect for them—has in many cases become irrelevant or even counter-productive. And rather ironically, another 'tradition' first promoted by the Meiji government, that of the remarkable work-rate of the Japanese, has probably also contributed to declining respect, for over time it has made the relative inefficiency of the elderly stand out. For the males in particular, if they are not productive workers, they risk ceasing to be treated as *shakaijin*. Along with the practical need to supplement their pensions, this is undoubtedly one reason why so many of them make desperate attempts to stay in the workforce in some form or other even well after official retirement—more than a third of men and a sixth of women in the 65 + group.[138]

In recent times, in addition to the Silver Columbia Plan to export the elderly, we have seen how some sons employ actors to visit their aged parents, which at best could be described as filial piety by proxy. Some aged parents, with sons unable or unwilling to fit them into their cramped urban apartment, are dumped in mental asylums or sent off to nursing homes of often questionable standards and intent,[139] though the figures here have also been the subject of exaggeration. Almost 60 per cent of elderly people in Japan still live with their children, which is significantly down on the almost 90 per cent of 1960 but is still a very much higher rate than in the west. A further 23 per cent live in an elderly couple household and 16 per cent live alone.[140] This means that only around 2 per cent live in institutions, at least on any long-term basis.

Thus, typically, the elderly still live with their children but are very conscious of being a burden. That they are generally very unhappy is seen among other things in their very high suicide rate. This is one of the highest in the world and is proportionately much more of a problem than the over-publicised child suicide rate. In 1992 Japan's overall suicide rate, of 17.8 per 100,000 population, was the eighth highest in the world. However, its rate for those in the 65–74 age group was 34.1, which was sixth highest in the world, and for 75 and over was 61.4, which was third highest in the world.[141]

The unhappiness of the elderly is also seen in visits to so-called *pokkuri-dera* ('pop your clogs' temples), which are temples where aged people go to pray for a quick and painless demise.[142] This practice is in fact nothing new, and has been going on for many centuries, but it has become particularly popular in recent years. More than 80 per cent of such temple visitors are women, and temple donations are the second biggest item of 'pocket money' expenditure among elderly women (after presents for grandchildren). Since women live longer than men, and thus have a lonelier old age, their prominence among temple visitors is understandable. Moreover, it also seems that women are more inclined than men to fear becoming a burden, which may reflect male accustomedness to being looked after.

In the end, of course, everyone dies. Before the war the great majority of old people died in their family home, but now, although most still live with their children, they spend their very final days in a hospital or similar institution. This too is understandable, as cancer and heart problems are the biggest causes of death and elderly patients would in most cases be receiving intensive medical treatment immediately prior to their death, as in other countries. Funerals are normally held with Buddhist rites, cremation being followed by various stages of mourning (nowadays effectively one week).[143] According to Shintō beliefs—and most Japanese follow both Buddhist and Shintō practice—death is the ultimate impurity, and the family of the deceased is considered polluted for a period of forty-nine days, during which they are not allowed into a Shintō shrine. Memorial tablets are normally kept for fifty years, after which they are destroyed in the belief that the deceased has now become a *kami*, or ancestor-god. In recent times, however, adherence to both Buddhist and Shintō traditions is weakening.

Life for the elderly, then, is not kind in Japan. They are seen as fundamentally removed from Japan's preferred aesthetic ideals. At a more mundane level, even if they are neither a burden in need of care nor still working, but healthy and financially independent, they still suffer more than most age groups from the infrastructural problems that beset life in Japan. Unlike many elderly in western nations, they cannot expect to spend their days enjoying green parks or recreational facilities such as golf courses or bowling clubs. They cannot potter around in their own car, going for a leisurely drive or a quiet picnic. Even visits from their sons and daughters—hopefully the real ones, and not actors—happen with less frequency than in the west, thanks to all the pressures of working-age life.

The imminent changes in working life, which will also mean changes in family life, together with a greater recognition of leisure, should help make life easier for the elderly. If nothing else, it will mean that their families will have more time to spend with them, and if necessary look after them. However, infrastructural changes still seem a long way off, despite talk about decentralising government and business offices and even relocating the official capital. More likely, some entrepreneur will develop some sort of artificial leisure centre for them, a sort of Disneyland for the elderly. (It is surprising that this has not already happened.) This is not a happy prospect, but, in the near future at least, it is more realistic than major infrastructural change. And even if a miracle happened and appropriate infrastructural changes did take place, it would still take another miracle to change fundamental aesthetic attitudes.

It is little wonder, then, that the young in Japan are reluctant to grow up. Though they hardly enjoy a stress-free life thanks to the pressures of the education system, they are still relatively well off. Life as a working-age adult is very demanding. The next stage of life, for the elderly, though less demanding, is in many ways worse still. All things considered, better to stay young.

3.4 BEING ONESELF: THE INDIVIDUAL IN A 'GROUPIST' SOCIETY

Japan has often been described—especially by the Japanese themselves—as a group-oriented society, in contrast to the individualistic society typical of the west. Though the nature of this 'groupism' is yet another exaggeration, it is true that in the main the Japanese do seem to prefer to belong to a group rather than be freewheeling individuals. Their concept of self-identity includes the group to a greater extent than in the west. And more so than westerners they seem to be uncomfortable on their own, and to need the reassurance of the presence of others, or more exactly others of their kind and particularly intimates such as family and friends.

One scholar has referred to a Japanese 'meta-level group orientedness',[144] meaning that people there are so accustomed to being in a group that if they are not already in one in any given situation, then they will feel impelled to form one. Another has referred to the Japanese concern to relate to others as 'social preoccupation' and treated it as an expression of a basic Japanese anthropocentrism[145]—a prioritisation of human beings in social organisation in contrast to the legalism or rationalism of many societies.

Various explanations have been put forward for this group-orientedness, this prioritisation of relations with others. Most seem to have some merit but to be insufficient in themselves. Japanese themselves usually stress the traditional need for group-based teamwork in the production of rice, their staple crop. However, this overlooks the fact that rice was introduced into Japan later than any other Asian nation, and moreover that other rice-based cultures are not necessarily group-oriented.[146] There is also a theory that Japan's population density has naturally led to groupism as a style of social organisation, for it minimises tensions between individuals. It is true that Japan is one of the most densely populated nations on the planet, and has long been so, but it is also a fact that other densely populated societies are not necessarily groupist.[147] A further theory is that Japan's potentially hazardous natural environment has over time produced in its people a latent sense of insecurity, which is conducive to seeking the security of the group for both psychological and practical reasons. There may be some particular truth in this argument. Group-orientedness is also seen for example in the Maori of New Zealand, which has an extremely similar geo-environment to Japan. On the other hand there are many other hazardous natural environments in which groupism is not seen, including long-settled parts of the United States.

At a deep level, the very concept of the individual self in Japan has been claimed to be muted, with people only finding a sense of existential identity in relationship with others. Whereas the delineation of western individuals from one another has been described by some westerners as 'interpersonal discontinuities', the term *kanjin,* meaning 'contextual person', has been used by some Japanese scholars to describe the Japanese individual.[148] *Kanjin* stands in contrast to *kojin* ('separate person'), a term used to describe the western-style independent individual. *Kojin* does in fact have negative connotations of social immaturity and self-centredness in Japan, and *kojinshugi* (individualism) is by no means seen as desirable. Among other things, this has significant bearing on Japanese perceptions of democracy and individual rights.

According to some Japanese linguists, the Japanese language illustrates the contextual person. One theory has it that the wide range of pronouns used to refer to oneself in the Japanese language is far from being a numeric indication of an obsession with the self, as many westerners might imagine. The pronouns vary according to the person being addressed, showing a flexible and relational concept of the self. This so-called 'other-oriented self-designation' is said to involve a form of conceptual fusing with others in a given situation. Where there are no others, then the self is left vague and undefined. The linguist Suzuki Takao writes:

The Japanese ego may be construed as being in an indefinite state, with its position undetermined, until a specific addressee, a concrete person, appears and is identified by the speaker.... Other-oriented self-designation is, to put it another way, the assimilation of the self, who is the observer, with the other, who is the observed, with no clear distinction being made between the two. It is frequently pointed out that whereas Western culture is based on the distinction between the observer and the observed, in the opposition of the self versus the other, Japanese culture and sentiment show a strong tendency to overcome this distinction by having the self immerse itself in the other.[149]

Such fusing of individuals is also said to be seen in *amae*, Japanese-style dependence in which individuals presume and depend upon others in the same way that a young child does upon its mother. The psychiatrist Doi Takeo, who popularised the theory of *amae*, has referred for example to the 'indivisibility of subject and object, self and others'.[150]

Amae and the contextual person, like so many claims about the Japanese, have been exaggerated by *Nihonjinron* writers and earned a bad press as a result, often being summarily dismissed. However, there does seem to be some merit to the basic argument that in their interpersonal relationships Japanese do have a greater tendency than westerners to 'merge' with others, to be interdependent rather than independent, to take the views of others into account and be less assertive of the self.

In decision-making, for example, there does seem to be a genuine belief that as far as possible the views of the group as a whole should have priority over the views of any one individual. There is a genuine recognition that the group is generally stronger and wiser than any one individual, a genuine acknowledgement that the most effective leader is one who can draw together the members of a group rather than dictatorially impose a decision. This preference for synthesising and adjusting views and arriving at essentially compromise decisions is known as *awase* (literally 'matching up').[151] It has been contrasted with a perceived western preference for *erabi* (selection), which refers to the presentation of a range of distinct views by respective individuals from which one is chosen.

Unfortunately, this too has become unhelpfully exaggerated. Group decisions have been portrayed by some as manifestations of some sort of natural Japanese instinct for harmony and consensus, one that effectively prevents conflict. Such exaggerated claims are easily disproved by evidence throughout history of at times quite serious conflict in Japan.[152] And in Japanese groups, as in groups anywhere in the world, the wishes of senior influential individuals inevitably carry more weight than those of juniors in the group. What appears outwardly to be balanced harmony and consensus is often a case of juniors deferring to seniors. In reality no group could survive for long unless it had some form of authoritative leadership and direction, and Japanese groups are no exception. At times of crisis in particular, Japanese have been prepared to accept quite assertive leadership. However, in general, they prefer that authority to be more subdued, more accommodating.

Recognition of others in a personalised, accommodating way is also seen in the preferred pattern of social exchange in Japan. Social exchange refers to interaction between people in society for the mutual exchange of benefits, as seen in the saying 'you scratch my back, I'll scratch yours'. As many scholars have noted,[153] exchange patterns in western societies tend to be relatively impersonal, explicit, and specific, and often temporary as a result. Specific benefits are exchanged subject to specific conditions, as embodied in the idea of contracts. By contrast, Japanese exchange patterns tend to be personal, implicit, and rather vague, with a long-term orientation. That is, whereas westerners tend to focus on the item that is the object of the transaction, Japanese tend to focus on the people involved in the transaction.[154] They prefer a broad and on-going personal relationship with 'give and take' that can accommodate the particular and possibly changing circumstances of those involved, with human understanding being shown all round.

All these theories about muted individualism and groupist pre-disposition have a certain truth to them. However, they risk over-essentialising matters. In particular, they tend to mask the fact that historically Japan has had many displays of strong individualism and self-interest. Medieval samurai were typically anything but the loyal and selfless servants of their masters that popular legend portrays them as. Though there were some over-romanticised excep-tions, more often than not they looked after 'number one' first, and pragmatically went whichever way the tide of victory was flowing.[155] And medieval warlords such as the twelfth-century Minamoto Yoritomo, who established the shōgunate as a permanent institution, and the three 'national unifiers' of the sixteenth century, Oda Nobunaga, Toyotomi Hideyoshi, and Tokugawa Ieyasu, can as indi-viduals in their own right comfortably be placed alongside western individuals such as Napoleon and Nelson and George Washington. In fact, Oda Nobunaga had such a massive ego that he was convinced of his own status as a deity, built temples where he could be worshipped, and declared his birthday a national holiday. Some historians even term him a 'solipsist' (one who believes that only the self exists).[156]

More likely, as a cogent if simpler explanation of Japanese 'groupism', is that it is in large part the result of political conditioning from the early seventeenth century on. Though there do certainly seem to be factors suggesting a longstanding degree of socio-psychological readiness among the Japanese to seek the company of others, in a manner conducive to groupism, this does not seem to have been strong enough to suppress individualism during the medieval period in particular. This is one main reason why the Tokugawa shōgunate, which became established in a country finally reunified after centuries of chaos and warfare, sought to suppress potentially disruptive self-interest. To maintain social order and facilitate political control, in addition to specific practical measures[157] the Tokugawa implemented a general policy of harsh orthodoxy and enforced conformism. This included peer pressure in the form of group accountability. If one member of a group stepped out of line (moreover a tightly prescribed line), the whole group risked severe punishment. It is easier to control groups than individuals, especially if they are very conformist groups that regulate themselves in fear of dire consequences if they fail to do so.[158]

In Tokugawa Japan, a person other than those in the samurai class could be executed on the spot by a samurai for 'rude' behaviour. The definition of 'rude' behaviour, as articulated by Shōgun Tokugawa Ieyasu himself, was 'acting in an other-than-expected manner'.[159] It is hard to imagine a more effective means of enforcing conformity and suppressing individualistic behaviour.

People's lives were prescribed down to the finest detail. Everyone knew their place, and what was expected of them. At a broad level, mainstream society was divided into four hierarchical classes. In descending order these were warriors/nobles (*shi*), peasants/farmers (*nō*), artisans (*kō*), and merchants (*shō*), and there were subclasses of outcasts beneath these. Movement between the classes was theoretically banned but in practice was not unknown, though it was difficult. At a more detailed level, there were prescriptions for type and place of work and residence for particular classes. At a finer level still, there were prescriptions for the type of clothing that a person of a particular class could wear, the type of present they could give to a child of a particular gender and a particular age, the type of food they could eat, and even where they could build their toilet.[160]

Conformity was particularly enforced in urban areas, most of these being directly under the shōgunate's control. Residents of each street were divided into groups, usually of five families, and the head of each of these neighbourhood associations was responsible for the behaviour of all in the group. If there was any misdeed, both miscreant and head—and in some cases all members of the association—would be punished. In rural areas, in domains under the control of the 250 or so *daimyō* (lords), life was a little easier, but collective responsibility was still maintained. If anyone in a village caused trouble, either the village head or other innocent members of the village could suffer too.

On the other hand, if there was no apparent problem, and the village duly and properly paid its taxes (collectively assessed and gathered), then domain officials rarely bothered about what was going on. In practice this meant that villages could experience quite serious inner conflict, but would not draw the attention of the authorities provided they preserved outward harmony.[161] Similarly villagers could enjoy considerable freedom 'behind the scenes' provided they outwardly paid deference to authority and to expected form. It was a type of lip-service, permitting freedom within limits.[162]

The consequences of this practice of lip-service are still seen today in the important distinction between outer form (*omote*) and inner substance (*ura*), and between what is stated in public (*tatemae*) and what is felt in private (*honne*). To some extent all cultures have a similar duality, but it is particularly marked in Japan, leading some commentators to refer to 'socially sanctioned deceit' and to the 'management of reality'.[163]

Another on-going consequence is the strong distinction between in-group (*uchi*) and out-group (*soto*). Again this is not in itself unique to Japan, but is particularly pronounced there. In the Tokugawa period an outsider could cause serious and indeed fatal trouble. Restrictions on movement meant that an outsider was anyway highly likely to be in trouble with the authorities, and moreover their behavioural potential was unknown to any group they might try to associate with (and which would suffer the consequences of any wrong behaviour). Given that these practical concerns were combined with a deeper spiritual equating of the outside with impurity, it is not surprising that the Japanese learned to be less than welcoming to outsiders.[164]

The rigidity of prescriptions in the Tokugawa period is still visible in the idea that everything has a proper form, known as a *kata* ('form' or 'model'). This is not a simple visual aesthetic: it has become a type of ideal to strive for in almost every aspect of behaviour. It is not the type of ideal that is far removed from everyday life, but an attainable one, a sort of 'functional ideal' that is very much normative. The *kata* has long been standard in the martial arts, but as a result of lifestyles in the Tokugawa period it has become broadened in its application. The basic notion of 'keeping to form' and 'doing the done thing' is found in any society, for it represents a useful means of preserving social order and is naturally encouraged by social elites. In Japan's case, however, once again its society is distinct in the matter of degree. In Japan *kata* even moulds personality. As one Japanese scholar has written:

> The notion of personality is quite different to a Japanese from what it is to a Westerner. Whether he will become an electronics worker, a teacher of English in a high school, or a fish-processing worker on a whaler, the young Japanese studies his assigned role till he perfects it. His worth will be measured by his approximation to the ideal of his type (*the* teacher, *the* electronics worker, *the* fisherman).... Personality is thus not a valued seed to be nurtured into flower, but a bud that must be 'withered' (*kareta*) as soon as it shows itself. At maturity, having been tamed in this way from early childhood, the Japanese 'personality', like an age-old redwood bonsai, ought to be a truly balanced and pleasing form.[165]

We see here not only the prioritisation of the *kata* over free expression, and the prioritisation of the role over the individual, we even see the taming and forced withering of the individual personality.

The metaphoric reference to nature is not coincidental, for the Japanese like to tame nature. They like to tame anything potentially disruptive and threatening, and this can obviously include people. And it is not just the wild and earthy woman who has to be tamed, in her case into the doll-like ideal of the geisha. All people have to be tamed into a non-disruptive, non-threatening form. Naked individuality is a threat, and—since the Tokugawa period at least—it cannot be tolerated. As the popular saying has it, 'The nail that sticks up gets hammered down' (*deru kugi wa utareru*).

This is, in effect, the process of growing up in Japan, of having one's potential for wilful independence as an individual contained, moulded within the social context. The *kata* is a major agent of social constraint and conformity. It is not just social order and stability in a political sense that are aided by it. Social relations, that mean so much to the Japanese, are also made easier for the people involved if they know what to expect of others.

And, as all truly mature Japanese adults have also learned, if for some reason the *kata* is not perfectly applicable in a particular situation—such as where one of the persons involved has a sudden and major change of circumstances—then the 'give and take' ethic of *yuzuriai* can come into play, pragmatically permitting a little latitude. Inevitably, human behaviour, even or especially in a social context, cannot be absolutely comprehensively prescribed by form, however much the Tokugawa shōguns might have wanted it so. There are simply too many permutations, too many variables. Moreover, humans cannot live by prescription alone. It is simply too constraining. Nor can they all attain the prescribed norm, the *kata*, with the same degree of mastery. For these reasons it would be an over-simplification to think of Japanese behaviour during and after the Tokugawa period as entirely one of *kata* alone. Rather it is a case of *kata* as the normative ideal, but in reality with a degree of latitude permitted through *yuzuriai* and through the distinction between outer form and inner reality (itself a sort of *yuzuriai*).

In the Meiji period that followed the Tokugawa period, when Japan was opened up to the west and was desperately trying to modernise and industrialise and catch up with it, the concept of the individual was revived somewhat. To some extent this was inevitable, as Japan was now suddenly exposed to an influx of western ideology that included individualism. But the nation's leaders realised that, if suitably controlled and guided, individualism could be helpful to Japan's cause by encouraging people to perform to their maximum. In particular the nation needed to stimulate entrepreneurialism, for this had been stifled under the Tokugawa. The fact that in the early stages the Meiji government had to take the initiative itself in most ventures is testimony to this legacy. The individualism that was fostered was therefore harnessed towards national efforts,[166] particularly through the *Imperial Rescript on Education* of 1890 that promoted a combination of Confucian ethics and Shintō reverence for the emperor.[167] Becoming a strong individual was one and the same as becoming a strong contributor to national success. Figures such as the entrepreneur Shibusawa Eiichi, a major industrialist and strong nationalist, and Fukuzawa Yukichi, a self-help educationist and nationalist, became role-models of 'successism' (*risshishugi*)—self-help that also helped the nation.

However, by the turn of the century, when in remarkably short time Japan had largely achieved its aims of modernisation and industrialisation, there were many who openly lamented the advent of individualism. It had served its purpose, and it was now time to get rid of it. Though considerably modified in Japan, it was still seen as too western. It gave people too much freedom, made them too self-interested and competitive, split up relationships between them. Japan's most popular novelist of the day, Natsume Sōseki, spoke for many—but not all—when he wrote (in 1906):

The people of today have become too self-conscious.... With self-consciousness as strong as it is, how can true peace be possible? ... There is always a constant struggle going on between men....

Because of our newly developed individuality, there is now no peace between man and man. We strain ourselves to the utmost to prove our individual strength, so we are living in agony. Because of this constant conflict, we have tried to find ways of separating ourselves from others....

Once you give man freedom of individuality, their relations with each other become cramped.... That is why Western civilisation is not as admirable as it appears.[168]

The government agreed that individualism had gone too far. From around this time, the balance between relatively free individualism and social control shifted inexorably towards the latter. The fact that the years immediately following Sōseki's comments saw the birth of the genre of the autobiographical 'I novel' (*watakushi-shōsetsu*)—an almost pathological obsession with the self that continues in Japanese literature to this day—is no coincidence. In most cases it was not a simple positive celebration of the self, but rather a desperate voicing of the self by those who had tasted and liked individualism but now faced the prospect of having it taken away from them. The self of the 'I novel' is essentially introverted and passive, not extroverted and assertive. It is a confused self, a self that has been (re-)awakened but denied an identity.[169]

Socialism was vigorously suppressed, and so too were labour movements, and democracy as a whole. By the eve of World War Two, thanks to government texts such as *Kokutai no Hongi* (The Cardinal Principles of National Polity) of 1937, Japanese were indoctrinated to believe that the very aim of their life—not merely their duty—was to sacrifice it for the emperor.[170] The individual as a concept was also sacrificed. *Kokutai no Hongi* refers explicitly to corruption of the nation by 'Occidental individualism and rationalism', and states that 'we must sweep aside the corruption of the spirit and the clouding of knowledge that arises from ... being taken up with one's "self", and return to a pure and clear state of mind'.[171] By this, it meant more exactly a return to a Tokugawa-style state of affairs wherein the individual did not cause trouble and obeyed the nation's rulers without question.

Attempts by the Occupation forces to revive ideas of the individual and democracy after the war met with limited success in practice, though on paper Japan has—thanks to the Americans who drafted it—one of the most liberal and democratic constitutions in the world. In practice individual rights, such as those of women, have not necessarily been respected. And though a form of successism was once again promoted after the war, it was more in the sense of working hard for the nation than becoming a successful nationally minded individual. In the postmodern period from the 1970s, and in particular during the upheavals in the workplace of the 1990s, there has been some degree of lessening of constraints on the individual, but basically, the *kata* mentality still prevails and there is little room or respect for western-style individualism.

Of course, though there is undoubtedly a link, individualism is not the same as individuality. Japanese people do have some scope for individuality, or 'personality', but again this is limited by the *kata*. Some scholars have claimed that Japanese can express their individuality through their choice of pastime, which is undoubtedly true as a generalisation.[172] Yet more so than in most countries choice of these pastimes can be limited by convention, and some can even be virtually obligatory. Women from 'cultured' backgrounds, for example, are expected to be at least familiar with the principles of flower-arranging. Golf is listed by many Japanese males as their favourite pastime, yet it is also *de rigueur* for any aspiring businessman in Japan to play golf. Is the businessman-golfer showing real individuality, or is he on the contrary showing the strength of the *kata*?

Other scholars have claimed that in Japan the materially affluent economic superpower it has become possible to express an individual identity through consumerism.[173] It is certainly true that in earlier times, when Japan was on the hard road to becoming a superpower and even before that, the individual's worth, and therefore to some extent their sense of self (such as it was), was in no small part based on what they produced. That they should in more recent affluent times change that basis to what they consume is only natural. There is undoubted evidence of a considerable association of self with product in Japan since the war. Among other things there is a practice of putting the prefix *mai-* (my) in front of a variety of products or material items, to form a compound noun. Thus one has *mai-hōmu*, *mai-kaa*, *mai-kon* (my computer), and so forth. It is an undisguised linking of self and product, a material and externally driven statement about the self.

Yet the consumption-defined self needs to be put in context. In any society, clothes and other material items have always expressed a certain individuality, especially if they are eccentric. Yet someone who simply wears or acquires the latest fashion—which is over-whelmingly the case in fad-obsessed Japan—is simply following the crowd, and is surely demonstrating the inadequacy of their individuality rather than the strength of it. They are no different from the teenage 'rebel' who joins a gang and conforms to its often demanding army-style rules, misguidedly thinking they are rejecting authority and experiencing freedom. By identifying with a fad they are really stating that their 'individuality' conforms to a group preference. It is just another form of group identity.

Of course, when this is extended across a wide range of items, even if they are all faddish brands, each individual may well build up a distinctive profile of sorts. They wear clothes of trendy brand X rather than alternative trendy brand Y, drive a car of brand A rather than brand B, and so forth. However, this is individuality selected from a menu. Though many people worldwide, especially teenagers, define at least part of their personality in such a way, what is concerning about Japan is that the menu selection often seems to actually form much of the personality, rather than merely express it. This is testimony to what seems to be 'the inadequacy of the Japanese personality'.[174]

As in any society, each Japanese individual has emotional and attitudinal factors that help make up their personality profile. In relative terms they may be lazy or diligent, or quick-tempered or patient, and so forth. But even these aspects are to a large extent prescribed by form. There is a behavioural *kata* for each type of situation, based on expected emotional reactions, and any individualistic emotion that might produce something different from this should be kept below the surface. Those whose behaviour falls too far from accepted norms and standards—that goes too far beyond the latitude permitted by *yuzuriai*—are likely to be seen as having psychological problems, and subjected to the *naikan* or Morita therapies aimed at making them realise their selfish shortcomings and the debt they owe society.

Though it may not be a realisation of true individuality, Japanese can at least stand out from the crowd—with society's approval—in one particular way, and that is excelling. In much the same way as that expressed by the English term 'outstanding', they can *kiwadatsu* (be outstanding) by exceeding expected standards in a positive way, and be for example more diligent than average, or more patient, and they will earn praise for it. The excellent student will be praised, and not be cut down as is so often the case in the west. Paradoxically, one can also be outstanding by the very degree to which one fulfils one's expected role, showing complete mastery of the *kata* while most others just come close to it. This is not unlike the concept of professionalism in the west. However, it remains an open question as to how far one can equate such thoroughness and even excellence with genuine individuality.

To some extent Japanese can also achieve a sort of indirect or vicarious individuality, entailing a partial escape from constrictive norms. This can be done in a number of ways. They can escape into a world of artificial fantasy where they can give free rein to their imagination and even play out roles to match their desires. Japan has plentiful means of providing such escapism, ranging from fantastic comics and toys to the virtual reality of computers, from Disneyland-type entertainment centres to the more bizarre establishments that cater primarily for sexual fantasies. Or they can identify with more exotic aspects of the real world, but a world outside their own small corner. They can travel overseas, identifying briefly with those living in a different environment and even experiencing the thrill of it themselves. To an extent they can also identify from a distance with individuals who deviate from the norms in Japan, not only foreign residents but even certain Japanese, such as the *yakuza*. However, such second-hand identity is not the same as the real thing, and very few go so far as to deviate themselves.

The individual in Japan, then, finds himself or herself in a web of constraints, with what are by western standards limited opportunities for self-expression. The individual has responsibilities to his or her group, and to society as a whole. They cannot easily act as a free agent. Independent individualism could destroy the delicate balance of things, and to guard against this the individual is put under pressure to conform to a set of norms, prescribed by the *kata*. They know their place, both in society and the group, and this is made easier by the fact that both the group and society as a whole are relatively clearly structured.

The structure of both the group and general society strongly reflects hierarchy, which in turn reflects rank. Japan has in fact been described as a 'vertical society' (*tate shakai*), a term popularised from the 1960s by the anthropologist Nakane Chie, who has had very considerable influence in the forming of popular images of Japanese society.[175] When groups form in Japan, according to Nakane they rarely do so on the basis of attribute—a shared characteristic, such as

the same interests or professional background or religious affiliation—as is common in many groups in the west. Rather, Japanese
groups form overwhelmingly on the basis of 'frame' (*ba*), meaning
place or situation, such as a company. The rare attribute-based
groups tend to be relatively egalitarian to start with, but eventually,
within both types of group, verticality orders the relationships of its
members, for 'in Japan a group inevitably and eventually develops the
vertical type of organisational structure', and 'rank is the social norm
on which Japanese life is based'.[176]

These vertical rankings reflect essentially Confucian ideas of
seniority, and mirror as closely as possible the family group. The key
element is the vertical relationship between parent (*oya*) and child
(*ko*), and indeed these same terms are often used to describe relationships within groups outside the family proper. She writes that 'an
organisational principle in terms of parent-child relationships consti-
tutes the basic scheme of Japanese organisation', and she extends this
to the organisation of society in general.[177] Each *oya* from any one
group or context is in turn *ko* to someone more senior in another
(higher) group or context. This is extended throughout the nation, in
pyramid style, with all people ultimately answerable to the pinnacle of
the social pyramid, the emperor. Nakane admits that this type of
structural organisation produces a number of problems, such as
'headless' disorientation when an *oya* suddenly dies. It also produces
a strong potential for factionalism, and difficulty in lateral relations
between various vertical groups.

Like so many claims about Japan by its *Nihonjinron* writers, her
theory of vertical relations has produced a simplistic and exaggerated
picture. It has been criticised by many scholars,[178] who among other
things point out the importance of horizontal relations such as 'old
school boy' networks (known as *kone* from the English term 'connections'), and more egalitarian community groups. Moreover, though
not to the extent of India (which Nakane sees as a society where
attribute is especially important), Japan does endorse the idea of an
attribute-based caste system in its marginalising of groups such as
burakumin and ethnic Koreans on the basis of birth. Japan also does
have quite a number of western-style attribute-based groups, particularly at community level, such as *rōjinkai* (old folks' clubs) and *fujinkai*
(women's clubs) and 'common interest associations'.

Nevertheless, exaggeration aside, it is undeniable that Confucian-
style rank and hierarchy are key organisational agents in Japan.
Hierarchy particularly dominated the social structure of Tokugawa

Japan, in its *shinōkōshō* system, which also reflected considerable Confucian influence. Although, unlike the Japan of earlier centuries, present-day Japan is not especially regarded as a formal class-based society—certainly in comparison with many European ones—it is still very much characterised by hierarchy at the level of interpersonal and intergroup relations. One scholar observes that 'hierarchy remains fundamental and pervasive throughout Japanese society', and another that 'hierarchy is inseparable from orderliness'.[179] Japan's notorious 'respect language' (*keigo*) is another clear illustration of the importance of rank. Though becoming a little more relaxed in recent years, it is still important to get the right level of language, the right polite term, the right honorific prefix, the right self-depreciatory term to reflect the relativities of rank in any given situation.

In modern times hierarchy in Japan has the potential both to encourage and discourage 'equality'. On the one hand, it is egalitarian in that most people nowadays—though not all—have a chance to rise through the ranks. But on the other hand it is anti-egalitarian, for it recognises inequality at any given moment and in any given situation. That is, for all its seeming rigidity, it too has a certain ambivalence and even flexibility to it, scope for manipulation and accommodation in the degree to which the balance is regulated, the emphasis applied. Certainly, the Japanese do not seem to like western-style egalitarianism. If anything, they see the equal treatment of essentially unequal people as a source of potential social unrest and imbalance. It is not the 'natural order'.

In this idea of 'natural order', Confucianism is also still strong. In essence, Confucianism promotes the idea of stability and 'proper and natural order' in all relationships. It focuses in particular on five specific ones—ruler and subject, husband and wife, father and son, elder brother and younger brother, friend and friend—but in Japan's case at least (where it has been somewhat modified) it is more the general idea that has been influential. That is, it has helped ingrain in people a sense of 'knowing their place' in a relationship and in society as a whole, especially in the sense of juniority and seniority of rank. This has obviously found favour with ruling elites, for in general it legitimises and safeguards their superior status.

Verticality is not the only structural element in interpersonal or intergroup relations in Japan. The universal distinction between in-group and out-group, given particular meaning under Tokugawa rule, has retained a special importance in Japan.[180] In addition to the vertical axis in a group, Nakane also observes—and others such as Doi Takeo have argued more strongly—that groupings in Japan are also generally characterised by concentric circles or zones based on this distinction.[181]

The core is the *uchi*, meaning both 'inside' and 'home'. It comprises intimates, especially family but also very close friends, and, in modern times, close colleagues from the workplace. In the *uchi*, one can relax and be oneself, and show one's real feelings (*honne* or *ninjō*). One can behave without pretence and feel only minimal need to consider such things as reputation (*menboku* or *mentsu*), restraint (*enryo*), and the feelings of others in the *uchi* group. It would be incorrect, however, to say that these considerations can be entirely dispensed with. Verticality is still present, and relativities of ranking cannot be totally ignored. It is simply that rules can be relaxed a little.

Next comes an intermediate zone of people with whom it is necessary to relate, and who cannot therefore be treated as total strangers, but who at the same time are not intimates. Such people include, for example, professional acquaintances in other companies, neighbours, teachers, shopkeepers, and so on. They represent considerable variety and dimensionality, for they range on a horizontal axis from reasonably close acquaintances to virtual strangers introduced by a friend of a friend, and on a vertical axis from the senior and very important to the junior and relatively unimportant. This is the zone of *enryo* (reserve or restraint) and *giri* (duty), and it is the zone that causes most difficulties in relations. It is also a principal source of the notoriously intricate Japanese web of social obligations and protocol described, and perhaps to some extent over-stated, by early western scholars of Japan.[182]

A major factor here is the incurring of *on*, meaning indebtedness for a favour given or kindness shown. It entails an obligation to repay this (*ongaeshi*) in some form or other. *Giri* is the protocol that controls the interaction. One scholar has defined *giri* as 'the obligation to act according to the dictates of society in relation to other persons', and as 'a norm that obliges the observance of reciprocal relations—to help those who have helped one, to do favors for those from whom one has received favors, and so forth'.[183]

Uncomfortable in this zone, with its various obligations and restraints, many Japanese prefer where possible to try either to bring an intermediate relationship into the *uchi* zone or to push it out into the outer zone. This means that boundaries between the zones can often become blurred. There seems in particular a blurring between the *uchi* and intermediate zones, with many in the latter being treated as a sort of second-tier of intimates with whom it is very possible to be on quasi-*uchi* terms.

The outer zone is known as *soto* (outside), and the people one meets in it are *tanin* ('others' or 'strangers'). As outsiders, they are from the outset associated with potential threat and impurity.[184] Relations with them are therefore viewed negatively and are not exactly encouraged. When total strangers do meet, as they inevitably must on occasion, then to some extent, depending on the nature of the situation and those involved, a simplified form of the same basic protocol as in the intermediate zone may apply. However, as often as not relations with total strangers will by western standards be very cold, and even rude and callous and seemingly selfish. (The pushing and shoving of fellow commuters being a well-known illustration of this.)

Many Western observers have remarked critically on this behaviour towards strangers, and the standard Japanese response is that cold-ness is not selfishness but the very opposite. It is argued that to do a favour for a stranger, such as helping out in a crisis, will actually do more harm than good to the recipient, since it will place the burden of *on* upon them. Moreover this will bring both the recipient and the giver of the favour into an intermediate-level relationship, an undesirable burden for all parties. In recent years there has been an increase in volunteer work and so forth, and people are starting to help strangers more than in the past. However, the *soto* mentality is still strong, and it is still not unusual to see victims of misfortune, especially elderly ones, wave away well-intentioned helpers.[185]

Though it has perhaps been over-stated, obligation is nevertheless very important in Japan. One reason for this is the great importance of 'face', or reputation—in Japan's case not just one's own personal reputation but also that of one's group.[186] This is a reflection of the importance of both external appearance and group accountability, in very large part legacies from the Tokugawa period. As the Tokugawa rulers would no doubt have appreciated, even without knowledge of the specifically appropriate *kata*, it is to some extent theoretically possible to broadly predict Japanese behaviour in interaction with others by combining a simplified *uchi–soto* distinction with that of the inner substance–outer form (*ura-omote* or *honne-tatemae*), to produce a schema of basic behavioural permutations.[187] This is illustrated in Table 3.3.

Table 3.3 Broad Situation-Based Behavioural Permutations

	Uchi (inner circle)	Soto (strangers)
Omote ('face' important)	(doesn't arise)	ritualised behaviour (conventional protocol)
Ura ('face' unimportant)	intimate behaviour	anomic behaviour (disregard for others)

The difference in patterns of Japanese behaviour depending on the situation helps explain why short-term visitors to Japan often seem to form confused and even polarised views about it. Some see the Japanese as polite yet aloof, others see them as rude and coarse, still others see them as warm and friendly. It all depends on what exposure they have had to Japanese behaviour, and in what situations.

A key concept here is the 'situational ethic', meaning that behaviour is determined by the protocol appropriate to a given situation rather than by a universal moral code. Role-playing is also related to this. A person who is in a junior role in one situation may well be the senior in the next (or even in the same situation if multiple people are involved), and vary his or her behaviour and language accordingly. Foreigners who are not aware of these variables—and even some who are—can end up dismissing the Japanese as erratic and inconsistent, or even duplicitous and 'two-faced'.

Though the policies of the Tokugawa authorities contributed much to the situational ethic, the relativity of morality is an even deeper underlying factor. Most cultures have a universal morality, usually based on religion and also enshrined in law. The morality–religion–law combination gives a cohesiveness and order to a society—though serious difficulties can and do arise when there are multiple cultures and religions in the same society. In Japan's case this nexus of morality and religion and law is all rather vague and weak. The nation achieves social order and cohesion largely through other means. These include the marginalisation of 'misfits' and undesirables to a perhaps greater extent than in most societies. They also include tapping into a homogeneity and national identity aided by insularity, and controlling behaviour by the promotion of orthodoxy and enforcement of conformity.

In some regards it may seem strange that a nation so keen on orthodoxy has not developed a universal moral code, for this might at first consideration seem to be a useful political tool. However, such a code would in practice be too binding to the Japanese—or more especially the Japanese ruling elite. They prefer to leave options open where possible. Paradoxically, for all its orthodoxy and conformity, Japan is a pragmatic and in many cases flexible nation. It prefers rules to morals,[188] for these are more easily adjusted to suit the situation, especially if the give-and-take ethic and the situational ethic are also applied. Though it may sound a contradiction in terms to talk of a flexible orthodoxy, rule-based orthodoxy is more flexible than morality-based orthodoxy.

From its earliest days, Japan's native religion, Shintō, has never made any explicit division between Good and Evil. 'Good' has always tended to be determined as basically that which is 'right' in the sense of appropriate to the circumstances.[189] A western-style concept of 'evil' hardly seems to have existed. Instead, there is 'wrong', in the sense of inappropriate and disruptive. There is also the concept of impurity (*kegare*), which in some ways fulfils a societal role similar to that of the western evil but is by no means the same as it, for its avoids moral judgement. The Shintō gods, as depicted in ancient mythologies such as the *Kojiki* and *Nihon Shoki* of the early eighth century, are extremely human, and demonstrate numerous human foibles. Their behaviour, judged by western moral standards, is far from the embodiment of universal moral perfection. It is particularised, varying from situation to situation. It also shows a broad-mindedness that avoids high moral ground. Even serious disruption, such as caused by the Storm God Susano-o when he harasses his sister Amaterasu the Sun Goddess, does not merit moral censure from the other gods. Instead, he is simply removed—a pragmatic solution, not a moralistic one.[190]

It is true that Buddhism, first introduced in the sixth century, does have a concept of evil. Indeed, the Buddhist association of women with evil was one reason—or perhaps more exactly one male justification—for women's decline in status in Japanese society. However, in broader terms the concept never really took hold. Nor did the Christian concept of evil when the religion was later introduced to Japan. In fact, along with the unappealingly uncompromising and transcendental nature of the Christian God, it was probably a major reason why Christianity as a whole never took root. Its dichotomy between good and evil was simply too inflexible, and the whole thing lacked 'give and take'.

Rather, the Japanese have preferred the social code of Confucianism, which has certain theoretically universal principles but is not a religion and is more easily adjusted. This does not mean that religion itself cannot be adjusted or manipulated. In Meiji Japan Shintō was deemed to be an 'expression of nationalist sentiment' rather than a strict religion. This paved the way for it to be forced on the people as so-called State Shintō and to be used for political ends to indoctrinate reverence for the emperor.

Basically, the Japanese have used religion either for nationalistic purposes, or for situation-specific purposes. It is a case not just of the situational ethic, but the situational religion. Put simplistically, Shintō is the religion of national spirit and life, Buddhism the religion of death, and Christianity the 'religion' of wedding ceremonies and pretty churches. Each have their own festivals and rituals, in which Japanese participate in great numbers but with questionable religious zeal. Religion in Japan, like the expression of individuality, is another select-from-a-menu type of affair. Surveys repeatedly show that just over 80 per cent of the population are Shintō adherents, just under 80 per cent are Buddhist, and 70 per cent profess no real religious conviction.[191] Clearly, it is a society of religious pluralism. In the main the Japanese are religious role players, interested in ritual rather than doctrine, and they are not concerned if the rituals happen to involve more than one religion.[192]

This is not necessarily a bad thing. Though there are undoubtedly some in Japan who hold deep religious convictions, there has rarely been serious inter-religious conflict there, and never the wars of religion that have torn apart many countries.[193]

The lack of religious conflict should not be taken as indicating that there is no conflict of any sort in Japan. Such absence of general conflict is yet another exaggeration by *Nihonjinron* writers keen to stress harmony. (Some critics argue that their very enthusiasm to do so suggests a need to keep reiterating that the Japanese are harmonious to help keep in check a significant potential for conflict.) It is invariably accompanied by a reference to the low rates of litigation in Japan, as 'evidence' of Japanese harmony.

It is true that harmony is a genuinely respected ideal in Japan, and it is also true that the Japanese do a better job than many of peacefully coexisting with each other in crowded and stressful conditions. In addition, it is true that many Japanese see recourse to the law as a failure in human relations, and where possible prefer informal conflict resolution. They see the law as impersonal, rigid, black-and-white, with winners and losers, good guys and bad guys. This is not particularly appealing to people who prefer 'give and take', have a relative morality, and a concern with face. Since the Tokugawa period in particular, they are accustomed to sorting out their own problems, and are usually very efficient at it. They are undoubtedly aided in this by their high degree of cultural homogeneity. Widespread concurrence of values and expectations means that relative to more culturally diverse societies, sources of potential conflict are fewer and more quickly able to be identified and addressed, and that where conflict does occur, agreement and reconciliation can be achieved more easily.

However, the situation has been distorted by excessively narrow comparison with the United States, one of the most culturally diverse of all nations, and one of the most litigious. It is understandable that in the United States law should acquire such a high profile in society, for it is a universally applicable means of conflict resolution—though not to everyone's liking, for law too embeds specific cultural values that are not necessarily shared by all. In comparison with the United States, Japan appears a very non-litigious nation. However, in comparison with other countries, the picture changes. For example, Japan has twice the rate of civil litigation of the typical Scandinavian country.[194]

The situation has also been distorted by what appears to be a misunderstanding of the legal system in Japan.[195] Figures are often quoted that show far fewer lawyers per capita in Japan than in most western countries. In 1990, for example, there were just over 14,000 attorneys-at-law in Japan, as opposed to 700,000 in the United States and 60,000 barristers and solicitors in the United Kingdom. The ratios relative to population were approximately 1:9,000 for Japan, 1:350 for the US, and 1:900 for the UK. This would seem to suggest that the Japanese are twenty-five times less in need of the law than Americans are, and ten times less than the British are. However, many of the tasks performed by lawyers and solicitors in western countries are actually carried out in Japan by para-legal specialists who are not formally classified as lawyers (even though they might use the term 'attorney'), such as tax attorneys, patent attorneys, and judicial scriveners (who prepare documents in a fashion similar to solicitors). When they are included in the reckoning, the number of 'lawyers' in Japan jumps to around 80,000, and the ratio per capita drops to 1:1,600. This is still fewer than in many western countries, but not dramatically so.

There are additional factors dissuading the Japanese from litigation, factors that do not necessarily provide evidence of natural harmony. There are, for example, the practical considerations of time and cost, which are both very considerable in Japan.[196] There is also a traditional deep-seated view of the law (as in many Asian nations) as something used by the government to punish people rather than something that people can use to their own advantage. Many people still have a basic suspicion of legal authorities, not helped by the brutality of the prewar thought police (still vivid in the memories of some) and ongoing questions about Japanese arrest, interrogation, and prosecution procedures.[197]

In short, for a variety of reasons, the Japanese do not particularly like having recourse to the law, but they will do so if necessary—as many foreign companies have found out in commercial matters. However, it is also fair to say that, although the police have a more visible everyday presence in Japan than in many countries thanks to the system of local police-boxes (*kōban*), in terms of legal action the law does not feature as prominently in Japanese life as in many countries. There appears to be a greater tolerance—or perhaps more exactly in some cases non-reporting—of behaviour that would result in criminal action in many other countries, such as sex offences and corruption. Authorities have also traditionally shown a greater tolerance towards organised crime than would be the case in most countries. (In recent years, however, attitudes have been changing and more cases are going to litigation, and the authorities are also showing less tolerance towards organised crime.)

By international standards Japan's crime-rate in most categories is low, typically a fifth or so of most western nations. And when crimes are committed (and reported) and criminal convictions follow, very few people are imprisoned.[198] In keeping with a general Japanese accommodating policy of give and take, expression of contrition counts for a great deal, and there is a genuine attempt to reintegrate offenders wherever possible. Provided the crime was not an extremely serious one, then if a criminal has learned his lesson, that is the main thing. Both he and society stand to gain from his reintegration.

Such attitudes to the law and its transgressors partly reflect the basic Japanese tendency to interpret 'wrong' as socially disruptive rather than evil. They also reflect a genuine attempt to keep society functioning with a minimum of divisiveness, and according to accepted norms of behaviour, with a minimum of involvement by legal officials.

Mainstream Japanese society, then, is not kept in order by morality, or religion, or law—at least not to the extent of many societies. Order is maintained largely by conformity to behavioural rules, rules which are particularised to a given situation but in general centre on each person understanding their place in the context of interpersonal relations. Notwithstanding a distinction between outer form and inner reality, and the importance of give and take, which together permit a certain freedom of movement, there is genuine respect for position, rank, and hierarchy, respect for doing the right thing in the right way, and respect for the maintenance of orderly relationships. Though conformity was initially imposed and harshly enforced, among other things to suppress potentially disruptive self-interest, in modern times it appears to have become in no small part self-regulating. People appear to understand the disruptive potential of excessively assertive western-style individualism and individual rights, and seem prepared to sacrifice some rights in return for the security of a more-or-less assured place in society. It is a type of 'social contract', not at all unknown in the west but again different in the matter of degree.

It is a society that does not give individuals the same degree of freedom most westerners would like, but then again the very concept of the 'individual' is open to question. Although Japan has shown itself at various points in history to be perfectly capable of producing strong western-style individuals, for some centuries now the Japanese individual seems to have developed a sense of identity that very much includes the group. Belonging means a great deal to Japanese, and many of them have made it clear that they see the western individual as a lonely, alienated creature.

3.5   BEING JAPANESE: A RACE APART?

The Japanese may not have a strong sense of religion in the usual sense of the word. Instead, according to one Japanese writer, they have a faith in their Japaneseness, a faith in the very state of being Japanese that fulfils the same role for Japanese that religion does for others.[199] It is a faith known as Nihonism, or Japanism. Indeed, it is the very strength of this Nihonism, we are told, that prevents religion in the normal sense from taking root, for 'it is futile to attempt to transform a faith as deeply rooted as Nihonism into another religion', and 'the entire Japanese nation is a body of faithful followers of Nihonism'.[200] It is moreover a very exclusive 'religion', for it is self-evident that 'only Japanese can become Nihonists'.[201] Those of other nationalities are left to seek salvation by other means.

Clearly, though it is questionable whether they actually go into religious ecstasy over it, the Japanese would appear to have a very strong and distinct national identity. So distinct, according to the same writer, that it is almost beyond the comprehension of non-Japanese. Japanese are so utterly unique that 'the peculiarity of their background and abilities makes it impossible to judge them on the basis of the criteria suitable to the evaluation of other peoples'.[202]

National identity is formed by a variety of factors, and it is undeniable that in each of them the Japanese—insofar as it is possible to evaluate them on the basis of criteria suitable to the evaluation of other peoples—score highly. One of them is geographical. If a nation's boundaries are neatly delineated by natural features, such as mountains or the sea, then this is a natural aid to the development of a sense of 'shared fate' and togetherness among those who live there. In this regard Japan has benefited from being an island nation reasonably distant from any continental land mass and from any other heavily populated islands.

Boundaries can, of course, be changed for political ends, usually by military means. When boundaries keep changing to include or exclude various regional minorities, it is harder for a distinct national identity to develop. In particular, large countries such as China and Russia have historically suffered from this. Japan's boundaries too have changed over time to include such minorities, as seen in the case of the Ainu and Okinawans. This has obviously had considerable impact on the minorities involved but for most Japanese it has not significantly affected their perception of the entity 'Japan'. Compared with many nations, Japan's boundaries have not moved all that much.

Political unity is also important. Japan achieved a reasonable degree of political unity by around the sixth century, with the hegemony of the Yamato clan and the emergence of the Yamato state. It weakened somewhat during the middle ages, but was restored by the beginning of the seventeenth century. It did suffer practical administrative problems till the modern development of efficient means of communication and transport, but in this it is little different from many other nations. Overall, it has done better than most nations in achieving and maintaining political unity.

It is also helpful in the formation of national identity if there is some specific stimulus to prompt and strengthen a sense of nationhood. Japan has experienced a number of such prompts, particularly the attempted invasions by the Mongols in the thirteenth century, the arrival of Europeans in the sixteenth century, and fears of colonisation by western powers in the nineteenth century. In the early twentieth century it was further prompted to consider its own identity when it suffered a number of rebuttals from the west on blatantly racial grounds.[203] And during the postwar Occupation Japanese inevitably contrasted themselves with the Americans who were suddenly thrust upon them and whose ways they had to accept (at least outwardly).

Cultural and ethnic commonality are also factors in national identity. Generally, the more ethnic groups and cultures there are in a nation, the weaker the sense of nationality. Japan is distinct in being the most ethnically homogeneous of all nations, not 100 per cent as claimed in the mid-1980s by then prime minister Nakasone, but very close to it at around 99 per cent.

In earlier times nations were often conceived of as race-based entities, with race itself being seen as essentially biologically determined. Nowadays it is widely accepted that 'race' is largely a political construct. Genetically, the Japanese are closely related to other Asiatic peoples and to a lesser extent Polynesian and Micronesian. They are not quite as unique as they would like to imagine. Nor are they totally unmixed, for they represent a mix of at least two genetic strands, those of the indigenous Jōmon people and those of the subsequent Yayoi people, who arrived around 2,000 years ago. However, the Yayoi and Jōmon, though distinct, were not all that far removed from each other in a broader context of worldwide mapping of genetics. Moreover, given that the Japanese have had no significant new input to their gene pool since the arrival of the Yayoi, it is not entirely meaningless to talk of a certain biological commonality. Such commonality is also conducive to the formation of a national identity.

In addition, very recent research in genetics has revealed that certain genes appear to have a significant bearing on certain behavioural predispositions and by extension personality.[204] Though it would of course be an exaggeration to think of behaviour and personality in terms of simple genetic determinism, particularly at a national level, it does nevertheless mean that in Japan's case, with its long-shared gene pool, one has to be careful about summarily dismissing the old-fashioned concept of 'national character' (*kokuminsei*). It may well prove to have some degree of genetic support to it. If so, this would obviously be an important factor in the emergence of a national identity.

But perhaps the major factor in the formation of national identity is indoctrination. This is almost always for political ends, and this was clearly the case in Japan in the Meiji period and prewar years. Indeed, prewar Japanese suffered the most extreme form of nationalistic indoctrination imaginable, when they were taught to believe that the very aim of life for a Japanese—not just their duty—was to give up that life for the emperor and his nation-family. That is, being Japanese meant dying Japanese. (Though this was conveniently overlooked in the case of Koreans who, as naturalised Japanese, gave their lives up for the emperor only to be posthumously disqualified as Japanese.)

Politically, a national identity has also served to bind Japanese society together, to give it a cohesiveness that the situational ethic does not. In modern times it has fulfilled a role filled in former times by harsh authoritarianism. In that sense, Nihonism has a strong socio-political role.

Not all indoctrination is primarily political, however. During the 1970s and 1980s in particular, when Japan was at the peak of its economic superpower status, Japanese had their sense of national identity virtually constructed for them by *Nihonjinron* writers seeking to explain the reasons for Japan's success. Though the government undoubtedly smiled favourably upon their flattering theories—at least before they started to cause an international backlash—it does not seem to have actually initiated the phenomenon. The writers were mostly a mix of academics and businessmen (who in the course of international business dealings often found themselves called upon to explain Japan's economic success). Though they were overwhelmingly Japanese, they included a number of westerners. Ezra Vogel, a Harvard professor who wrote *Japan As Number One* in 1979, is widely seen as an example of a western *Nihonjinron* writer. Well-known Japanese writers associated with the *Nihonjinron* approach to describing Japan include Nakane Chie (professor) and Doi Takeo (professor and psychiatrist), but there are many dozens more.[205]

The *Nihonjinron* approach has been widely criticised, especially by westerners, as academically weak. It is characterised by such flaws as over-simplification, exaggeration, stereotyping, unsupported claims, leaps in argument and logic, ignorance of actual fact, and use of selective data to prop up assumptions. It is rarely that one proceeds more than a few pages in any *Nihonjinron* text without encountering such major problems, even in the case of writers who in other contexts display admirable academic rigour. It is as if, when writing about Japan, otherwise respect-worthy writers become carried away by their enthusiasm—their mission—and tragically thwart the achievement of their aims by abandoning discipline and authority.

One writer, for example, claims that the Japanese have always hated western-style analytical logic and categorisation and instead think in an intuitive, integrated, holistic way.[206] He conveniently omits discussion of the fact that the main Japanese word for 'to understand', *wakaru*, means literally 'to de divided up'. That is, contrary to his argument, it could equally well be claimed that there is a clear conceptual link in Japan between analysis and thought processes. Another writer claims that, unlike the Japanese language, western languages lack a word that can be used of both the self and others, 'proving' the rigidity of the western duality between self and others, and by extension between self and society.[207] His understanding of English, the major western language, would not appear to extend to the pronoun 'one' (and equivalents in other western languages), which can be used of first, second, or third person singular or plural and even of society as a whole. Theoretically, if this line was pursued, it could be argued that western languages show a closer relationship between self and others than the Japanese language does.

Some scholars in the west have in fact set out to demonstrate the weakness of the *Nihonjinron*-style of argument by using it against itself, deliberately applying similar 'reasoning' to produce entirely the opposite conclusions to the *Nihonjinron* writers.[208] For example, by selectively citing a few strong Japanese individuals (such as Oda Nobunaga) and a few well-known western groups (such as the Three Musketeers), it can be emphatically proved—by *Nihonjinron* standards—that Japanese are individualistic and westerners are group-oriented.

The *Nihonjinron* assumptions are basically that Japan is a special and unique (and superior) nation, and that it is inherently and monolithically characterised by such things as harmony, consensus, loyalty, homogeneity, diligence, familialism, and groupism. These are all contrasted with a greatly over-simplified 'west'—a contrasting that is in itself something of a contradiction to *Nihonjinron* claims of a Japanese dislike of dichotomy. The tragedy is that there is often a degree of truth to these assumed characteristics, but proper balanced consideration of them has been impeded by *Nihonjinron* misrepresentations and academic shortcomings.

One scholar has made a particular study of the contrast between Japan and the west according to *Nihonjinron* writers, and produced a list of as many as forty or so pairs of major claimed differences.[209] The main generally claimed differences are outlined in Table 3.4.[210]

Table 3.4 Japan vs West according to *Nihonjinron*

West	Japan
mixed races	racial purity
individualism	groupism, contextualism
horizontality	verticality
contract (*keiyaku*)	'kintract' (*enyaku*)
private	public
guilt	shame
rights	duties
independence	dependence
inner-directed	other-directed
intolerant	tolerant
logical, either/or	ambivalent, both/and
rational	emotional
objective	subjective
rigid principle	situational ethic
universality	particularity, uniqueness
heterogeneity	homogeneity
absolutism	relativism
rupture	harmony, continuity
donative	receptive
active	reactive

The Japanese have not been alone in this wedge-driving between Japan and the west. Westerners too—and not just those typically associated with *Nihonjinron*—have quite happily exaggerated the differences between a simplified east and simplified west, and Japan has been a particularly useful illustration to them of the exotic Otherness of the Orient.[211] Particularly prior to the war it was often, on the basis of little or no actual knowledge, seen as a topsy-turvy land where everything was done back to front—mounting a horse the 'wrong' side, drawing a bow the 'wrong' side, washing *before* getting in the bath, and so on.[212] Studies during and shortly after the war were more realistic but still focused on differences. Ruth Benedict's classic study *The Chrysanthemum and the Sword*, originally written in 1944, referred to the Japanese in its opening sentence as 'the most alien enemy' of the United States.[213] It went on not only to focus on differences, but to draw attention to paradoxes, thereby helping—despite its scholarly endeavour to explain the nation to western readers—to reinforce an image of Japan as mysterious and exotic.

It is not surprising that some commentators have felt that *Nihonjinron* discourse about the specialness and uniqueness of Japan is in no small part a case of the Japanese deliberately playing up western perceptions of difference.[214] This is very probably true in some cases, but *Nihonjinron* should not be seen as primarily some sort of political tactic. The Japanese genuinely like to believe that they are different, and even if the west had never treated the Japanese as in any way different from westerners, then the *Nihonjinron* phenomenon would still have occurred. The Japanese would still have proclaimed their own specialness and uniqueness.

This is not to deny that *Nihonjinron*-style claims about Japanese uniqueness have ever been used politically. In international affairs it has been very convenient for the Japanese to claim that they are misunderstood and need special treatment, or even that they have unique physical considerations. One of the most classic examples was in discussions in the late 1980s over beef imports. Minister of Agriculture Hata Tsutomu—later to become prime minister—explained to Americans that Japan could not possibly import greater quantities of beef because Japanese intestines were different in length from Americans' and could not easily cope with it.

The obsession with uniqueness is such that the Japanese, when making a generalisation about human behaviour, will very often say 'we Japanese' (*wareware Nihonjin wa*) instead of using a nationality-neutral term such as simply 'people'. One western commentator on Japan, a long-time resident there, tells of being vividly reminded of this tendency when he spotted a book on evolution, written by a Japanese scholar, entitled *From the Fossil Apes to the Japanese*.[215] This immediately begs the question whether the Japanese feel they have evolved to a stage beyond that of the rest of humankind, or are yet to catch up.

There is also the well-known matter of 'the Japanese brain'. In the late 1970s Tsunoda Tadanobu, an audiologist, claimed that the Japanese brain was unique in that it processed natural sounds, such as the calls of crickets, with the same hemisphere of the brain that processed human speech.[216] This was immediately seized on as proof that the Japanese lived in special harmony with nature. His findings have never been confirmed. It is true they do not appear to have been disproved either, by neurophysical means, but they can quite easily be challenged from a linguistic perspective.

If Japanese really had a special affinity with nature, this would presumably show up in language related to natural objects, including the insects that featured particularly prominently in Tsunoda's claims. In fact, a simple comparative analysis of the connotations of terminology associated with such objects in both Japanese and English, while revealing certain specific differences of detail, shows a remarkably similar basic pattern.[217] For example, of metaphoric references to insects, a similar majority have negative connotations, a similar intermediate proportion have neutral connotations, and a similar minority have positive connotations. Moreover, English has at least as many—if not more—examples of personification of natural features, such as a babbling brook, a sighing breeze, and so forth.

In other words, the case of the Japanese brain has been subject to the same over-simplified and unauthoritative presentation by *Nihonjinron* writers as many other claimed unique aspects of the Japanese. Very few now take it seriously.

It is unfortunate that *Nihonjinron* claims have ended up with what is in effect an automatic disqualification from many later commentators on Japan. As indicated earlier, in many cases the claims do appear to have some truth to them, but they have been discredited through exaggeration and poor presentation that at times borders on the absurd. Moreover, however unauthoritative the claims may be, they are in themselves an important indication of ideas—and ideals— that Japanese have about themselves, and also of the images they have of the western Other. We should not 'throw the baby out with the bathwater' by totally dismissing *Nihonjinron*.

The Japanese may not be all the things they claim. They may not be unique, a race apart. But it seems they would like to be, and the intensity with which they feel this is in itself something relatively distinctive about them. All peoples like to feel they have their own unique identity, and in the weak sense of the word 'unique', they do. The English are not the French, and the French are not the Japanese, and so on. Each have their own set of distinguishing characteristics that make up their Englishness, their Frenchness, their Japaneseness. But, as with so many things about Japan, it is in the matter of degree that the Japanese distinguish themselves. More than most nations, they seem to have a passionate wish to see themselves as fundamentally different from the rest of humankind, as 'unique' in the strong sense of the word. Their preference for group identity does not seem to extend to an identification with the global human race, with the global community of nations (though 'globalism' has, like 'internationalisation', been a buzz-word for some years now).

As the age of internationalisation proceeds, this will be a major challenge to the Japanese. If they wish to join the world, they will have to give up a little bit of their Japaneseness—the bit that tells them they are somehow more special than the rest of us.

Conclusion: Japan as Itself, and the Aesthetics of Purity

Japan does, after all, make sense. It may do things differently. It may confuse us, frustrate us, challenge us, but ultimately it proves not to lie beyond the frontiers of human understanding. Probably to the considerable disappointment of many Japanese, it is not destined to be eternally veiled in mystery. It is knowable, even to westerners.

But it has at least forced us to move sideways to arrive at that understanding. We should be grateful to Japan for that. It has opened our minds to other ways of social organisation, other ways of considering how human beings can order their affairs and regulate their behaviour. Some westerners may not necessarily like the ways Japan has of doing things, but at least it has made the west think about its own ways, perhaps to change a little in some areas, perhaps in others to feel reassured that western ways are best.

It has made us consider in a fresh light cosy western assumptions about the individual and democracy, about the self, and about the meaning of maturity. To the Japanese, the western-style independent individual risks breaking the social contract. He or she threatens wilfulness, selfishness, arbitrariness, and disruption to social order and stability. These are all signs of immaturity. Better to have more socially mature 'contextual individuals', who can relate to each other—for the most part at least—with shared values of interdependence and a mutual understanding of their place. Indeed, some Japanese would maintain that as an ideal they should have but a muted sense of otherness between themselves and those around them.

They are helped in this by what to westerners seems an unappealingly normative social context, one filled with prescriptive rules of conduct and form, one that constrains and discourages difference. There is a certain freedom, beneath the outer form and in the cracks between the norms, but it is probably not a freedom satisfying to the western individual. And yet it is the Japanese who in some regards may feel the freer. The westerner is constrained by a rigid universal morality, nagged by anxieties about moral rectitude and offending

God—or if not God directly, then at least the more terrestrial authority of the law in its role as guardian of the Commandments. Western
behavioural codes based on morality are, to the Japanese, far more
constraining than those based on mere rules and regulations. That is
why, for all the undoubted orthodoxy of Japanese society, it is also in
some ways more flexible and pragmatic than the typical western
society. For the situational ethic—once something almost unknown to
westerners—can be very flexible indeed if it has to be. And it explains
with an almost embarrassing simplicity many of the paradoxes of
inconsistent behaviour that were once associated with Japan.

Japan has also shown us with great clarity how gender is more than
a mere biological duality. It has been known in the west for some time
that political, economic, ideological and other factors have also
played a part in the construction of gender, but there have been few
such clear examples as Japan. In particular, Japan has shown us the
importance of aesthetics in the formulation of gender—not just the
simple aesthetics of being good-looking, or even Japan-style 'cute',
but higher aesthetic ideals that challenge the very concept of gender
itself. How much greater a challenge can there be than the ideal
representation of one gender being seen in its portrayal by its
supposed opposite?

That very aesthetic of artificiality is another eye-opener for many
westerners, especially those who simplistically thought the Japanese
to be worshippers of nature. It may solve for them the baffling riddle
of how a people who supposedly love nature could so damage it with
their notorious industrial pollution of the 1960s, how they could get
so carried away by economic development as to hideously scar their
natural environment. That love is indeed just supposition. The
Japanese do not love raw nature as westerners do, they fear it. Nature
has to be tamed by human hand, its beauty retained only in miniature,
along with its symbolism of life's vital forces, but its destructive potential reassuringly subdued—for the moment at least. For all the
rhetoric of nature-worship, to the Japanese it is the human world that
matters most. Their supposed harmony with nature is in actual fact a
harmony with the human-tamed version of it, the artificial version of
it.

The aesthetic of artificiality meshes nicely with the situational
ethic, for it supports role-play. Not only does the individual become
an actor with a different repertoire for each situation, the actor can
substitute for the real. This is not only in the matter of gender
portrayal, but also in other supposedly basic matters such as visiting

one's aged parents. Confucian duty may well have a place in Japanese society, but that duty does not necessarily have to be acted out by any specific individual—or so the Japanese see it. The main thing is that the duty gets done, the aged get visited, and who better at it than hired actors who specialise in such a thing? In fact, as specialists, they are probably better able than the real son to achieve the *kata*—the ideal form—of the expression of filial piety. For again, though westerners too know the importance of form and outer appearance, the Japanese have shown us that it can have a far greater role in human affairs than we might have imagined. In fact, the artificial, the outward, the display can mean more than the real itself. The artificial can be cultured, moulded, made to harmonise. The real, the untamed raw, has far too much disruptive potential.

The aged suffer anyway, much like the sick and disabled, from the ugliness of imperfection, of degeneration. If they were not so numerous, and so much a part of normal life, they would be classed as marginals, and indeed in some regards they are treated as if they actually were. Their decrepitude is far removed from the aesthetic ideal of beautiful youth. The autumn leaf does have a certain beauty in the Japanese eye, but it is a wrinkly beauty symbolic of the imminence of death, the ultimate impurity. Far better to admire the cherry blossom, pure and fresh even as it falls. Death is inevitable, but far better, like the Cherry Blossom suicide pilots, to meet its sullying arrival with the full bloom of youthful purity. To die pure means that one's existence has been pure to the end. The sacrifice of teenagers is not an abuse of life, but an exaltation of it. Death is denied an opportunity to encroach, to defile the purity of life through the decrepitude of aging. It is met full on, with the full force of pure vitality.

Aesthetics, particularly of purity, have a far greater importance in Japanese life than in the west—or at least, than we acknowledge about life in the west. Westerners have the duality of Good and Evil. The Japanese, for all their claims to a dislike of dichotomy, also have a duality, but it is not that of a morality-based Good and Evil. It is the dialectic of Pure and Impure. Moreover, it is not the relatively simple idea of purity–impurity that most westerners have. Purity in Japan does not just mean undiluted or clean, it can include such concepts as perfection and normalcy. Impurity can include not just the mixed and the dirty, but also the sick and impaired, the spiritually or ritually tainted, the primitive, the selfish, the failure and others who fall from the grace of perfection, and even those who fall from the grace of idealised normalcy. In the west too we can define impurity as something mixed in that shouldn't be there, but in Japan it extends to the idea that anything abnormal and/or imperfect can disrupt and pollute the normal flow of things, and should be avoided.

More than anything else it is impurity, in one form or another, that underlies marginalisation in Japan. Though it may seem to be at a level of mundaneness incompatible with the lofty realm of aesthetics in the western mind, the adult male in Japan who fails to obtain a regular job is aesthetically impure. Of course, in more practical terms, he is seen as a bludger, a drain on the economy, just as in western societies, but it is more than just that. The failure helps define the successful, the abnormal helps define the normal. Success and normalcy may seem a contradiction in terms to the westerner, who only sees success as something more than normal. Japan's idea of success is broader. It can—and in fact very much does—include the western concept, as seen in its successism of the Meiji period and the race to succeed in the world of education. However, it also treats as success the achievement of normalcy, the attainment of the *kata* of doing the expected. Normalcy is equated with the pure and possesses an aesthetic significance at a socio-psychological level. Of course reverence for the normal is also a practical way of achieving social order and facilitating political control, but it is more than that. In Japan's case, aesthetics and practicality are merged.

The impure marginals are Japan's internal Other. Since they fulfil both practical and particularly aesthetic roles, they are not easily going to be accepted into mainstream society. The mainstream is the abode of the Pure Self. If it embraces the Impure Other, it jeopardises that very purity essential to its identity and survival. The mainstream will necessarily maintain relations of a sort with the margins, but such relations will only be for its own purposes, essentially relations of contrast. The Other is always needed. Even if the treatment accorded certain marginals is made more positive (as it seems to be in recent years), even if some current marginals are eventually accepted, then it is highly likely new marginals will be made. Japan can teach us much, but it seems it cannot teach us how to dispense with the idea of Otherness. Perhaps, though, it can make us think more about our own processes of marginalisation, our own ways of separating our Self from Others. In particular, it can make us think about our own ideas of Good and Evil, and even whether we too might not, deep down, have ideas of Pure and Impure not dissimilar to Japan's.

At a national level, Japan has in fact on occasion partly embraced the Other, the Foreign Other. It has recognised that sometimes a particularly strong potential threat is best dealt with by identification with it, by learning its ways and thereby strengthening itself against it. This is in a sense a form of inoculation, taking in some of the threatening impurity of the Other in order ultimately to strengthen the powers of resistance of the Self and thereby the purity of the Self. When the situation calls for it, Japan will set about this process quite intensely. It is in part driven on by a wish to learn, a curiosity, a fascination for that very same Other it is trying to keep at bay. It is further driven by a need to feel itself the stronger, to be Number One in the hierarchy, and if the situation comes down to a test of strength it will not easily back down. But, like anyone, in the final analysis it does not particularly enjoy being inoculated. It would be easy to say that it would be better to have no disease, no contaminant to contend with in the first place, but this is not possible, for at a national level the Foreign Other is just as needed as the marginals are within Japan's own society. However, Japan would like to keep as healthy a distance as possible from it.

Japan's distance to date has certainly helped provide it with a distinct identity. It is patently inappropriate to say that there is nothing Japanese about Japan. Though obviously it is not characterised by values and behaviours entirely unknown elsewhere in the world, its patterns of priorities and preferences do make it distinct, and in a sense unique. But it is not absolutely unique, and it does need reminding from time to time that it is a member of the human community.

The age of internationalisation is, however much Japan might dislike it, inexorably catching up with it. Defining the values of internationalisation is, of course, another matter. For better or for worse the western world dominates the international arena, and assumes its ways to be right. Those western ways are themselves dominated by American ways. Perhaps this is the natural right of the victor, who gave us a Pax Americana rather than a Pax Nipponica. But perhaps we should strive to think in terms other than victors, other than winners and losers. The world community—or American community, as one will—does not necessarily condone some of Japan's habits, but that should not prevent us learning from them.

Japan is facing certain difficulties in this new climate. It is, for example, unacceptable nowadays for an advanced nation to have an authoritarian regime. Yet it was authoritarianism that for much of its history helped keep Japan together. The situational ethic is not especially good as a binding agent. Unless the various particularised norms relate meaningfully to each other, the cohesiveness of society can be lost. In earlier times conformity was harshly imposed by an authoritarian government, and those who fell from the way were punished severely. In more modern times, and particularly as a result of Japan's defeat in the war, authoritarianism has been replaced by a high degree of self-regulation, a widespread acceptance of the importance of obeying conventional rules loosely held together by the fabric of Confucianism. But self-regulation and convention are not especially robust or dynamic. As a result, in some ways Japan could be likened to a leaky, drifting ship of state with no real authority for its rudder, no really binding universal code to seal its beams, no fundamental morality for its anchor.

This is one reason why the so-called 'national character' has been so emphasised. It is a sense of being Japanese, a sense of shared Japaneseness, that more than anything else keeps Japan together nowadays. It has been helped in this by a number of factors conducive to a national identity, not the least of these being its insularity and an extremely high degree of ethnic homogeneity, but it is something that is going to come under increasing threat as the age of internationalisation gathers pace. The maintaining of national identity in a world community is another case of the importance of the balance between the universal and the particular.

It is to be hoped that Japan will not lose its character, but will at the same time become a constructive and educative participant in world affairs. It would be nice to think that the *Encyclopaedia Britannica* of 1797 got it wrong again when it said of Japan that: 'It looks as if Providence had designed it to be a kind of little world by itself.'

Notes

PART ONE: THE ESSENTIALS OF SOCIETY: MEN AND WOMEN

1. In terms of fixed wages, Labour Ministry figures for 1994 show men to earn more than half as much again (161 per cent) as women (*Asahi Shimbun Japan Almanac* 1997, p. 100). After recruitment (when the gap in pay is smallest) men generally go on a 'career escalator', whereas women go on a 'clerical escalator'. Career path and promotional opportunities are affected, among other things, by educational attainment. Whereas numerically a smaller percentage of matriculating male students (43 per cent) than female students (48 per cent) proceed to some form of tertiary education, a majority of females (52 per cent)— and almost no males (5 per cent)—merely attend a short-term junior college as opposed to a regular university, meaning that males typically have much stronger qualifications (Ministry of Education figures, in *Asahi Shimbun Japan Almanac* 1997, p. 240).

2. Management and Coordination Agency figures, in *Asahi Shimbun Japan Almanac* 1997, p. 48.

3. See for example Okonogi 86, p. 1.

4. See Smith 83, p. 128, for a vivid illustration of the often extreme degree of prioritisation of the company over self. Smith recounts an incident in 1979 when a male worker successfully tackled a robber. He had not realised that the robber was in fact armed with a knife, and when asked by the television news reporter if he would still have tackled the robber if he had known this, he replied that he wouldn't have, because he might have been injured, had to take time off work as a result, and thereby inconvenience his company.

5. The *kōha* and other types are also discussed in Buruma 85, esp. Chapter 8.

6. Van Wolferen 89, p. 251.

7. Seward 72, pp. 103 and 142, Taylor 85, p. 201, and Okonogi 86, p. 1.

8. Taylor 85, p. 45.

9. Buruma 85, p. 128. Note also the longstanding Japanese saying that 'The womb is a borrowed thing' (see Paulson 76, p. 5).

10. Leupp 95, p. 3, his italics. (Leupp does not necessarily discuss homosexuality in a *kōha* context.)

11. Female impurity is discussed in the following chapter.

12. Leupp 95, pp. 20–1.

13. Leupp 95, p. 4.

14. Leupp 95, pp. 178–82.

15. See, for example, Woronoff 81, passim, Fukutake 82, p. 148, or Okonogi 86 for discussion of the gradual replacement of hard men such as the *mōretsu-gata* (fiercely determined type) by soft men such as the *mai hōmu taipu* ('I value my home' type) and *datsu-sara* ('escaped

salaryman'). Repeat surveys conducted by the Prime Minister's Office also show a similar trend, with those prioritising work over private life decreasing slowly but steadily over the last twenty years. According to these surveys, the number of people in the early–mid-1990s clearly prioritising family life over work (39 per cent) exceeded those clearly prioritising work (23 per cent), but it should be noted that the respondents include women. (See the *Japan Times*, Weekly International Edition, 22–28 August 1994.)

16. A government report in 1992 indicated that 39 per cent of men felt that males should help more around the home (*Japan Times*, Weekly International Edition, 7–13 Dec. 1992), and a survey conducted in 1994 by the Tōkyō Metropolitan Government indicated that around one-third of husbands actually do help around the home with cleaning, shopping, meal preparation and so on (*Tōkyō Metropolitan News,* vol. 44, no. 3, Autumn 1994). A 1995 government white paper also noted that males now spend 60 per cent more time (122 minutes as opposed to 76) 'home-making' at the weekend than twenty years ago—a trend no doubt also reflective of the increasing spread of a five-day working week as well as a change in male attitudes. (See the *Japan Times*, Weekly International Edition, 15–21 April 1996.)

17. Tobin 92b, p. 19.

18. Figures are for 20-year-olds, recorded annually by the Ministry of Education since 1900. See *Asahi Shimbun Japan Almanac* 1997, p. 218. Women have shown a similar increase. Since 1991 heights have levelled off and, in the case of males, even declined slightly, adding a physical dimension to widespread concern over the perceived spiritual decline of the young.

19. The Toronto-based Harlequin publishing company conducts regular international surveys on this topic among women in twenty or so nations. The figures given here are selected and edited from survey results released early in 1996. Questions are multi-choice, with only one reply permitted in each case. Turkey is included here as a non-(Anglo)western control, all other countries in the survey (except Japan) being western.

20. The two main texts embodying this mythology are the *Kojiki* (Record of Ancient Things) of 712 and the *Nihon Shoki* (Chronicle[s] of Japan, also known as the *Nihongi*), of 720. Though produced in the early eighth century they had been commenced in the late seventh. Both are available in English translation, by Philippi (68) and Aston (1896/1972) respectively.

21. An account of Himiko is given in the *Wei Chih* (History of Wei), a Chinese chronicle written in AD 297. See the translation in Tsunoda et al. 64, vol. 1, pp. 4–7.

22. Sei Shōnagon is known for her notebook-style *Pillow Book* (Makura no Sōshi) of around 1002, and Murasaki Shikibu for her novel *Tale of Prince Genji* (Genji Monogatari) of around 1004. Both works are available in several versions of English translation.

23. Hōjō Masako (1157–1225) was the widow of Japan's first permanent shōgun, Minamoto no Yoritomo (1147–99), and effectively ruled the

country after his death, a feared and formidable figure.

24. I follow in particular Ehrenberg 89.

25. The best-known reigning empress, Suiko (554–628, r.593–628), had a male regent, her nephew Prince Shōtoku (574–622), acting on her behalf for much of her reign, in fact from 594 till Shōtoku's death in 622. She was not suffering from any known incapacity.

26. Paulson 76, p. 10.

27. William and Helen McCullough comment that 'As far as we know, no Heian [794–1185] woman ever wrote a single piece of prose in Chinese', and also mention 'unflattering references in tales to Sinitically learned ladies' (W. and H. McCullough 80, vol. 1, p. 10).

28. Paulson 76, esp. pp. 7–9.

29. Smart and Hecht 82, p. 256.

30. Paulson 76, p. 7, and Pharr 83, p. 258.

31. See Paulson 76.

32. Derived from the teachings of Confucius (Kung Fu-tzu, c.551–479 BC), Confucianism stresses harmony, hierarchy, and proper order in human affairs and relations. Not surprisingly, it has often been endorsed by rulers in Japan and elsewhere wishing to promote stability and thereby safeguard their own rule.

33. Pharr 83, p. 258.

34. Hoshino 83, p. 186.

35. See *Japanese Women Now*, pp. 72–3, which also lists other places 'off-limits' to women, such as *saké* breweries and fishing boats. It seems that even today there is at least one mountain which women are not allowed to climb, Mt Omine. Some mountains have been barred to women for Shintō reasons, others for Buddhist, since many Buddhist temples have been located on mountainsides.

36. See Aston 1896/1972, p. 13, and Paulson 76, p. 2.

37. One of the six reigned twice under different names, as Kyōgoku 642–5 and as Saimei 655–61, giving seven reigns by empresses in those early days. The two later reigning empresses were Meishō (1630–43) and Go-Sakuramachi (1762–70). Both reigned in a period when the imperial position was extremely nominal.

38. See Pharr 83, p. 258 and Paulson 76, pp. 5–8 regarding inheritance and the matrilocal marriage pattern known as *mukoirikon* (literally 'son-in-law moving-in marriage'). See also Hane 88, pp. 4–5. Hane observes (p. 5) that even into the Kamakura period (1185–1333), daughters still had the right of inheritance, and a widowed mother controlled the family property.

39. Paulson 76, p. 6.

40. Pharr 83, p. 258, Paulson 76, p. 5, and Ackroyd 59, p. 32.

41. Pharr 83, pp. 258–9.

42. See Paulson 76, p. 11.

43. See Paulson 76, p. 11.

44. See Paulson 76, p. 11.

45. See Leupp 95, p. 184.

46. Hane 82, p. 79.

47. Pharr 83, p. 258.

48. See Leupp 95, p. 186.
49. See Leupp 95, p. 186.
50. Less is known about rural male sexual behaviour, but from various literary references it would appear that a similar pattern to that of the urban male prevailed—frequenting of pleasure quarters in the local town, purchase of both female and male prostitutes, bisexual behaviour, and so on. See Leupp 95, p. 63.
51. Leupp 95 contains a convenient selection of such prints.
52. For a detailed study of Yoshiwara see Seigle 93, and for details on Ponto-chō see Dalby 83.
53. Liza Crihfield Dalby, an American, has the rare distinction for a westerner of having actually worked as a geisha. See Dalby 83 for a detailed discussion of the life and history of the geisha, and esp. pp. 54–7 regarding matters discussed here and in the following paragraphs.
54. Dalby 83, p. 55, makes the same point in very discreet language.
55. Dalby 83, pp. 109–10, and Seigle 83, pp. 179–80. The defloration ceremony has long been important in the geisha world. In most cases virginity was simulated, and the client was usually aware of this, but the symbolic honour of carrying out the 'defloration' (*mizuage-shiki*) was nevertheless considerable.
56. See Tsunoda et al. 64, vol. 2, p. 66, and also Hane 82, p. 3.
57. Hane 82, pp. 209–13. See also Leupp 95, p. 134, regarding boys being sold into prostitution.
58. Hane 82, p. 213.
59. One of the more interesting illustrations of this in an East Asian context is the fact that the Sino-Japanese character for 'trade' (*akinau* in Japanese) is almost certainly derived from an ideographic representation of copulation. See Henshall 88, Character No. 317.
60. Dalby 83, p. xiii. See also p. xiv and p. 8.
61. For details of the shift from male to female geisha, see Dalby 83, pp. 54–7, and Seigle 93, pp. 170–2.
62. A few male geisha did in fact continue in business till after World War Two, at least until the 1970s. So strong has the association now become between geisha and the female that the geisha has for some time been seen as one sort of ideal female type, and many present-day young Japanese react with incredulity when told that originally geisha were male.
63. A useful brief overview of reforms in the Meiji period is given in Paulson 76, pp. 13–17, and for a fuller overview of women from the Meiji Restoration to World War Two see also Hane 88, pp. 7–28.
64. Paulson 76, p. 15.
65. Paulson 76, p. 16.
66. Hane 88, p. 14.
67. Hane 88, p. 13.
68. Iwao 93, p. 11.
69. See Hane 88, p. 12.
70. Tayama Katai 1907/81, p. 42.
71. Tayama Katai 1907/81, p. 44.
72. Hane 88, p. 15.

73. This may seem to suggest that men were much quicker to 'modernise' than women. This is certainly not untrue, but in this particular regard the wearing of western clothes by males was in many cases not so much a reflection of personal taste but a sort of social duty as part of Japan's attempt to be taken seriously by the west. The emperor himself almost always wore western dress in public, and thereby set the standard. Women were not considered important enough to be included in this social obligation.

74. In her 1904 poem *"Kimi Shinitamō Koto Nakare"* (You Must Not Die, My Brother) she openly criticised the emperor for sending young men like her own brother to risk their lives in the Russo-Japanese War while not going to the battlefront himself. Uproar followed its publication, and there were accusations of treason, but somehow—perhaps because she was a woman and not taken too seriously—she avoided serious recrimination.

75. Condon 85, Part IV.

76. I have used the translation given in Hane 88, p. 21. (The translation of the title, however, is my own.)

77. The story of Sirota's drafting of her part of the constitution, and its final acceptance, is truly remarkable, as indeed is the whole story of the constitution. Despite her Japanese-sounding name she was the daughter of a Russian pianist teaching in Japan before and during the war. Because she was a woman and had experience of life in Japan—both rare attributes among the Occupation forces—Sirota was picked as a member of the Occupation team asked by General MacArthur to draft the constitution during a mere six days in February 1946, and was given responsibility for covering women's rights. Though she had little or no formal knowledge either of constitutions or of women's rights, she did have many ideals in mind, and to carry out her task she made a mad dash around libraries to gather relevant material. Her initial draft was too lengthy and detailed, and many of its proposals were consigned for consideration for the subsequent Civil Code (though not all were accepted). When her final draft was presented to the Japanese representatives on the constitutional steering committee (chaired by Colonel Charles Kades) for their approval, there was great alarm at its radical nature. Sirota had been acting as an interpreter for the Japanese and they were kindly disposed towards her. They did not realise that she herself had drafted the proposal they were now considering so late in the day, after sixteen exhausting hours spent mainly debating the new constitutional role of the emperor. Kades said to them, 'Miss Sirota has her heart set on the women's rights, so why don't we pass them?' As Sirota herself recalls succinctly, 'And they did.' When subsequently placed before the Diet lively debate again ensued, but her clause on women's rights was finally accepted along with the rest of the constitution, being formally promulgated on 3 November 1946 and becoming effective 3 May 1947. Sirota and Kades are interviewed in the video "Reinventing Japan", and a reasonably detailed interview with her is also given in the *Japan Times*, Weekly International Edition, 31 July–6 August 1995 (pp. 10–11).

78. Iwao Sumiko, a specialist in Women's Studies. See Iwao 93, p. 12.
79. According to Labour Ministry figures for 1994, in terms of fixed wages women earn only 62 per cent as much as men. (See *Asahi Shimbun Japan Almanac* 1997, p. 100.) Suzuki (96, p. 58) remarks that if all workers, including part-timers, are taken into account, then women earn only 51 per cent of male earnings. ILO figures for 1992 suggest that the wage discrepancy between male and female workers in Japan is the worst among the world's developed nations (Suzuki 96 p. 58).
80. See, for example, Koike 95, pp. 147–9, or Suzuki 96.
81. Suzuki 96, p. 55.
82. The *Japan Times*, Weekly International Edition, 25–31 December 1995.
83. The *Japan Times*, Weekly International Edition, 22–28 September 1997. The survey was by the Tokyo-based publishing company Tōyō Keizai Shinpo-sha.
84. The *Japan Times*, Weekly International Edition, 25–31 December 1995.
85. *Facts and Figures of Japan* 1997, p. 56.
86. See Shimoda (96), a university academic who was herself once in broadcasting.
87. For doctors, Ministry of Health and Welfare figures given in the *Japan Times*, Weekly International Edition, 16–22 March 1998. For lawyers and accountants, Ministry of Labour figures given in *Japan: a Pocket Guide*, 1996, p. 149.
88. The *Japan Times*, Weekly International Edition, 29 Sept.–5 Oct. 1997.
89. One widely reported example of the sexual harassment of a senior woman professional was that of the molestation of Kitaguchi Kazuko, a municipal assembly-woman in Kumamoto. In 1991, in front of multiple witnesses, Kitaguchi had her breasts fondled then (following her protestations) twisted in anger by a fellow assembly-man. She brought charges against the offender, but the District Prosecutor's Office decided not to indict him, on the grounds that he was drunk at the time and had anyway suffered 'social punishment' since. When she subsequently protested to the Kumamoto Municipal Assembly about their lack of action to address the issue of sexual harassment, she was formally reprimanded by the Assembly for her action. See the report in the *Japan Times*, Weekly International Edition, 22–28 March 1993.
90. Iwao 93, p. 204. An idea of the scale of the problem is that in a recent survey of 1,500 women, no fewer than 90 per cent said they had been sexually harassed. (See the *Japan Times*, Weekly International Edition, 22–28 March 1993.) However, one factor obstructing a positive and speedy remedy is that incidents are rarely reported. According to the feminist author Saitō Reiko, 'most [Japanese] women take sexual harassment for granted'. (See the *Japan Times*, Weekly International Edition, 10–16 February 1992.)

That Japanese companies pay far less attention to sexual harassment in Japan than do their overseas subsidiaries/affiliates is seen from a 1996 survey conducted by the Japan Overseas Enterprises Association, which revealed that 53 per cent of Japanese affiliates in the United States had instructions to prevent sexual harassment, whereas at their headquarters in Japan only 7.2 per cent of companies

received such instructions. (See the *Japan Times*, Weekly International Edition, 8–14 July 1996.)
91. See, for example, Lam 92.
92. Suzuki 96, p. 55.
93. See *Asahi Shimbun Japan Almanac* 1997, p. 240.
94. For more details on female students in two-year colleges, see McVeigh 95 and 97.
95. In 1995, the fiftieth anniversary of female suffrage in Japan, only 2.7 per cent (14/511) of parliamentarians in Japan's Lower House were women, and only one cabinet member was a woman. The major exception to the low profile and presence of women politicians is Doi Takako, who has on several occasions been leader of a once-major political party, the socialists (the first such woman leader in Japan's history). She has also been Speaker of the House.
96. Kumagai 96, pp. 97–8. In the July 1993 Lower House election, for example, 68.1 per cent of women voted, as opposed to 67.1 per cent of men, and this pattern is typical too of Upper House elections, and local elections.
97. The *Japan Times*, Weekly International Edition, 28 October–3 November 1996.
98. How good or effective they actually are at carrying out household tasks is another matter. In 1991, according to a survey by the Prime Minister's Office, women still did more than 90 per cent of basic household tasks such as washing, cleaning, and meal preparation. See Kumagai 96, p. 103.
99. Data given in the *Japan Times*, Weekly International Edition, 15–21 April 1996.
100. Kumagai 96, pp. 100–1.
101. Ministry of Health and Welfare figures. See the *Japan Times*, Weekly International Edition, 2–15 January 1995.
102. Data published in the *Yomiuri* newspaper and released in English by Reuters. My source is the *Waikato Times*, 25 January 1993.
103. Atsumi 97, esp. p. 282.
104. Sakamaki 97, p. 36.
105. See, for example, Hasegawa 84, esp. p. 58, and also Fallows 90, pp. 74–5, and Lebra 84, pp. ix–x.
106. See Rayner 80.
107. For example, out of a total international attendance of 40,000 women at the NGO Forum on Women held in Beijing in 1995 on the eve of the United Nations Fourth World Conference on Women, 5,000 were Japanese.
108. See Hakim 95. Hakim does not refer to Japanese women, but does refer to the existence among British and other European women of a view of a woman's role similar to that still widely held in Japan, to the effect that women should stay at home and concentrate on the family. According to Hakim this view has equal support to that of the opposite view, but has been ignored by feminists, whose purpose it does not suit. Her article has aroused considerable controversy.
109. Iwao 91, p. 7. See also Iwao 91, p. 2, and Iwao 93, p. 16.

110. The *Japan Times*, Weekly International Edition, 25–31 July 1994.
111. Condon 85, p. 295.
112. Iwao 91, p. 2, and see also Iwao 93, p. 15.
113. Iwao 91, p. 2, see also Iwao 93, pp. 13–15.
114. See, for example, the 1908 work *Tsuma* (Wife) by Tayama Katai, in which he writes 'The blossoming of the beautiful flower of love is simply to bring two physical bodies together, simply a means of nature to bring about reproduction' (quoted in Henshall 77, p. 285). The subsequent discovery of bio-chemical agents such as pheromones and hormones would clearly have strengthened his opinion.
115. See Doi 73. Doi is the person most associated with the identification of *amae*. However, some decades before Doi (though not published till the 1970s), the Japanologist Kurt Singer had identified a similar dependence syndrome. See Singer 73, esp. pp. 35–6.
116. See, for example, Dale 86, p. 120, regarding the actual male focus of *amae* and many other theories on the Japanese.
117. Buruma 85, p. 19.
118. Taylor 85, pp. 200–1.
119. The translation is my own, and is deliberately literal. 'Snuggle against this warm breast of mine' is '*atsui mune ni amaete*'.
120. Buruma 85, p. 101, refers to prostitutes as acting like 'highly trained mothers'. See also his discussion of the *manga* (comic) heroine Sachiko, a prostitute who describes her genitals to one (albeit special) client as a 'man's home'. He calls her 'Mummy'. (Buruma 85, pp. 205–6.)
121. See Buruma 85, p. 104.
122. For discussion of the Japanese preference for the Ajase Complex (from the Indian Ajatasaru), see Dale 86, pp. 117–18, and Davis 92, pp. 260–3.
123. The term used for 'madonna' is *seibo* ('holy mother'), with the reading 'madonna' in phonetic script. It is clearly intended in a pseudo-religious sense.
124. Iwao 93, p. 150. See too Allison 96, who describes mother–son incest as a part of the mother's attempts to help the son grow successfully into manhood, thereby confirming her effectiveness as a mother.
125. For example, Shigekane Yoshiko's 1979 Akutagawa Prize-winning work *Yama-ai no Kemuri* (Smoke in the Valley) features a mother who, as part of her maternal duties, acts as lifelong sexual partner to her unmarriageable but highly sexed son. The 1969 short story *Sai* (Rhinoceros), by the Naoki Prize-winning author Atōda Takashi, is about a father repeatedly having sex with his young daughter.
126. Pharr 83, p. 258.
127. Doi 73, p. 105, and see also Iwao 91, p. 8.
128. Okonogi (86) is another who sees *maza-kon* as pathological. On the other hand, one wonders whether it really can be considered pathological when it is characteristic of so many men and supported by so many women. For example, realising that women seem to positively enjoy their role as 'mothers' to their lovers, Japan's *Popeye* magazine, which is aimed at men in their late teens and twenties, recently encouraged men to exaggerate their *maza-kon* so as to attract women.
129. The desire for cuteness in women may well originate in men but many

women themselves also help promote it. This does not only apply to very young women, either. In the late 1990s, many older women in their twenties and thirties are part of the 'Hello Kitty' craze, associating themselves with a vast range of objects bearing a white kitten motif. See the report by Naoko Aoki in the *Japan Times*, Weekly International Edition, 19–25 January 1998, p. 7. For a detailed academic discussion of cuteness and its role in femininity in Japan, see McVeigh 96.

130. This male preference for much younger females may also have a bearing on the clear female preference for much older male partners seen in Table 1.1. However much women might wish to 'mother' their male partners, in practice they would only very rarely envisage marriage to a younger male.

131. See, for example, the *Japan Times*, Weekly International Edition, 29 April–5 May 1995. Among ongoing examples of laxness, Japan's Criminal Code still allows sex with children aged as young as 13, despite recent agreement on the need for change to the law. Regional governments can apply their own regulations, but it was not until late 1997 that the Tōkyō Metropolitan Government introduced tougher if still limited legislation (banning sex with minors under 18 when goods or money are given in return for sex). See the *Japan Times*, Weekly International Edition, 1–7 September 1997 and 20–26 October 1997.

132. For a recent discussion of this, see Oshimo and Court 97, and the *Far Eastern Economic Review*, 12 December 1996, pp. 49–50.

133. The survey was by the Tōkyō Metropolitan Government. See the *Far Eastern Economic Review*, 12 December 1996, pp. 49–50.

134. See the *Far Eastern Economic Review*, 12 December 1996, pp. 49–50.

135. Such a sense of male inadequacy, especially in a sexual sense, is quite common in literature, such as for example many of the works of the modern novelists Tanizaki Junichirō, Kawabata Yasunari and Oe Kenzaburō (the latter two Nobel Laureates). As an extreme example, note also Oshima Nagisa's 1976 film about nymphomania, *Ai no Korida* (Realm of the Senses).

136. Christopher 84, p. 61, makes a similar point about conflicting messages being received by the male, who is taught that as a male he is superior yet in actuality owes so much of his life and well-being to his mother— a female. See too Iwao 93, p. 3, for comment on male awareness of their dependence on and hence inferiority to women.

137. For fuller discussion of the male taming of the potentially fearsome female, see Buruma 85.

138. For example, Lent, 89, p. 234, remarks on the great increase in fanta-sised sex and violence in cartoons since the 1960s.

139. Seward 72, p. 94.

140. See Taylor 85, p. 201.

141. See the report in the *Japan Times*, Weekly International Edition, 20–26 May 1996, which confirms both the lack of official research and the continuation of the problem. An earlier report in the same publication, 26 April–2 May 1993, refers to a survey conducted by a concerned private group that found only 171 out of almost 1,000 female respond-ents (out of 4,675 questionnaires distributed) reported no violence

against them. More than half said that they were frequently beaten and/or sexually assaulted, but almost none of them had reported the attacks to the police. About 300 of the women said that they had required hospital treatment. Even allowing for the fact that those women who chose to respond (less than a quarter of those approached) may not be fully representative of women in general, this is a figure which clearly indicates a scale such that medical authorities must be aware of the problem.

142. See, for example, the *Japan Times*, Weekly International Edition, 24–30 July 1995, Reingold 92, p. 101, and also Taylor 85, pp. 193–4.

143. Condon 85, p. 83.

144. *Pacific Friend*, 24/1, May 1996, p. 34. See also Schodt 83, p. 12.

145. See, for example, Woronoff 81, p. 276, Seward 72, p. 65, Buruma 85, p. 54, and Condon 85, p. 76. The Japanese definition of pornography and obscenity has long baffled westerners. It has traditionally largely been confined to pubic hair. While the most outrageous material by western standards has been freely available, anything showing pubic hair, such as *Playboy*, has been banned or had the offending illustration removed. Until recently, even many Japanese comics and magazines aimed at a general readership would include material that was obscene to westerners.

146. One extremely disturbing publication, the adult comic *Kaijin Akkaaman* (Akkaaman the Mystery Man), was given to me (in the 1980s) by a Japanese woman, who had knowingly acquired it. Akkaaman literally lives to spread sex around the universe, a universe peopled with a mix of ordinary humans, sci-fi movie figures, and fantasy characters based on genitalia (such as the ET with a head formed from a foreskin). He copulates whenever, wherever, aided not only by a variable-size penis that can fit any hole (not necessarily a vagina) including the orifices of large animals, but by the ability of his very thoughts—as indicated graphically by the thought balloons in the cartoon—to take on phallic form and penetrate any woman who takes his fancy. Women walking down the street are thus 'raped' by an unseen—but certainly not unfelt—assailant. He can also disseminate sexual frenzy, causing ordinary families to throw off their clothes at the breakfast table and stage orgies which challenge one's perception of incest and child sex. Akkaaman runs a (boys only) school to pass on his wisdom. Among other tests, his students have to pierce a concrete wall with their penis, bring the world's most frigid woman to a climax (on the teacher's desk), and play a version of hoopla in which women have to be stacked on top of each other, the head of each in the vagina of the woman above her.

To move around the universe, his wonders to perform, Akkaaman has a collection of vehicles ranging from a phallic dinosaur to a carriage pulled by a team of women. The carriage is steered by a wheel whose column is firmly rooted in the rectum of the 'lead woman'. Among other adventures, Akkaaman survives an attempt on his manhood by a Tibetan witch who disguises herself as a nubile virgin. Her hymen turns out to have superglue qualities and attaches itself to his organ during deflowering. Unable to urinate, he suffers for a while but eventually his urine bursts through in a spectacular ejaculation, taking the roof with it.

This particular story of *Kaijin Akkaaman* is in the *Action Comics* series, Part 5, published in 1981 by Sōyōsha. I have been unable to ascertain the connotations of the name 'Akkaaman'.

147. Sengoku 87, p. 1.
148. Schodt 83, pp. 125–6.
149. Referred to here are four comics in the *Koro Koro* series, Numbers 48, 50, 51, and 52, published in 1982 by the highly regarded educational publisher Shōgakukan. They are random acquisitions, given to me as language teaching material by a Japanese friend whose young son was a regular reader. Each issue contains about twenty stories spread over some 600 pages.
150. The club members themselves explain to readers that their name is formed from *kintama* (testicles) and *chinpoko* (a children's word for penis). The KP Club's badge is an artistically arranged set of *kintama* and *chinpoko*. The male KP Club members have an unusual but imaginatively appropriate form of distance communication, which entails stretching the foreskin out over the glans of the penis to make a sort of echo chamber so as to amplify the call to gather. It is not clear how the female members of the club (for there is at least one) communicate.
151. There are numerous adventures with *unko* (turd) in the same June 1997 issue of *Koro Koro*. A sculpture is made out of a giant turd. A man who accidentally shaves off his moustache uses a straightened turd as a substitute, only to suffer the torment of having to endure the smell right under his nose. In "*Gakkyūō Yamazaki*" one of the students defecates dramatically on a desk in Yamazaki's classroom. In Yamazaki's 'agony column', in which this streetwise hero offers advice to young readers, one reader asks how he can become an Olympic champion without being very athletic. Yamazaki's advice is to practise hard at something yet to be recognised as an Olympic sport, becoming proficient 'in advance' in the sport in the expectation that it will eventually be included in the Olympic agenda. The sport he suggests is the 'long-turd'—the sport of producing the longest *unko*. His advice comes complete with a picture of Olympic officials measuring a still-emerging turd of at least a metre, just as if they were measuring a long-jump.

There are even more *unko* scenes in the four *Koro Koro* comics of the 1980s referred to earlier. Even robots produce *unko*. A motor-bike rider escapes his pursuer by lifting his bared buttocks and blasting *unko* over the unfortunate's visor. Little boys are forced out of bed by *unko* bigger than they are. Little girls who dare to protest about the quality of their school meals are tied up by the principal and forced to eat *unko*. One child plays a trick on another one hot summer's day by freezing a mixture of *shonben* (urine) and *unko* then grating it to look like the traditional Japanese summer treat of shaved flavoured ice—though the trick backfires when it is consumed with relish by the blissfully ignorant victim. The KP Club use the school toilets as their clubrooms, and graphic representations of these clubrooms never fail to include *unko* in various stages of production—the cross-section diagram being particularly dynamic as it shows the *unko* in free fall. Another story, about a hero-figure called Kintaman (a pun on *kintama*/testicles), seems to contain more *unko* than it does people. In fact, they seem crucial to plot development.

152. See, for example, Schodt 83. See too Leupp 95, who refers to modern Japan continuing to be a 'faeces-friendly society' (p. 118). This is despite the fact that excrement is supposedly *kegare* (impure) in Shintō beliefs.
153. See, for example, Buruma 85, p. 110, Christopher 84, p. 144, and Taylor 85, p. 207.
154. Though the figure is now rather dated, Mouer and Sugimoto 86 (p. 330) refer to an estimated usage in the year 1981 by 1.1 billion [sic] persons. This would be equivalent to more than once per month per adult nationwide.
155. Though this too is a little dated, see Woronoff 81, p. 276. One Tōkyō survey revealed that more than two-thirds of middle managers had had extra-marital sex during the previous year.
156. The *no-pan kissa*, or *no-pantsu kissaten* ('no panties coffee bar').
157. The general trade in schoolgirls' soiled knickers is known as the *buru-sera* trade (from the Japanised pronunciation of 'bloomers' and 'sailor suits', the uniform of schoolgirls). See the *Japan Times,* Weekly International Edition, 28 February–6 March 1994. The extension of the trade to vending machines is a recent development.
158. See Condon 85, p. 80.
159. See, for example, Leupp 95, who refers to Japan's 'ancient roots of gender blending' (p. 174).
160. Leupp 95, p. 52.
161. Reingold 92, p. 98.
162. Doi 73, p. 114.
163. Doi 73, pp. 113–21. Doi recognises that *amae* operates inter-sexually as well as intra-sexually, but still feels that 'the essence of homosexual feelings is *amae*' (p. 118).
164. Doi 73, p. 116.
165. Though nature in Japan is usually benign, the nation's location on the Pacific 'Ring of Fire' means it is prone to natural disasters such as earthquakes and volcanic eruptions, as well as monsoons and tidal waves. The Kōbe Earthquake of January 1995, which killed over 5,000 people and caused massive damage, was a poignant reminder of the potential threat of nature.
166. See, for example, Kalland 95, esp. p. 246 and p. 250, and Buruma 85, Chapters 4 and 5, esp. p. 65.
167. For further discussion of this line of argument see Buruma 85.
168. An all-female theatre founded in 1913 in the resort town of Takarazuka, near Osaka. Its musical performances are aimed primarily at a female audience. A number of other theatres are also all-female, but Takarazuka is the most famous. For more details on Takarazuka see Buruma 85, pp. 113–22, Anderson 83, or Robertson 92.
169. See Leupp 95, p. 177. The italics are mine.
170. See Reingold 92, p. 98.

171. Leupp 95, p. 178.
172. Leupp 95, pp. 130–1.
173. Kondo 92, p. 190.
174. Buruma 85, p. 118.
175. Buruma 85, p. 125, and see also Aoyama 88, p. 196, and Schodt 83, p. 101.

PART TWO: ON THE FRINGES OF SOCIETY: MINORITIES AND OTHER MARGINALS

1. The government officially claims there are just over 1 million *burakumin*, whereas *burakumin* representatives themselves claim 3 million. See Neary 93, p. 242, and Ministry of Foreign Affairs 84.
2. Distribution details in de Vos and Wetherall 83, p. 3.
3. Though a little dated as an illustration, in a 1965 government survey 70 per cent stated that they believed *burakumin* were of a different race and lineage from the Japanese. See Hane 82, pp. 139–40. The 'different race' is invariably a reference to assumed Korean origins. There is absolutely no scientific evidence to support this, and the Japanese are aware of this, but many still prefer to believe it.
4. See also Ohnuki-Tierney 84, p. 46.
5. Hanami 95, p. 124.
6. De Vos and Wetherall 83, p. 4.
7. Hane 82, pp. 141–2. The four main classes of the day, in descending order, were warriors (*shi*), peasants (*nō*), artisans (*kō*), and merchants (*shō*).
8. Hane 82, p. 142. The reasoning behind this specific fraction is not clear, but there are similarities with, for example, class-based monetary values placed on human lives (*wertgild*) established under Danelaw in pre-Norman Britain.
9. See de Vos and Wetherall 83, pp. 8–9, for details of these various investigations.
10. See Cornell 67, and Wagatsuma and de Vos 67. General society is formally known as *ippan shakai*, but is better known to *burakumin* as *soto* ('outside') or *atchimae* ('over there').
11. See Reingold 92, p. 162. See also Cornell 67, p. 352.
12. A translation of one of Nakagami's works, the short story "The Immortals" (*Fushi* 1984), is found in Gessel and Matsumoto 85, Vol. 2, pp. 412–28. Some useful studies of him, by various scholars, are found in Vol. 8, Nos. 1 and 2 (1996), of the *Japan Forum*. One of Nakagami's approaches is to use his *burakumin* status as a marginal to bluntly address the deeper forces repressed beneath mainstream culture, such as male violence against women (a significant element in "The Immortals"). Unfortunately, for many readers this may perpetuate some of the stereotypes about *burakumin*. In other words, Nakagami's marginal status is something of a double-edged sword—he can see things and express things in a way not possible for a 'mainstreamer', but at the same time he runs the risk of only ever being seen as a marginal

reflecting marginals' values.

Though not a *burakumin* herself, the novels of the *burakumin* sympathiser Sue Sumii have also done much to highlight discrimination. She too died recently, in 1997, aged 95.

13. Yoshino and Murakoshi 83.

14. Van Wolferen referred in his book to some of the forceful tactics of the BLL. When the Japanese translation appeared in 1990, his Japanese publisher was put under pressure by the BLL to withdraw the book. However, it was kept on sale in no small part due to the insistence of the author, who refused to bow to BLL pressure.

15. See Wagatsuma and de Vos 67 for further discussion of this stereotype of violence.

16. De Vos and Wetherall 83, p. 5.

17. For example, in 1991, at considerable cost, Japan Airlines scrapped 280,000 copies of its in-flight magazine containing an article on *burakumin* (written by an American scholar), because of the sensitivity of the '*dōwa* problem'. And as Makiko Hanami comments (95, p. 132), 'Today, *buraku* issues are taboo for the Establishment. Major publishing companies rarely publish material that includes even a few lines of opinion on *buraku* issues.'

    Ironically, attempts to avoid *burakumin* issues, and in particular to avoid being deemed to provoke negative public criticism of the *burakumin*, may in some cases have brought about problems for the *burakumin* themselves, as well as society as a whole. For example, the major outbreak of food-poisoning in the Osaka region in the summer of 1996, which saw around a dozen deaths and more than 10,000 people fall ill, was from an early stage believed to be linked with meat and slaughterhouses, where almost all the workers were *burakumin*. As Shimada Toshio, head of the intestinal-infection laboratory at the National Institute of Health commented, despite this belief inspections of slaughterhouses were delayed because of 'historically sensitive issues'—that is, the *burakumin*. For the same reasons, newspapers were also told by their editors not to mention slaughterhouses as a probable source of the contamination. In the meantime, people not only continued to fall ill as a result of the lack of thorough investigation, many people came to suspect meat as the cause anyway, and, unable to be reassured by any inspection that might have given clearance, stopped buying it, adversely affecting *burakumin*-run meat companies. See the *Far Eastern Economic Review*, 8 August 96, p. 21.

18. For example, such a view was frequently encountered in a recent survey of students. See Hanami (95, p. 131), who also draws attention to students' ambivalent views on the matter, first denying there is still a *burakumin* problem, then advising researchers against probing too deeply since it is dangerous. Among other things this contradictory response confirms that many Japanese have more opinions about *burakumin* than they initially acknowledge.

19. The definition of 'Japan' varies with time and place, but the nation is generally seen as emerging with the formation of the Yamato state by the sixth century, centred on Yamato in the Nara Basin. 'Yamato',

along with 'Nippon/Nihon', was often used as a name for Japan, which at the time did not include Hokkaidō (then known as Ezo). The term 'Yamato Japanese' is thus often used by the Ainu and other outlying regional groups such as the Okinawans to distinguish between themselves and the 'mainlanders'.

20. See also Morris-Suzuki 96.

21. See, for example, Bird 1881, who devoted half her writings on Japan to the Ainu (Aino) and was very clearly fascinated by them.

22. The name of Japan's most famous mountain, Fuji (in central Japan), is believed to be derived from the Ainu word for 'fire', *fuchi*.

23. Records of the time refer to primitive people called Ezo or Emishi. These were once believed by scholars to have been one and the same as the Ainu, partly because Ezo was also the early name applied to Hokkaidō by Yamato Japanese. However, it is now considered more likely that these terms were used generically to refer to a range of 'barbarian' peoples. (See Barnes 93, p. 51, and Kōno and Bowles 83, p. 35.)

    The title *shōgun*, established since the days of Minamoto no Yoritomo in the twelfth century as the designation of the military ruler of Japan, was earlier still used as a temporary title (*seii tai-shōgun*, 'barbarian-subduing generalissimo') for generals conducting campaigns to subdue these barbarians.

24. In a 1986 survey, the number of self-identifying Ainu in Hokkaidō was 24,381 (Neary 93, p. 244.) There are probably several thousand Ainu elsewhere in Japan (approximately 1,000 of these in Tōkyō), and in Russian territory. Kayano Shigeru, the noted Ainu writer and activist, estimated in 1994 that there might be as many as 50,000 nationwide — a high figure which apparently includes 'hidden' Ainu who prefer to conceal their ethnicity in similar fashion to *burakumin* who have 'passed' into mainstream society. See the *Japan Times*, Weekly International Edition, 22–28 August 1994, and see also de Vos and Wetherall 83, p. 13. In 1902, 70 per cent of births were unmixed (that is, pure Ainu), yet by 1957 this had dropped to zero. In 1980, it was estimated that fewer than 200 pure Ainu remained (Kōno and Bowles 83, p. 35).

25. See, for example, Ossenberger 86, Dodo 86, and Katayama 96.

26. The immigrants who arrived around 300 BC were (later) known as the Yayoi people. Though there was some degree of inter-breeding between Yayoi and Jōmon, the Yayoi prevailed and were in substance the ancestors of the Yamato Japanese.

27. Ossenberger 86, pp. 211–12, Dodo 86, pp. 157–8, Katayama 96, and Kōno and Bowles 83, p. 35.

28. Philippi 79, pp. 1–3.

29. Watanabe 73, p. 73.

30. See Philippi 79, pp. 59–63, for further details of Ainu gods.

31. Even Philippi (79, p. 59), an authority on Ainu, treats *kami* as the older term. The issue may be confused by the fact that *kami* also exists as a homophone in Japanese meaning 'above', suggesting some fundamental link with a celestial heaven and divinity. However, such a connection

cannot be assumed. The etymologist Ono Susumu (1974, *Nihongo o Sakanoboru*, Iwanami, Tōkyō, pp. 189–93, in Japanese only), points out that *kami* in the sense of 'god' or 'spirit' is not as ancient as other Japanese terms with similar meaning (such as *tama*, *chi*, *hi*, and *mi*). However, he too concludes—albeit tentatively—that the Ainu term is probably derived from the Japanese. This is unconvincing. Unless the Ainu dual world-view evolved subsequent to contact with Japanese, which is extremely unlikely, it simply does not make sense that they could have a name for one half of that duality (*ainu*) but not the other. A far more likely scenario is that prior to their arrival in Japan the Yayoi people (later to become the Yamato Japanese) had a range of types of gods, each with a term of its own. After their arrival, and contact with the Ainu, they applied the term *kamui* to various local natural objects already deemed by the indigenous Ainu to be imbued with godhood. When Shintō became codified shortly afterwards, the use of the (by now shortened) term broadened and eventually prevailed. The ramifications of this scenario would be unappealing to most Yamato Japanese.

32. Philippi 79, p. 50.
33. The following description of the traditional Ainu lifestyle draws heavily but not exclusively on Watanabe 73.
34. Morris-Suzuki 96, p. 91.
35. In particular, the Saru River region in the south of Hokkaidō is widely seen by Ainu as the point of origin of their culture. See Kayano 94, p. 7.
36. Among other things, the Ainu felt the Japanese to be treacherous both in trade and war. This is made clear in a number of their epics. See Philippi 79, esp. p. 13, for a description of the Japanese tactics of feigning peace then striking by surprise.
37. See Hanazaki 96, p. 118, and Siddle 95, p. 79. As Siddle points out (pp. 74–9), the Japanese view of them as less than human was in part based upon their hairiness, for this has long been associated by the Japanese, as also by the Chinese, with barbarian and subhuman (demon) status. A popular story among Japanese was that Ainu were descended from dogs, which may be a derogatory Japanese variant of an Ainu self-identification with wolves or more likely a pun on the similarity of the term *Ainu* with the Japanese *A! Inu!*, meaning 'Ah! A dog!' Such attitudes and stereotypes were to continue into the modern period.
38. Morris-Suzuki 96.
39. For details of this event, see Hanazaki 96, pp. 117–19.
40. Morris-Suzuki 96, esp. pp. 90–2.
41. Morris-Suzuki 96, p. 92.
42. Hanami 95, p. 126.
43. Western observers of Ainu during the Meiji period, though they rarely went so far as to consider them subhuman, still treated them as extremely inferior. For example, the American scholar Edward Morse, otherwise noted for his pioneering contribution to an understanding of Japanese prehistory, described the Ainu as 'low unlettered savages without moral courage, lazy, and strongly given to drunkenness' (see Siddle 95, p. 84). Basil Hall Chamberlain and Isabella Bird also basically

viewed the Ainu as uncivilised savages (though Bird did find some noble qualities in them). Henry Landor, after describing them as 'malformed, ill-natured, and often idiotic', concluded that their physical features 'strongly support Darwin's theory of evolution, and the hairy arboreal ancestor with pointed ears from which the races of men are descended' (see Siddle 95, p. 85). Darwinian views, which were very popular in Japan, only served to strengthen pre-existing Japanese views of the inferiority of the Ainu.

44. Philippi 79, p. 15.
45. Hanami 95, p. 135.
46. See, for example, Wetherall 93.
47. See Kayano 94, pp. 57–61 regarding his father, and pp. 33–4 regarding his grandfather.
48. Kayano 94, pp. 59–60.
49. McCormack 96, p. 290.
50. The *Japan Times*, Weekly International Edition, 7–13 April 97.
51. Reischauer and Craig 79, p. 12. See also de Vos and Wetherall 83, p. 9, for reference to a similar peerage a century or so earlier.
52. 'They look like us but they aren't us' was an unsolicited response featuring repeatedly in an informal survey on Japan–Korea relations that I conducted in Japan in 1977.
53. Taylor 85, p. 60, and Neary 93, p. 243.
54. The earthquake struck on 1 September 1923. It was Japan's worst natural disaster, killing over 100,000 people, mostly in fires, and making more than 3 million homeless. Rumour had it that Koreans had started some of the fires, that they were looting, and poisoning wells to kill off more Japanese. Some Japanese even believed the Koreans had actually caused the earthquake by upsetting the gods through their very presence in Japan. As a result, more than 6,000 are estimated to have been murdered by vigilantes in the days of relative lawlessness immediately following the earthquake. For further details see Stanley 83. For a personal insight into this 'Korean hunt' I am indebted to Okamoto Yoshio, of Kōbe, whose father, though a Japanese, was initially mistaken for a Korean and barely escaped with his life.
55. Toyotomi Hideyoshi, one of Japan's great warlords who achieved virtual hegemony over the nation, appears to have had grand schemes of conquering all Asia. As an initial step he twice (1592 and 1597) tried to invade Korea, only to be repelled by a combination of Korean and Chinese forces. The behaviour of his troops caused considerable bitterness towards Japan. For example, the ears of captives were sliced off almost as a matter of course and brought back to Japan as trophies. It was not until four centuries later in the 1990s that some 20,000 of these were finally returned to Korea.
56. As early as 1873 one of the new government leaders, Saigō Takamori, proposed an invasion of Korea. This was ostensibly intended as punishment for Korea's reluctance to approve the new government, but in reality was intended both as an outlet for samurai frustration at their impending disestablishment and as an early step in Japan's acquisition of colonies to match the western powers. Saigō's proposal itself was not

approved, but Japan soon started blatantly interfering in Korean domestic affairs. Among other things it removed the Chinese presence from Korea through the Sino-Japanese war of 1894–5, and the possibility of Russian presence through the Russo-Japanese War of 1904–5, after which Korea became a Japanese protectorate till its formal annexation in 1910.

57. Neary 93, p. 243, and see also Choe 93, p. 10.
58. See, for example, the *Japan Times*, Weekly International Edition, 14–20 August 1995, p. 3, and again 21–27 August 1995, p. 8. For further discussion of Japanese behaviour in Korea, see the various works by Frederick McKenzie, such as McKenzie 80. For a treatment relatively sympathetic to Japan, see Duus 95.
59. Choe 93, p. 11.
60. De Vos and Wetherall 83, pp. 9–10.
61. For an account of the experiences of some of these women, see Howard 95. In 1995, as a Japanese government initiative, a private fund (largely from business interests) was set up to offer some compensation to them, but this has proved a further source of grievance, for the government itself is still refusing to take official responsibility.
62. Hoffman 92, p. 480.
63. Hanami 95, pp. 127–9.
64. Lee 83, p. 291.
65. The *Japan Times*, Weekly International Edition, 2–8 December 1996, p. 7.
66. The *Japan Times*, Weekly International Edition, 3–9 April 1995.
67. For example, a monument recognising Korean casualties in the Hiroshima bombing, built by Korean donations in 1970, currently stands outside the Peace Park, while other monuments are inside. Its location is often seen as a symbol of anti-Korean discrimination. In 1990 the Hiroshima municipal authorities agreed to build a new monument inside the park, but this has been continually delayed by a disagreement between North and South Koreans over the wording. (See the *Japan Times*, Weekly International Edition, 18–24 August 1997.)
68. For fuller details of this and other cases, see Hanami 95, pp. 140–1.
69. See Hanami 95, p. 139, and also Lee 83, pp. 291–2.
70. The *Far Eastern Economic Review*, Fiftieth Anniversary issue, 1996, p. 206.
71. Hanami 95, p. 143.
72. Hoffman 92, p. 489.
73. The *Japan Times*, Weekly International Edition, 3–9 March 1997. Yu is in fact the third Korean to win the Akutagawa Prize. She is a symbol of anti-Korean discrimination in other ways too. Though born and raised in Japan, with Japanese as her mother tongue, and though a high-profile celebrity in Japan, she was still not allowed to sign a contract to rent her current apartment. This had to be done by a Japanese.
74. The *Japan Times*, Weekly International Edition, 20–26 January 97.
75. Inami 92, p. 354.
76. For further details of the history of the *yakuza* see Kaplan and Dubro 87, Part I, or, in brief, de Vos and Mizushima 67.

77. See also Thayer 83, p. 286.
78. Kaplan and Dubro 87, pp. 16–21.
79. See, for example, Kaplan and Dubro 87, pp. 190–2. These films have, like the *yakuza* themselves, become 'harder' and more nihilistic in character in recent years. However, though they have declined as cinema features, they are still very popular as TV films. See Schilling 96 and Buruma 85, pp. 170–95, for a useful overview of trends in *yakuza* films.
80. Raz 92, p. 230.
81. Raz 92, p. 225.
82. Buruma 85, p. 188.
83. Contrary to the popular image of industrial harmony associated with Japan there was actually considerable unrest in the early postwar period, culminating in 1960 in a nine-month strike at the Mitsui-owned Miike coalmines in Kyūshū. The dispute, over planned lay-offs and rejected wage claims, represented a major confrontation between the labour movement as a whole and government-backed big business. 10 per cent of the national police force was used to help break up the strike, along with hired *yakuza*. Considerable footage of the dispute is included in the video "Inside Japan Inc." in the *Pacific Century* series.
84. See Kaplan and Dubro 87, pp. 210–16, for discussion of the varied role of the *sōkaiya*. They comment (p. 210) that 'For years, virtually every company listed on Japan's stock exchanges dealt with them.' As one specific illustration, in 1979, 58 per cent of companies listed on the Tōkyō Stock Exchange admitted to police that they had hired them (Taylor 85, p. 156). *Sōkaiya* continue to thrive despite the passing as long ago as 1982 of a commercial law punishing any company that pays money under any circumstances to a *sōkaiya*. In 1997, for example, major companies such as Nomura Securities, Dai-Ichi Kangyō Bank, and Yamaichi Securities all featured in scandals involving huge payments to *yakuza*, and suffered various legal penalties as a result. It is sometimes difficult to draw a line between paying off and hiring. Similarly, companies would argue that short AGMs are the result of having to rush in order to prevent *sōkaiya* intimidation, not thanks to it.
85. See for example Kaplan and Dubro 87, p. 144, and de Vos and Mizushima 67, p. 306.
86. Kaplan and Dubro 87, p. 100. They name in particular Kodama Yoshio and Sasakawa Ryōichi as major fixers.
87. Some 120 or more members of the Diet and bureaucracy, many of them in very high positions, took 'money for favours' from the Sagawa company, which had links with the underworld.
88. De Vos and Mizushima 67, p. 307.
89. Such claims have been widely made, such as for example by Taoka Kazuo, former boss of the Yamaguchi-gumi (*Asahi Shimbun*, 25 February 1985). See also Van Wolferen 89, pp. 101–5.
90. Kaplan and Dubro 87, p. 202.
91. Eric von Hurst. See Kaplan and Dubro 87, p. 202.
92. Kaplan and Dubro 87, p. 26, and see also de Vos and Mizushima 67.
93. Kaplan and Dubro 87, p. 26.
94. Hayashi 92.

95. See, for example, Hayashi 92, Inami 92, p. 358, and Makihara 92.
96. The *Japan Times*, Weekly International Edition, 22–28 June 1992.
97. The *Japan Times*, Weekly International Edition, 19–25 September 1992.
98. See "Japan's *Yakuza* Go Legit" (1991), and see also Inami 92, and Kaplan 95 (who discusses in particular the business dealings of Ishii Susumu, boss of the Inagawa-kai during the bubble years).
99. Inami 92, p. 354.
100. The *Japan Times*, Weekly International Edition, 7–13 July 1997.
101. See, for example, Tayama Katai's novel *Country Teacher* of 1909 (English translation 1984).
102. Katayama 96, esp. p. 24, and Pearson 96.
103. See Sakai and Sakihara 83, pp. 85–6. Korean visitors to Yonagumi Island (in the far south of the group) in 1477 reported that the inhabitants lived in flimsy window-less huts, used primitive clay vessels, and were ignorant of iron.
104. Sakai and Sakihara 83, p. 86.
105. In 1871, fifty-four Ryūkyūan fishermen had been shipwrecked on the shores of Taiwan (Formosa) and killed by the aborigines. The Japanese government had claimed compensation from China for this ill-treatment of its 'nationals' but this was not forthcoming, so in May 1874 a force of some 3,500 men was sent on a punitive expedition to Taiwan. Significantly, the men were led by Saigō Tsugumichi, the brother of Takamori (who had the previous year proposed a punitive expedition to Korea). Things did not go as well as the Japanese hoped and it was the end of the year before they were to emerge victorious, having suffered heavy losses. They were, however, successful in finally gaining compensation from China and thereby also international recognition (except by China) of their suzerainty over the islands.
106. Sakai and Sakihara 83, p. 87.
107. See, for example, the accounts given by various Okinawans in H. and T. Cook 92. See also Reingold 92, p. 19, and the *Japan Times*, Weekly International Edition, 27 November–3 December 1995, pp. 10–11.
108. Reingold 92, p. 21.
109. Hanazaki 96, p. 129.
110. The following account of the Ogasawaras draws particularly on Stanley 94.
111. Stanley 94, p. 29.
112. Mayo 83. During the Tokugawa period Japan had entered a phase of relative withdrawal from the world, especially from contact with the west (with the exception of the Dutch). The western powers made various attempts to reopen contact with it, all unsuccessful until US Commodore Matthew Perry, backed by the authority of the American president, arrived in 1853 to settle the matter with 'gunboat diplomacy'. For more details see Pineau 68.
113. See Stanley 94, p. 31.
114. Kishida Yūji. See Buruma 87, p. 84.
115. Kitahara 89, esp. p. 144.
116. One well-known focus of attention was Ishihara Shintarō's 1989 work *The Japan That Can Say 'No': Why Japan Will Be First Among Equals*

(English version 1991). As a high-profile Diet member and novelist, Ishihara's advocacy of standing up to America (and by extension the west) and its 'Japan bashing' was particularly influential. The word *kenbei* ('dislike of America') came into fashion shortly afterwards.

117. See respectively the *Japan Times*, Weekly International Edition, 25–31 May 1992, and 13–19 June 1994.

118. See, for example, an article in the *Japan Times*, Weekly International Edition, 17–23 February 1992, p. 14, which discusses how publicly subsidised apartments in Kasai in Tōkyō's Kōtō Ward are not available to foreigners, owing to a legal situation which permits the landowner, despite receiving public money, to decide for himself whom he allows to take up residence in the apartments, and he has openly stated that he will not accept applications from foreigners.

119. Some local governments, such as Kawasaki and Osaka, have been pioneering the employment of foreigners for some years now. Initially this was opposed by the central government, but in November 1996 the Ministry of Home Affairs finally gave it informal approval. There has never been a clearly defined legal ban on foreigners in government employ, but a 1953 government decree stated that public servants with administrative authority or influence on the general public must be Japanese nationals. See the *Japan Times*, Weekly International Edition, 2–8 December 1996.

120. Probably the most remarkable example of this is the native Hawaiian and American citizen Chad Rowan, a sumō wrestler who in 1993, under the name Akebono, became *yokozuna* (grand champion), the first non-Japanese ever to achieve this hallowed rank. See the *Japan Times*, Weekly International Edition, 8–14 February 1993.

121. Buruma 92, pp. 185–6.

122. Buruma 92, p. 186.

123. For example, Japan modelled its Meiji Constitution and military structure on German precedents.

124. Dower 86, p. 207.

125. See Tokayer and Swartz 79. The plan was the brainchild of the industrialist and political adviser Ayukawa Gisuke (also known as Aikawa Genji, founding father of Nissan), but it had official Foreign Ministry approval. Documents were seized by the Occupation authorities but some copies found their way into private hands. The plan became public knowledge in the early 1970s when a copy was obtained by a Jewish resident in Tōkyō.

126. As described at the time by one of its supporters, Captain Inuzuka Koreshige: 'The plan is very much like *fugu*. If we are indeed skillful in preparing this dish—if we can remain ever-alert to the sly nature of the Jews, if we can continue to devote our constant attention to this enterprise lest the Jews, in their inherently clever manner, manage to turn the tables on us and begin to use us for their own ends—if we succeed in our undertaking, we will create for our nation and our beloved emperor the tastiest and most nutritious dish imaginable. But, if we make the slightest mistake, it will destroy us in the most horrible manner.' (See Tokayer and Swartz 79, pp. 52–3.)

127. See Tokayer and Swartz 79, Part 2. For briefer details, see the *Japan Times*, Weekly International Edition, 29 May–4 June, 1995, p. 10, or Reingold 92, pp. 178–9.

128. See Ben-Dasan (the alias of Yamamoto Shichihei), 72.

129. For details of this literature, and further discussion of general Japanese attitudes towards and treatment of Jews, see Reingold 92, pp. 176–82.

130. In September 1986, at a gathering of young Liberal Democrats, Nakasone remarked that the homogeneous Japanese were smarter than Americans because American intellectual levels were lowered by blacks and Hispanics. He seemed surprised that his comments ended up reaching western ears. Nakasone's comments about blacks and Hispanics have gained particular notoriety, but he was far from alone in his sentiments. Similar derogatory views were made a few years later by Aida Yūji, a well-known academic, who stated that America was heading for a problem because blacks and Hispanics would eventually outnumber the whites there but lacked the skills—in both education and personal qualities—to run a nation. See Aida 90, passim but esp. p. 4 and p. 6. See also Russell 91, p. 422, which contains a lengthy extract.

131. Russell 91, pp. 418–19.

132. See Russell 91, p. 423.

133. Taylor 85, p. 28.

134. Fields 83, p. 100.

135. Fields 83, pp. 99–100.

136. Miller 82, p. 156.

137. Taylor 85, pp. 31–2.

138. This reputation is shown to have considerable substance, at least in the case of the Filipinos, by Ray Ventura (himself an illegal Filipino worker) in his 1992 book *Underground in Japan.*

139. See Harnischfeger 93, and the *Japan Times*, Weekly International Edition, 27 April–3 May 1992. The estimate is almost certainly understated.

140. See Gill 96, p. 7.

141. Harnischfeger 93.

142. Based on figures given in Nakano 95, p. 62.

143. Harnischfeger 93.

144. Nakano 95, p. 62.

145. See Harnischfeger 93, p. 11.

146. Strong 83, p. 271. There are certain exceptions, however, notably in the entertainment industry.

147. The word *gaijin* (literally 'outside person') in fact applies almost always just to Caucasian westerners. The term *bata-kusai* (literally 'smelling of butter') is also sometimes used of westerners, being a reference to the buttery, soapy smell associated with them by Japanese. Though most Japanese claims about physical differences between themselves and westerners are at best highly questionable (such as the unique brain or unique intestines of the Japanese), in this particular case there is in fact some scientific support for it due to the relatively high amount of butyric acid in most westerners' perspiration as a result of high consumption of fatty meats.

148. According to Pearl Buck. See Seward 72, p. 275.

149. Strong 83.
150. In theory, even prior to recent law changes, they could apply for citizenship to be granted on special grounds, though in practice such applications rarely succeeded since a number of qualitative criteria had to be met (such as being of proven upstanding character, service to society, and so forth).
151. Fields 83, p. 130. Despite his surname George Fields has a Japanese father. His mother is Australian.
152. Macdonald and Kowatari 95, p. 249.
153. Akiko Kowatari, in Macdonald and Kowatari 95, esp. p. 249.
154. Macdonald and Kowatari 95, p. 250.
155. Sharon Traweek. See "Japanese Fear Loss of 'Soul' Abroad", *New Scientist*, 2 March 1991, p. 13.
156. Guzewicz 96, p. 45.
157. Benedict Giamo. See Guzewicz 96, p. 45.
158. The *Japan Times*, Weekly International Edition, 27 April–3 May 1992.
159. See Ventura 92, passim. See also Gill 96 for a brief further account of life in Kotobuki. Gill observes that since Ventura's book the Filipinos have declined in number (though still very much a presence), and it is now Koreans who predominate there. Interestingly, he also writes (p. 7) that not only the flophouses, but 'practically the whole of Kotobuki is owned by Japan-resident Koreans'.
160. Gill 96, p. 6.
161. Sakurai 96, p. 35.
162. See Sakurai 96, p. 35.
163. Gill 94, p. 273.
164. For detailed accounts of life in Sanya, see Fowler 96 and de Bary 97.
165. Guzewicz 96, pp. 43–4.
166. Gill 94, p. 274.
167. Gill 94, pp. 277–8. Gill covers welfare facilities in some detail.
168. Gill (94, p. 280) remarks that there are a dozen or so Christian missions in the Sanya area, whereas 'the Japanese indigenous religions are conspicuously absent'.
169. For a detailed account of the incident, see Sakurai 96.
170. The *Japan Times*, Weekly International Edition, 11–17 March 1996.
171. For example, Satō Hirotada was beaten to death by three youths in October 1995 in Tōkyō's Higashi-Jūjō Park. (See Guzewicz 96, p. 52.) See Matsuzawa 88 for earlier examples.
172. Ohnuki-Tierney 84, esp. p. 22.
173. See Farris 85, esp. Chapter 2, for details of the very serious effects of this and other 'imported' diseases.
174. See Johnston 95 for a detailed study of tuberculosis and its sociology in Japan.
175. See "The Lepers of Japan", in the *Economist*, 24 February 1996.
176. See "The Lepers of Japan", in the *Economist*, 24 February 1996.
177. For these and other details of discrimination, see the comments by Dr Shimazaki Kiyoko, long-time president of the Japan Leprosy Mission, in the *Japan Times*, Weekly International Edition, 19–25 February 1996, p. 16.

178. See for example the *Japan Times*, Weekly International Edition, 25–31 May 1992, p. 2, for a comment from an official of the Tōkyō Chamber of Commerce (Kamiya Kazuo) that many companies wanted to carry out AIDS tests on foreign employees.
179. The Ministry of Health and Welfare estimates that the actual number of HIV-positive persons is nine times the declared rate, but the same non-disclosure factor applies to all nations. See *Nippon: A Charted Survey of Japan 1994/95* (Kokuseisha), p. 310.
180. Health and Welfare Minister Kan Naoto, appointed to office in January 1996, was again instrumental in bringing the scandal to light. For further details on the scandal and Kan's approach see Itagaki 96.
181. Ikeda 95, pp. 29–30.
182. Ienishi was recruited into politics by the newly formed Democratic Party, of which Kan Naoto was co-leader, and ran for a seat in Nara. He failed to gain this, but was the party's number one proportional representative for the Kinki area, and won his seat on this party-list basis.
183. See the feature in the *Japan Times*, Weekly International Edition, 7–13 April 1997, p. 7. The book in question is entitled simply *Ryūhei*, published in 1996 by Kirihara Shoten, Tōkyō, and available in English translation.
184. Ikeda 95, p. 21.
185. According to Ministry of Health and Welfare figures for 1995, 263,000 people died from cancer, as many as the combined figure for those who died from Japan's two next principal causes of death, cerebrovascular diseases and cardiac diseases.
186. Munakata 86, p. 374.
187. See, for example, Yamazaki 96. Yamazaki Fumio, a cancer surgeon, is a noted advocate of telling patients the truth, and of better treatment of the terminally ill.
188. *Nippon: A Charted Survey 1994/95* (Kokuseisha), p. 309.
189. Data from *Japan 1997: An International Comparison*, p. 107.
190. Ohnuki-Tierney 84, Chapter 3.
191. See Chapter 1.2, p. 12. The boy, born to the descended gods Izanami and Izanagi, was seemingly born without limbs, for he was referred to as a 'leech child' (*hiruko*). He was set adrift in a small boat and pushed out to sea.
192. Mogi 92, p. 440.
193. Mogi 92, pp. 440–1. Does one, for example, treat as 'disabled' anyone who wears spectacles even occasionally?
194. The *Japan Times*, Weekly International Edition, 22–28 April 1996, p. 7.
195. The *Japan Times*, Weekly International Edition, 26 August–1 Sept. 1996, p. 16.
196. Honna and Katō 95, p. 272.
197. The *Japan Times*, Weekly International Edition, 11–17 August 1997.
198. Mogi 92, p. 441.
199. Revenge-killing, for example, is tolerated and even expected in some cultures, whereas in others it is deemed either an outright criminal act or a serious loss of self-control suggesting mental instability.
200. In fact, even if it is the result of a mental illness, deviancy can under

certain circumstances be accepted (after a fashion) by Japanese society, in an apparently similar way to the acceptance of the *yakuza*—that is, it provides a sort of vicarious thrill in a society dominated by orthodoxy. In that respect, the more outrageously deviant the better, provided it is of course not seriously disruptive and is unlikely to set a trend.

An extreme illustration of this is the case of Sagawa Issei. In 1981, when a 31-year-old student in Paris, Sagawa killed and partly ate a 25-year-old female Dutch student, Renee Harteveld, who had visited his apartment to help him with his studies. He was arrested and deemed insane by French authorities, who allowed him to return to Japan where he was placed in a mental institution. However, arguably as a result of pressure applied by his father, a wealthy banker with considerable political influence, Sagawa was released after less than four years, despite the pleas of the victim's family and despite writing boastfully during his confinement that he had found Renee very appetising and if freed he would eat another woman—fortunately a boast that does not appear to have been carried out. Since his release he has written frequently—including a best-selling book—about his deviant attitudes to women and their flesh. He has also appeared in pornographic and sensationalist films. In a clear display of values that would simply not be tolerated in the west, he even became a food critic for the Japanese magazine *Spa*. His fixation is with western women, which presumably makes him relatively non-threatening to the Japanese themselves.

201. This is also discussed in McCormack and Sugimoto 86a.
202. Munakata 86, p. 371 (re elderly), and Matsuzawa 88, p. 149 (re *furōsha*).
203. McCormack and Sugimoto 86a, p. 15.
204. Lebra 83a, p. 310. For further details on *naikan* see also Lebra 76 and Murase 86, and for a harsher view Dale 86, Chapter 12.
205. Morita therapy aims not merely at social reintegration, though this is certainly a key intention, but also at acceptance by the patient of life in general, with all its ups and downs—a form of fatalism felt by many to be a strong Japanese norm. For further details on Morita therapy, see (in brief) Lebra 83b, and (in more detail) Lebra 76. Again, for a harsher appraisal, see Dale 86, Chapter 12.
206. Dale 86, p. 168.
207. See Braithwaite 89, passim. Braithwaite's main thesis is that the Japanese try to reintegrate offenders wherever possible by using informal resolution methods such as apology and reparation to the victim, also relying on shame and guilt on the part of the offender, and labelling the offence rather than the offender as 'evil'. Braithwaite also points out (pp. 62–3) that fewer than 10 per cent of convictions in Japan result in a prison sentence, and that in turn only one-fifth of these sentences result in actual imprisonment. This 2 per cent rate of imprisonment relative to conviction contrasts greatly with the 45 per cent rate in the United States.
208. Munakata 86, pp. 373–4.
209. Munakata 86, p. 375.

210. The *Japan Times*, Weekly International Edition, 23 February–1 March 1998, p. 16.

PART THREE: THE MAINSTREAM OF SOCIETY: BEING A NORMAL JAPANESE

1. According to a 1995 survey by the Health and Welfare Ministry, 40 per cent of children under the age of 4 go to bed after 10 p.m. (*Japan Times*, Weekly International Edition, 3–9 March 1997). According to a recent municipal survey in Yokohama, 60 per cent of all elementary students go to bed after 10 p.m., and 30 per cent of junior high schoolers after midnight (*Yoke*, 14/80, January 1997, p. 14).
2. See Iwao, 93, Chapter 4 and p. 135.
3. See, for example, Christopher 84, p. 64, regarding the use of this tactic by mothers.
4. See, for example, Tobin, Wu, and Davidson 89, p. 70, regarding the use of this tactic by teachers.
5. In 1992 there were more than 400,000 abortions officially reported, with estimates being that in actuality there were up to four times as many as that. The politics of abortion and contraception (particularly the ban on the pill) are quite complex in Japan's case. For an informative overview, see Norgren 98.
6. Hanley and Yamamura 77, p. 226, and see also pp. 330–1.
7. See Chapter 1.3.
8. For example, the well-known warlord and shōgun Tokugawa Ieyasu (1542–1616) was, at the age of 5, sent to a neighbouring family by his father as a hostage to underpin an uneasy alliance. Ieyasu later killed his own allegedly rebellious son as proof of his loyalty in another alliance, and had the 7-year-old son of a defeated rival executed by beheading. This behaviour was by no means exceptional.
9. See, for example, Hane 82, p. 3 and p. 213.
10. So common has the practice been that there is rarely any stigma attached to it, nor any real attempt at concealment. Some of Japan's most prominent figures, such as the dominant Meiji period statesman Itō Hirobumi and the postwar prime minister Kishi Nobusuke, were adopted out.
11. Official Ministry of Health and Welfare figures for 1994 indicate 1,961 reported cases of physical child abuse, mostly perpetrated by parents on children under 4, but experts estimate that the real figure is closer to 20,000 per year. See Hashimoto 96 for further discussion.
12. See Ishida 93, esp. pp. 247–9.
13. On corruption in education see, for example, Miller 82, pp. 244–50, Woronoff 81, pp. 119–20, and Goodman 93, p. 248.
14. For example, Keiō Kindergarten, associated with prestigious Keiō University, has fourteen applicants for each place. Its entrance examinations, like those of similar institutions, take the form of interviews in which certain questions are asked that cannot be properly answered without preparation. As a consequence, there are special pre-kinder-

garten preparatory 'cram schools', of which the largest is the Nikken organisation. See Sakamaki 97, p. 37. In practice it is often the mother who has to pass the interview, rather than the child. In recent years, some private maternity hospitals have been guaranteeing a place at a desirable kindergarten to the offspring of their clients.

15. A 1996 municipal survey in Yokohama gave figures of 68 per cent for junior high and 59 per cent for elementary students (see *Yoke*, Vol. 14, No. 80, January 1997, p. 13).

16. See Benjamin 97. Despite noting this, Benjamin is more favourable than many western observers in her assessment of schooling in Japan.

17. See Stevenson 89, pp. 90–1. In one international comparison, whereas 58 per cent of American elementary students of mathematics rated themselves as average or higher, only 29 per cent of Japanese students did so. Moreover, American children had to do less well than Japanese children for their mothers to be satisfied. Stevenson's thrust is to criticise Americans for complacency rather than to criticise the Japanese.

18. According to the earlier mentioned municipal survey in Yokohama in 1996, as many as 30 per cent of high school students did not even consider school to be 'passable', let alone 'enjoyable' (*Yoke*, Vol. 14, No. 80, January 1997, p. 13). Also, a recent international survey among fifth-graders in six countries found youngsters in Japan 'the least likely to find school "fun" by a wide margin' (*Japan Times*, Weekly International Edition, 18–24 November 1994, p. 20).

19. Amano 90, p. 5.

20. For discussion of the *naishinsho* see Horio 88, pp. 279–87. See also Sugimoto 86, p. 70, who among other comments on the manipulative use of the *naishinsho* remarks that it is generally weighted as equivalent to one-quarter of a student's marks.

21. Horio 88, note on p. 280.

22. A good example of the type of question in a university entrance examination is given in Goodman 93, p. 248. The question is on world history, specifically on Kuwait, and has six blanks in a descriptive passage which have to be filled in by choosing from a pool of twenty-two items—all proper nouns and dates. That is, an examinee who could memorise passages from the appropriate school text, like an actor learning lines, would be able to score full marks without displaying any actual understanding of matters such as causality, or any analytical ability. And as with any such test, sheer guesswork can have a significant bearing on the result. Moreover, history ends up packaged as something closed to alternative interpretation.

23. In recent years *kanji* (character script) learning at elementary level appears to have become one part-exception, for in addition to the repetitive learning of fixed pronunciation and stroke order etc., students are also encouraged to analyse the component elements of the *kanji* and to make up stories to help remember them. See Bourke 97.

24. Rohlen 83, p. 316.

25. The 1980s saw a major controversy over the Ministry's attempts to replace the word *shinnyū* (invasion) with *shinshutsu* (advance). The leading Japanese academic in the ongoing fight against textbook

interference has been the historian Ienaga Saburō. See NLSSTSS 95.

26. See, for example, the video "Risen Sun" in the BBC's *Nippon* series. See also Schoolland 90, p. 172, for evidence of similar ignorance among high-school students. Moreover, in a 1996 survey of 1,900 students in twenty-two public high schools in Tōkyō, only 15 per cent could name the year in which the Pacific War started, and only 50 per cent the year it ended. See the *Japan Times*, Weekly International Edition, 20–29 January 1997.

27. Even at Tōkyō University, Japan's most highly rated tertiary institution, 42 per cent of some 1,000 students surveyed in 1990 said they were unhappy with lectures. (Reported in the 11 February 1992 issue of the Japanese-language magazine *AERA*.) Poor teaching was also one of the grievances of rioting students in the 1960s.

28. See, for example, Gold 88.

29. Reverse engineers specialise not in constructing a new item but in deconstructing an existing item with a view to being able to improve it bit by bit, usually to give a market edge.

30. For a brief but useful discussion of how Japanese education benefits corporations rather than individuals, see the *Economist*, 21 April 1990, pp. 51–6. For a more detailed discussion of the merits of the Japanese education system for Japanese industry, see Duke 86.

31. Some of these more commonly encountered rules are featured in the video "The Learning Machine" in the BBC's *Nippon* series, while some of the more extreme ones are highlighted in the 25 December 1991 issue of the Japanese-language magazine *Spa!* The latter examples include a Tōkyō high school that requires students to obtain a 'conversation permission slip' if they wish to engage in conversation with members of the opposite sex; and a Nagano junior high school that requires students when walking down a corridor to keep 10 cm from the wall and to turn corners at a 90 degree angle. See also Sakamoto 86 for further examples.

32. This, along with other illustrations of rules and the enforcement of conformity, is shown in "The Learning Machine" in the *Nippon* video series.

33. Hendry 89, pp. 46–7.

34. Hendry 89, p. 41.

35. See, for example, Hendry 84, esp. p. 218, and Caudill and Weinstein 74, esp. p. 229.

36. According to Ministry of Education figures there are typically around 200 incidents of bullying reported each day in the 1990s, less than half the rate of the 1980s. For an overview of bullying in Japanese schools, see Sakamaki 96.

   In 1994 there were, according to Management and Coordination Agency figures, 396 reported cases of violence against teachers by junior high students, and 124 by senior high students (*Asahi Almanac 1997*, p. 242). Very occasionally deaths result. For example, in January 1998 a female junior high teacher in Tochigi was fatally stabbed by a 13-year-old she had just reprimanded for being late, an incident which also highlighted the problem of fashionable butterfly knives being brought to school.

By contrast, the National Education Association of America estimates that every day 100,000 students carry a gun to class; and every
day, 6,250 teachers are threatened with violence and 260 are actually
injured. That is, in a mere two days in America there are more incidents of pupil violence against teachers than in an entire year in Japan.
(See "The Knife in the Book Bag" in *Time*, 8 February 1993, p. 22.)

37. One particularly well-known case of (mental) bullying involving teachers was that leading to the suicide of 13-year-old Shikagawa Hirofumi
in 1986, which after many years of legal action was finally adjudged in
1994 to be the result of bullying. Among other torments his classmates
had held a mock funeral for him some months before he finally took his
own life, and no fewer than four teachers had participated in this mock
funeral. (See the *Japan Times*, Weekly International Edition, 30 May–
5 June 1994.)

There are a number of cases where a student has actually been killed
as a result of physical violence by a teacher, but such cases appear to
result from attempted physical punishment rather than classic bullying.
Corporal punishment is officially banned, but each year there are
several hundred cases—436 in 1995—of teachers being disciplined for
it.

38. The overall child and youth suicide rate has long been comparable to
many western countries. For example, in 1982 Japan had a suicide rate
of 10.6 per 100,000 in the 15–24-year-old group, as opposed to 12.3 in
the United States (see Schoolland 90, p. 128). In fact, among young
people the rate is highest among those in their twenties (12.4), who are
legally adults (perhaps reacting to the trauma of the adult world). In
1993 the rate was a mere 0.7 among 10–14-year-olds, and just 4.2
among 15–19-year-olds (see the *Asahi Shimbun Japan Almanac, 1996*,
p. 54). The latter compares markedly with the world high of 15.7 in
New Zealand, where youth suicide is obviously a far more serious
problem than in Japan.

39. Although truancy rates are only about one-fifth of those of the USA,
they have been increasing steadily ever since Ministry of Education
records were first kept in 1966. About 1.5 per cent of all junior high
students skip school regularly. (See the *Japan Times*, Weekly
International Edition, 28 August–3 September 1995 and 12–18
February 1996.) Although about 96 per cent of junior high students
continue to senior high, that is, beyond compulsory levels, about 5 per
cent of senior high students drop out before completion. Some
portraits of 'drop outs' and their lifestyles are given in Greenfeld 94.

40. Drug and alcohol abuse among teenagers is increasing. In 1996 a
record 214 high school students were arrested on drugs charges. In
1997, in the nation's first ever survey of student attitudes to drug-
taking, 16 per cent of male high school seniors thought taking drugs
was acceptable and within the boundaries of their personal freedom
(*Japan Times*, Weekly International Edition, 20–26 October 1997).
Regarding alcohol, a survey of 14,000 high school students in 1992
found that 80 per cent of them drank regularly, with a remarkable 25
per cent of boys and 11 per cent of girls drinking to the extent of

passing out at least once a week. These figures represent a ten-fold increase over figures from ten years earlier. (See Hashimoto 95, p. 136, who adds that out of the total population there are now 2.2 million people with recognised drinking problems.) See Greenfeld 94 for some detailed accounts of the lives of young drug and alcohol abusers.

41. In 1997 almost 18,000 minors were arrested for crimes of violence, up 15 per cent from the previous year.

42. Things done for kicks or trivial reasons include schoolgirls selling their soiled knickers for pocket money, and school students beating vagrants to death. In addition, there is the recent increase in *enjo kōsai* ('financially assisted relationships'), which is effectively a form of child prostitution. (See also Chapter 1.4.)

43. *Facts and Figures of Japan 1997*, p. 85.

44. In recent years notices have been put up in Harajuku banning dancing. This is apparently an attempt to restrict the numbers of young people in the area, largely as a reaction against the appearance of more sinister activities such as drug-dealing. However, some dancing still takes place despite this ban. Moreover, even if dancing there entirely disappears, Harajuku will always retain a place in Japan's social history as a major symbol of 'conformist non-conformity'.

45. Students did riot quite violently in the 1960s, confronting police and causing some campuses to be closed. Their grievances included poor teaching, the tightly controlled and often corrupt nature of education, and Japan's relationship with an America at war in Vietnam. However, broadly speaking, their aims were diffuse and lacked constructiveness. Fragmentation soon set in, extremists emerged and damaged support (some later forming the notorious Red Army), and the movement petered out.

46. For example, the various 'coming crisis' books by Jon Woronoff (such as Woronoff 81, esp. p. 253), and the only slightly less pessimistic opinions expressed by Sengoku Tamotsu, director of Japan's Youth Research Institute (such as Sengoku 87). See also Naka 77.

47. Reported in the *Japan Times*, Weekly International Edition, 4 February 1989.

48. The *Japan Times*, Weekly International Edition, 20–26 January 1992.

49. In 1987 more than 70 per cent of Japanese high school students read comic books, as opposed to fewer than 20 per cent of their counterparts in the United States (see Sengoku 87, p. 1). Tanaka's book even explains its brand-name references in a 41-page glossary. I am not aware of any English translation of it.

50. The *Japan Times*, Weekly International Edition, 13–19 January 1992, p. 15.

51. See the feature in the *Japan Times*, Weekly International Edition, 10–16 March 1997, p. 16. See also Oshimo and Court 97. The term *tamagotchi* derives from *tamago* (egg, a reference to its oval shape) and *uotchi* (watch).

52. Mita 92, p. 511 and p. 500 respectively.

53. See the feature "Dark Sci-Fi Cartoon Taps into the Ennui of Youth", in the *Japan Times*, Weekly International Edition, 19–25 May 1997, p. 16.

54. Shinji Miyadai. See the *Japan Times*, Weekly International Edition, 19–25 May 1997, p. 16.
55. For example, for both girls and boys aged 16 the average power of their grip was down 2 kg, their reach in touching their toes was 3 cm shorter, the distance they could throw a ball was down 1.7 metres, and their distance in the long jump was down 20 cm for boys and 27 cm for girls. Reported in the *Japan Times*, Weekly International Edition, 28 October–3 November 1996.
56. Koyama 87, p. 7.
57. The *Japan Times*, Weekly International Edition, 9–15 June 1997, p. 6.
58. See, for example, the features in the Japanese-language magazines *Days Japan* (October 1989) and *AERA* (19–26 August 1996).
59. For example, in May 1995 there were 53,847 foreign students in Japan, of whom 7,371 were on programmes sponsored by the Japanese government. 92 per cent of all foreign students were from Asia. (See the *Japan Times*, Weekly International Edition, 15–21 July 1995.)
60. See, for example, the *Japan Times*, Weekly International Edition, 3–9 February 1992, which reports on a Management and Coordination Agency survey in which more than half of junior and senior high students said they did not want to grow up.
61. Buruma 85, p. 122.
62. For example, official statistics for maximum height are based on this age. As in many societies, certain specific legal rights associated with 'growing up', such as to obtain a driver's licence or to marry (though with parental consent), are conferred some years earlier.
63. Hendry 92, p. 64.
64. Kawakami Hajime. See Dale 86, pp. 209–10.
65. Korea mostly uses Hangul but does also use characters.
66. See, for example, Nakane 70, esp. p. 7, and Van Wolferen 89, pp. 166–7. However, such a view is not necessarily confined to Japan: writing in general terms, the renowned early sociologist Emile Durkheim remarked on the company replacing the family as the source of social solidarity. (See Lincoln and Kalleberg 90, p. 11.)
67. See Wilkinson 81, p. 221.
68. Typically, Japanese in the 1980s in manufacturing industries worked around 2,100 hours per year (now around 1,900), as opposed to a western norm of around 1,800. Public holidays (that is, when the company is obliged to close for the day) accounted for 13 days per year, and paid vacation for around 15. The average 'take-up' rate of these 15 days was typically 8 in the 1980s (nowadays 11). Westerners, by contrast, had between 20 and 30 paid vacation days, and almost a 100 per cent take-up rate.
69. In 1980 only 5.6 per cent of all workers had two days off per week (Linhart 84, p. 213). Though the five-day week system has since been gradually implemented, at least as formal policy, by most large companies (usually defined as 300 or more employees), precise figures are hard to arrive at since many companies, though confusingly listed as having a five-day week system, actually operate the system only once or twice each month. In approximate terms, something like half of large

companies now operate a proper and regular five-day week (partly prompted by the recession), but the proportion is much less among smaller companies. One milestone was the adoption of a regular five-day week for government employees in 1992.

70. Morita 87, p. 184.
71. The *Japan Times*, Weekly International Edition, 3–9 June 1996, p. 16.
72. I also draw here on my own personal experiences.
73. The practice is known as *tanshin funin* (literally 'proceeding alone to one's post'), and it involves as many as 400,000 employees (almost all male) annually. See the *Japan Times*, Weekly International Edition, 7–13 February 1994.
74. According to a survey of 3,000 male salaried workers in the 30–54-year-old group carried out by the Tōkyō Metropolitan Labour Research Institute in 1990, 69 per cent said they went drinking with colleagues after work at least one night a week, the majority of these going on multiple occasions. Only 21 per cent of them saw it as relaxation. Conversation topics overwhelmingly centred on business. See the *Tōkyō Municipal News*, Autumn 1990, p. 8.
75. See, for example, the 1996 *White Paper on National Life*, which refers to 90 per cent of salaried workers believing that they make a bigger contribution to their company than their salary warrants. See also JETRO 93, p. 35, for a survey response indicating that the great majority of new recruits felt Japanese workers worked too much.
76. Lincoln and Kalleberg 90, esp. p. 60.
77. Linhart 84.
78. Article Eight of Shōtoku's Constitution starts 'Let the ministers and functionaries attend the court early in the morning and retire late' (see Tsunoda et al. 1964, Vol. 1, p. 49).
79. See also Linhart 84.
80. See also Mita 92, esp. pp. 244–7.
81. The Kyōto Ceramic Company is one example of a company that has arranged graves for its employees. The general policy of a company looking after the personal affairs of its employees is known as *marugakae* ('embracing everything'). Of course, western executives too may have their houses and their children's education and so forth arranged by their company, but this is generally only on transfer and only at top executive level. In Japan the involvement of the company is much broader.
82. Ouchi (81, p. 17), for example, writes that 'The most important characteristic of the Japanese organization is lifetime employment.'
83. The literature on Japanese management is truly vast. As a simplified generalisation, one can say that, until recently, most of it was divided into pro/endorsing on the one hand and anti/critical on the other. Pascale and Athos 82 might be felt to represent the former, Sethi, Namiki and Swanson 84 the latter. Whitehill 91, though somewhat inclined to the former, appears more balanced and is useful as an introduction. Since the effective collapse of Japanese management practices in the 1990s there have obviously been some red faces, and the output of literature has slowed, especially in book form. Most commentators,

not surprisingly, appear to be waiting to see what will happen.
84. See Dore 84, esp. pp. 23–4. Two particular models of personnel management were Krupp in Germany and National Cash Register in the United States.
85. Despite well-intentioned labour reforms enacted by the Occupation forces in the late 1940s, a considerable number of massive labour disruptions occurred during the first fifteen years or so after the war. The Nissan Strike of 1953, for example, lasted for some six months and saw the members of the All-Japan Automobile Industry Union—a 'trade union' rather than an 'enterprise union'—defeated and displaced by a company-oriented union. Following this, business leaders increasingly set up company unions in a largely successful attempt to stop workers in any given industry or trade uniting nation-wide. Company unions include all staff below middle management (who generally, until the 1990s at least, have not belonged to any union), and clearly run counter to the principles of industry-wide solidarity underlying unionism in the west.

The most notorious and bitter dispute occurred in 1960, at the Mitsui-owned Miike coalmines in Kyūshū (see Chapter 2.4, p. 67, and accompanying Note 83). For further details of Miike, and its repercussions for industrial relations, see Price 97; for discussion of unrest in the mining industry in general see Allen 94; and for a detailed account of unions in general see Kawanishi 92.

Essentially, after Miike unions were rarely to pose a serious threat again through strike action, with grievances mostly being aired in other ways and strikes usually becoming tokenised into brief stoppages—sometimes only one hour—at agreed times of the year. Thus the amount of days of production lost through industrial action was to be a fraction of that in most other major nations. *Nihonjinron* writers have used this as 'proof' of the claimed innate Japanese predisposition towards harmony.
86. A 'large' company is usually defined in Japan as having 300 or more employees, with 'medium' employing 30–300 and 'small' fewer than 30, but, confusingly, sometimes the definitions are 1,000 or more employees, 100–999 employees, and 10–99 employees respectively, with any below 10 considered family businesses. Relative to western countries, Japan in fact has a very large preponderance of small companies. According to Management and Coordination Agency figures, less than 1 per cent of businesses in Japan employ more than 300 people (*Asahi Almanac 1997*, p. 83), though obviously they occupy a far greater percentage of the workforce (more than 15 per cent). (See Fukutake 82, p. 189.)
87. Morishima 82, esp. pp. 192–3.
88. Naturally, this also affects the ability of government departments, which normally cannot expand, to implement a full seniority system for civil servants.
89. The *Japan Times*, Weekly International Edition, 13–19 June 1994.
90. For example, in a twenty-month period during the recession the formerly little-known Tōkyō Managers' Union experienced an

eighteen-fold increase in its members, and was consulted by some 1,500 dismissed or demoted managers, with legal action often being pursued against the company involved. See the video "Goodbye Japan Corporation", produced jointly in 1996 by Film Australia and—interestingly—Japan's state-run NHK.

91. The *Japan Times*, Weekly International Edition, 17–23 March 1997.
92. Moroi Kaoru in Esaka and Moroi 96, p. 40.
93. By the early 1990s there were more than 400 such agencies in Tōkyō alone. They often recruit not just for Japanese companies, but for overseas companies keen to take advantage of surplus managers in Japan. See the *Japan Times*, Weekly International Edition, 23–29 December 1991.
94. Nissan is one company that has been leading the way in this particular change. See the *Japan Times*, Weekly International Edition, 9–15 December 1996.
95. A good illustration of this 'making of company men' on video is "Being Japanese" in the BBC's *Nippon* video series, which follows new recruits at Fuji Film. Women were almost entirely treated as 'non-career track' and were not given the same training.
96. See also Esaka Akira in Esaka and Moroi 96, p. 39.
97. See, for example, JETRO 93, p. 35, which reports that two-thirds of new graduates about to enter the workforce said they would not feel committed to their company and would consider a change, and 90 per cent of them said they would not be willing to sacrifice their private life for the company.
98. Featured in TVNZ's *Foreign Correspondent,* 28 June 1990.
99. See the video "Being Japanese" in the *Nippon* series.
100. See, for example, Kamata 82, where, based upon his experiences at Toyota, he remarks that 'Each man is beaten down and his pride broken into pieces' (p. 191). See also Kawamura 94, where he writes: 'The concept of the enterprise as one large household concealed the actual exploitative relationships existing between the owners and workers.... The ideology of paternalism's function was to create docile workers' (p. 20). See also Van Wolferen 89, esp. p. 161 and p. 170.
101. Regarding the adoption of the suggestion-box system, which appears to have originally been pioneered by Eastman Kodak in America in 1898, see Whitehill 91, pp. 236–7. Quality control was introduced into Japan after World War Two by W. Edwards Deming, who is much better known and respected in Japan than in his home country of America.
102. For details see the report in the *Far Eastern Economic Review*, 25 April 1996, pp. 63–4. In late 1997 Wallace resigned and was replaced by another foreigner, the American James Miller.
103. *Far Eastern Economic Review*, 31 July 1997, pp. 46–51, esp. pp. 46–7.
104. See Murakami, Y., Kumon, S., and Satō, S., 1979, *Bunmei to shite no Ie Shakai* (*Ie* Society as a Pattern of Civilisation, Chūōkōronsha, Tōkyō). A condensed English-language version of this book is found in Murakami 84. See the *Journal of Japanese Studies*, Vol. 11, No. 1 (1985), for a series of criticisms of the theory from scholars such as John Whitney Hall, Takie Sugiyama Lebra, and Thomas Rohlen. See

also Nakane 83 for an overstatement of the traditional role of the *ie* and of its influence on modern corporate culture.

105. See also Ueno 96, pp. 213–14.
106. Ueno 96, p. 217, and Kumagai 96, p. 17.
107. *Facts and Figures of Japan 1997*, p. 18.
108. Yashiro 96, p. 22.
109. For 1995 figure, *Facts and Figures of Japan 1997*, p. 18. For 1920 figure, Kumagai 96, p. 17.
110. See the feature in the *Japan Times*, Weekly International Edition, 11–17 May 1992, p. 11. A briefer article was also released internationally that month by Associated Press, Tōkyō (my source the *New Zealand Herald*, 25 May 1992).
111. Kumagai 96, p. 22.
112. See Shida 96, esp. p. 4.
113. *Yoke*, Vol. 14, No. 79, October 1996, p. 7.
114. Yashiro 96, p. 26. Though current figures are not clear, in 1986 the average age of first marriage among Swedish women was 26.8 years.

   A Japanese woman who was still single after her 25th year used to be called a 'Christmas Cake'—an unflattering reference to having passed her 'sell by' date. In view of the increasingly later age of first marriage, the term has recently been changed to a 'New Year's Eve Cake', giving her another six years before social disapproval.
115. Management and Coordination Agency figures. See the *Japan Times*, Weekly International Edition, 17–23 February 1997.
116. Prime Minister's Office figures. See *Yoke*, Vol. 14, No. 79, October 1996, p. 10.
117. Ministry of Health and Welfare figures. See *Asahi Shimbun Japan Almanac 1997*, p. 54.
118. *Asahi Shimbun Japan Almanac 1997*, p. 54.
119. Yashiro 96, p. 26.
120. A particularly strong case is made in McCormack 96. McCormack also argues for other changes, such as to Japan's consumerism and obsession with economic growth.
121. Japan is to start with disadvantaged by having three-quarters of its land mountainous and effectively uninhabitable. However, industrialisation and urbanisation have meant that about half the population lives in just a couple of percent of the land area, in what is known as the Pacific Coast Industrial Belt from Kitakyūshū to Tōkyō. Space is so tight that residents in some major cities need to produce evidence of having space to park a car before they are granted a driver's licence. Residents of Tōkyō enjoy only 2.6 sq m of park space per capita, as opposed to 30.4 sq m in London, and 45.7 sq m in Washington. (See *Japan 1995: An International Comparison*, p. 86.)

   Commuting can take up to 90 minutes each way. Ministry of Construction figures indicate that 25 per cent of commuters in the Tōkyō area spend more than one hour each way. (See *Facts and Figures of Japan*, 1997, p. 79.)

   The average dwelling in Japan is barely half the size of that in the United States (90 sq m as opposed to 170), yet relative to income costs around four times as much (and more still in the major cities). See for example *Asahi Shimbun Japan Almanac 1997*, p. 204, or *Japan 1995: An International Comparison*, pp. 84–5. The famous description of these cramped dwellings as 'rabbit hutches' has already been mentioned.

122. Based on Management and Coordination Agency Figures.
123. Figures from *Japan 1997: An International Comparison*, p. 13.
124. Ogawa 96, p. 17, and Ministry of Foreign Affairs' *Official Information Bulletin*, No. 197 (October 1996).
125. Ogawa 96, pp. 17–18. For the actual number of centenarians, see the *Japan Times*, Weekly International Edition, 12–18 May 1997. The oldest person alive in Japan as of May 1997 was the 113-year-old Miyanaga Suekiku of Kagoshima Prefecture.
126. Nakamura 96, p. 49.
127. Nakamura 96, esp. pp. 48–9.
128. For further details see Wilson 86, from which the following comments are taken.
129. For details see *Japan Times*, Weekly International Edition, 9–15 June 1997, p. 7.
130. Okamoto Yūzō, of the Kōbe City College of Nursing. See the *Japan Times*, Weekly International Edition, 9–15 June 1997, p. 7.
131. For example, the administering of the system, along with financial responsibilities, is to be devolved to municipality level rather than being retained at central or prefectural level. Critics have pointed out that there are more than 3,000 of these municipalities, suggesting a great potential for complexity, inconsistency, and duplication of paperwork.
132. The *Japan Times*, Weekly International Edition, 4–10 March 1996.
133. See the *Japan Times*, Weekly International Edition, 23–29 September 1996, p. 7.
134. Regarding dislike of institutions, see Bethell 92a and 92b; regarding dislike of being a burden, see Wöss 84, p. 224, and the survey in the *Japan Echo*, Special Issue 1996, pp. 70–1.
135. See Keene 68, p. 43.
136. For example, Bethel (92a, p. 131) refers to a lack of solid evidence for it and dismisses it as mere 'myth'. By contrast, Plath (83, p. 99), feels it likely to have happened to particularly incapacitated elderly.
137. For example, it is referred to in the twelfth-century collection of instructive tales *Konjaku Monogatari* (Tales from Once Upon a Time), and the Nō drama *Obasute* by the renowned fifteenth-century playwright Zeami Motokiyo.
138. For figures see Kumagai 96, pp. 139–40. In the early 1990s 17 per cent of women and 38 per cent of men aged 65 or over were in the workforce. Figures were much higher still for the 60–64-year-old group. 76 per cent of men in this bracket were in the workforce, compared with 55 per cent in the United States, 35 per cent in Germany, and a mere 19 per cent in France.

In certain professions it is common to work beyond the standard retirement age. There has for example long been a practice known as *amakudari* ('descent from heaven') in which retired top civil servants, with valuable knowledge of procedures and even more valuable contacts, take up senior positions (often as consultants) in major corporations. As one illustration of the extent of this practice, 20 out of 63 senior officials who retired from the Bank of Japan over the last ten years took up positions in private financial institutions. (See the *Japan Times*, Weekly International Edition, 19–25 May 1997.) In very recent times the reverse is also happening (*ama-agari*, or ascent to heaven), with retired businessmen becoming consultants to government institutions.

139. There are various types of homes for the elderly in Japan, depending on factors such as age and financial standing. Bethel gives a brief discussion of these (92b) as well as a detailed account of life in one particular home (also in 92a). Some of the institutions are more concerned with profit than care, for example trying to extract as much money as possible from relatives by demanding medical expenses for the treatment of alleged afflictions. Such institutions are known in the vernacular as *sushiya byōin* ('squeeze hospitals', after the trade of the sushi-maker who squeezes his product). See Wöss 84, p. 227.

The first nursing home in Japan was started by an Englishwoman, in 1896. Before that, elderly people with no family support were placed in poorhouses along with orphans, the sick, and vagrants. (See Bethel 92a, p. 127.)

140. See Kumagai 96, pp. 147–9, and (for international comparison) her Note 1 on p. 154.

141. Kumagai 96, p. 134.

142. An account of these is given in Wöss 84, on which the following draws in particular. (See also Plath 83, esp. p. 99.) There is a popular saying 'Kuu toki nya tappuri, Neru toki nya yukkuri, Shinu toki nya pokkuri', which roughly translates as 'When you eat, eat heartily; When you sleep, sleep soundly; When you die, die quickly.'

143. A succinct description of funerals and memorial rites is given in Hendry 89, pp. 130–1.

144. Ben-Ari 91, p. 276. See also Smith 92, p. 19.

145. See Lebra 76, Chapter 1.

146. Rice was not introduced to Japan till around 1,000 BC, some 4,000 years later than China and several centuries later than Korea. It was not systematically cultivated until around 400 BC.

147. As early as the seventh century Japan had a population of around 5 million, 'an enormous figure compared to European populations of the time' (Farris 85, p. 8), and by the eighteenth century had around 30 million. At the time, Edo (Tōkyō), with a population around 1 million, was the largest city in the world. Japan's current population is around 127 million.

In terms of nominal density (total land area divided by population), Japan has 332 persons per sq km, as opposed to 237 in Britain, 27 in the United States, 13 in New Zealand, and 2 in Australia. The world average among major nations is 40 persons per sq km. However, far less of Japan's total land area—merely 20 per cent or so—is habitable in comparison with other nations. For example, Britain's population density in terms of habitable area is 250 persons per sq km, which is little different from the nominal density of 237. Japan, by contrast, has an effective population density five times its nominal density, in the order of 1,650 persons per sq km. This is beaten only by 'city states' such as Hong Kong and Singapore, which are both around the 5,000 persons per sq km mark.

148. The western term was popularised notably by Claude Lévi-Strauss, and the Japanese term by Hamaguchi Eyshun (see Hamaguchi 85).

149. Suzuki 78, p. 143.

150. Doi 73, p. 77.

151. See Mushakōji 76, esp. p. 44.

152. Clashes between workers and management/government during the early postwar period are just some illustrations of such conflict.

153. See Befu 90 and also Murakami and Rohlen 92.

154. There are of course exceptions. The well-known Japanese practice of gift-giving is often cited as a means of deepening the personal element of a relationship. Sometimes that is true. However, a gift is also sometimes used as the 'return payment' for a service rendered and a signal that there is no need for a relationship to continue. At other times, the need to reciprocate the gift exactly, even if it is intended as a bonding reinforcement, can ironically lead to a very intense focus on the item rather than the person.

155. See, for example, Katō 81, p. 301, for comment on massive defections. The career of the fourteenth century warrior-shōgun Ashikaga Takauji is also a classic example of naked self-interest.

156. Elison 83, p. 64.

157. For example, banning wheeled transport and restricting bridges in order to make movement difficult, banning foreigners, forcing warlords to attend upon the shōgun, redistributing feudal domains to minimise potential for neighbourly conspiracy, and so forth.

158. The horrific nature of punishments (which included roasting and boiling in oil), and the collective way in which they were often meted out, are illustrated by the contemporary accounts in Cooper 65. They shocked European visitors of the day, hardened as they were to horrific punishments in their own home nations.

159. See Hearn 1904, p. 193.

160. Satō 90, p. 41. See also Hanley and Yamamura 77, pp. 89–90.

161. Expulsion of a particularly troublesome member, though it sometimes did happen, risked drawing attention from outside. The ultimate 'in-house' punishment was therefore ostracism—being shunned by the group/village but not actually physically expelled from it.

162. For further discussion of this point see Haley 91, esp. pp. 57–62, and Haley 92, pp. 42–3.

163. Van Wolferen 89, p. 234 and p. 227.

164. See also Cooper 65, his notes p. 165.

165. Miyoshi 74, pp. 78–9.

166. See also Mita 92, pp. 244–7.

167. The full text of this is given in Tsunoda et al. 64, Vol. 2, pp. 139–40.

168. Natsume Sōseki 1906/61, pp. 405–19 passim.

169. The first recognised 'I novel' was Tayama Katai's "The Quilt" (*Futon*) of 1907, which described his abortive affair with a student. It is available in English translation. Much of Katai's literature deals with the clash between the individual and social constraints.
170. See Hall 74, p. 9, and *Kokutai no Hongi*, p. 100.
171. *Kokutai no Hongi*, p. 67.
172. For example, Reischauer 88, pp. 163–5.
173. See, for example, Tobin 92b, esp. p. 8, and Rosenberger 92, esp. p. 108.
174. A description used in a different context by the Korean philosopher Chung Kyungmo. See McCormack and Sugimoto 86a, p. 16.
175. See in particular her 1967 work *Tate-Shakai no Ningen Kankei: Tanitsu Shakai no Riron e* (Human Relations in a Vertical Society: A Theory of a Homogeneous Society), translated into English in 1970 with the rather prosaic title *Japanese Society*. Earlier scholars such as Aruga Kizaemon made similar observations about verticality.
176. Nakane 70, p. 63 and p. 31.
177. Nakane 70, p. 96.
178. A convenient summary of early works critical of Nakane, authors of whom include well-known scholars such as Harumi Befu, Ross Mouer, and Yoshio Sugimoto, is found in Hata and Smith 86. A majority of recent works by western scholars of Japan have been critical of Nakane.
179. Respectively Reischauer 88, p. 154, and Taylor 85, p. 42.
180. For a detailed discussion of *uchi-soto* in present-day Japan, see Bachnik and Quinn 94.
181. See, for example, Doi 73, Chapter 2.
182. For example, see Benedict 47.
183. Befu 83, p. 34.
184. See also Ohnuki-Tierney 84, p. 22.
185. Western visitors to Japan do not always realise this, for ironically a Japanese is often more likely to relate to a foreign stranger—and to be helped by them—than a Japanese one, especially if there is a strong probability that they will not meet again.
186. This has led to considerable and often over-simplified debate in the past as to whether Japan is a society characterised primarily by shame (Benedict 47) or by guilt (Doi 73). Clearly, shame features more prominently in Japan than in many societies, but it would be incorrect to assume that individuals had no conscience and felt no guilt. There is even a tradition of using guilt to socialise children, as discussed earlier. In view of recent recognition of the ease with which external pressures can become internalised, the debate now seems largely pointless.
187. The following is based on Lebra 76, Chapter 7.
188. See also Buruma 85, p. 160.
189. See also Christopher 84, pp. 63–4, who makes a similar point.
190. Among some of the 'bad' things done by Susano-o, he smears excrement on the walls of his sister Amaterasu's palace, destroys the ridges between her rice-fields, and throws a flayed pony through the roof of her weaving-shed (killing a weaver according to some versions).
191. See, for example, Tsushima 96 (p. 1 and p. 3), for recent *Shūkyō Nenkan* (Yearbook of Religion) figures that show Shintō organisation

membership in Japan numbers just over 100 million, and Buddhist membership just under 100 million. Tsushima also refers (p. 1) to surveys repeatedly showing that on average only 30 per cent of the population claim to belong to a religion. See also Reader 91, pp. 5–6 for a similar picture in the 1980s.

192. See also Reader 91, p. 13.

193. See also Shillony 90, esp. p. 127, and Ashkenazi 90, esp. p. 206.

194. Haley 91, p. 109.

195. The following draws on data in Oda 92, pp. 102–4.

196. In 1990 the average time to judgement in contested civil cases at district court level was 28 months, which was ten times longer than in criminal cases (Oda 92, p. 79). Legal aid is very restricted, with less than half of applicants being given aid. Moreover, even if the litigation is successful and costs are awarded, they still generally do not cover even attorney's fees (Oda 92, p. 82). In a recent survey in Japan, 85 per cent of respondents felt litigation was too lengthy, and 67 per cent felt it could well bankrupt them (Oda 92, p. 88).

197. A prosecutor's decision to go ahead and prosecute cannot be appealed, merely any decision *not* to prosecute. Prosecutions result in an astonishing 99 per cent conviction rate. The vast majority of prosecutions are based on confessions, obtained in circumstances that would not be permitted in most western countries (such as without a lawyer being present, or after protracted interrogation sessions without rest or food). These matters have repeatedly drawn western criticism. See also McCormack 86 and Igarashi 86.

198. Just 2 per cent of convictions actually result in imprisonment, as opposed to 45 per cent in the United States. See Chapter 2.10, p. 106, and Note 207 to Part Two.

199. Yamamoto Shichihei, writing under the pseudonym Isiah Ben-Dasan. See Ben-Dasan 72, esp. Chapter 7.

200. Ben-Dasan 72, p. 107 and p. 91.

201. Ben-Dasan 72, p. 113.

202. Ben-Dasan 72, p. 63.

203. America's Immigration Act of 1924 was deliberately tailored to ban further immigration by the Japanese, of whom there were by this stage more than 100,000 in California alone. (See Daniels 83, p. 164.) In addition, a founding member of the League of Nations in 1920, Japan suffered rejection of its proposal to have a racial equality clause inserted into the League's charter, largely due to opposition from Australia, which was maintaining its 'White Australia' policy. (See Frei 91, Chapter 6.)

204. For example, the receptor gene D4DR appears to have a strong relationship to levels of excitability.

205. See Dale 86 for a detailed critical discussion of these and other *Nihonjinron* writers.

206. Kunihiro 76.

207. Hamaguchi 85.

208. See especially Mouer and Sugimoto 86.

209. Dale 86, pp. 46–51.

210. This draws significantly upon Dale's list but does not necessarily follow it in every particular.
211. For a discussion of the general western tendency to view the Orient as Other, see Said 78. For detailed discussion of Japan as Other, see for example Befu and Kreiner 92, or in brief Befu 92.
212. A number of books have dealt in detail with western images of Japan. See for example Wilkinson 81, and particularly Littlewood 96.
213. Benedict 47, p. 1.
214. See for example Moeran 89, pp. 181–4. Moeran goes so far as to refer to 'the inverse orientalist trap laid by the Japanese' (p. 184).
215. Taylor 85, p. 41. The book is *Kaseki-Saru kara Nihonjin made*, by Suzuki Hisashi, published by Iwanami, Tōkyō, 1971.
216. He has subsequently published a number of works on this and related topics. For an English translation, see Tsunoda 85. See also *The East*, Vol. 26 No. 5, May 1991, pp. 38–40, for an indication of the way his findings have been taken up by Japanese.
217. See Henshall 92.

References

Abbreviations:

CEJ: *Cambridge Encyclopedia of Japan*, 1993, Cambridge University Press
FEER: *Far Eastern Economic Review*
JE: *Japan Echo*
JJS: *Journal of Japanese Studies*
JQ: *Japan Quarterly*
KEJ: *Kōdansha Encyclopedia of Japan*, 1983, 8 vols, Kōdansha, Tōkyō
NZJEAS: *New Zealand Journal of East Asian Studies*

Ackroyd, J., 1959, "Women in Feudal Japan", in *Transactions of the Asiatic Society*, 7 (Nov. 59), pp. 31–68.
Aida, Y., 1990, "America's Multiethnic Society: an Achilles' Heel?", available in English as an eight-page monograph from the Asia Foundation Translation Centre, Tōkyō. (Original in *Voice*, September 1990.)
Akazawa, T. and Aikens, C. (eds.), 1986, *Prehistoric Hunter-Gatherers in Japan: New Research Methods*, University of Tōkyō Press.
Allen, M., 1994, *Undermining the Japanese Miracle: Work and Conflict in a Coalmining Community*, Cambridge University Press.
Allison, A., 1996, *Permitted and Prohibited Desires: Mothers, Comics and Censorship in Japan*, Westview Press, Boulder, Colorado.
Amano, I., 1990, *Education and Examination in Modern Japan* (trans. W. Cummings), University of Tōkyō Press.
Anderson, J., 1983, "Takarazuka Kagekidan [Theater Troupe]", in *KEJ*, Vol. 7, p. 318.
Aoyama, T., 1988, "Male Homosexuality as Treated by Japanese Women Writers", in McCormack, G. and Sugimoto, Y. (eds.), 1988, *q.v.*, pp. 186–204.
Asahi Shimbun Japan Almanac, annually, Asahi Shimbun Company, Tōkyō.
Ashkenazi, M., 1990, "Religious Conflict in a Japanese Town: Or Is It?", in Eisenstadt, S. and Ben-Ari, E. (eds.), 1990, *q.v.,* pp. 192–207.
Aston, W., 1896/1972, *Nihongi: Chronicles of Japan from the Earliest Times to AD 697* (translation of *Nihongi*), Tuttle edition, Tōkyō, 1972.
Atsumi, R., 1997, "Dilemmas and Accommodations of Married Japanese Women in White-Collar Employment", in Moore, J. (ed.), 1997, *q.v.*, pp. 272–87.
Bachnik, J. and Quinn, C. (eds.), 1994, *Situated Meaning: Inside and Outside in Japanese Self, Society, and Language*, Princeton University Press.
Barnes, G., 1993, "The Nara Period", in *CEJ*, pp. 48–52.
Befu, H., 1983, "Giri and Ninjō", in *KEJ*, Vol.3, p. 34.
Befu, H., 1990, "Conflict and Non-Weberian Bureaucracy in Japan", in Eisenstadt, S. and Ben-Ari, E. (eds.), 1990, *q.v.*, pp. 162–91.

Befu, H., 1992, "Othernesses of Japan", *Japan Foundation Newsletter*, 20/3, pp. 6–9.

Befu, H. and Kreiner, J. (eds.), 1992, *Othernesses of Japan: Historical and Cultural Influences on Japanese Studies in Ten Countries,* Iudicium, Munich.

"Being Japanese" in the *Nippon* video series, BBC, London, 1991.

Ben-Ari, E., 1991, *Changing Japanese Suburbia: a Study of Two Present-Day Localities,* Kegan Paul International, London.

Ben-Dasan, I. (the alias of Yamamoto Shichihei), 1972, *The Japanese and the Jews* (trans. Gage, R.), Weatherhill, Tōkyō (orig. 1970, *Nihonjin to Yudayajin*).

Benedict, R., 1947, *The Chrysanthemum and the Sword: Patterns of Japanese Culture,* Secker and Warburg, London.

Benjamin, G., 1997, *Japanese Lessons: a Year in a Japanese School through the Eyes of an American Anthropologist and Her Children,* New York University Press.

Bethel, D, 1992a, "Alienation and Reconnection in a Home for the Elderly", in Tobin, J. (ed.), 1992a, *q.v.*, pp. 126–42.

Bethel, D., 1992b, "Life on Obasuteyama, or Inside a Japanese Institution for the Elderly", in Lebra, T. S. (ed.), 1992, *q.v.*, pp. 109–34.

Bird, I., 1881, *Unbeaten Tracks in Japan*, 2 vols., Putnam, New York.

Bourke, B., 1997, *Maximising Efficiency in the Kanji Learning Task*, Ph.D. thesis, University of Queensland.

Braithwaite, J., 1989, *Crime, Shame, and Reintegration*, Cambridge University Press.

Buruma, I, 1985, *A Japanese Mirror: Heroes and Villains of Japanese Culture*, Penguin, Harmondsworth.

Buruma, I., 1987, "The Right Argument: Preserving the Past to Reclaim Japanese 'Supremacy'", in *FEER*, 19 February 1987, pp. 82–5.

Buruma, I., 1992, "Afterword", in Ventura, R., 1992, *Underground in Japan*, Jonathan Cape, London, pp. 185–93.

Caudill, W. and Weinstein, H., 1974, "Maternal Care and Infant Behavior in Japan and America", in Lebra, T. S. and Lebra, W. (eds.), 1974, *Japanese Culture and Behavior: Selected Readings*, University of Hawaii Press, pp. 225–76.

Choe, K., 1993, "The Dilemma of Japanese Studies in Korea", in *Japan Foundation Newsletter*, 20/4 (February 1993), pp. 9–11.

Christopher, R., 1984, *The Japanese Mind: the Goliath Explained*, Pan, London.

Condon, J., 1985, *A Half Step Behind: Japanese Women of the '80s*, Dodd, Mead & Co., New York.

Cook, H. and Cook, T., 1992, *Japan at War: an Oral History*, New Press, New York.

Cooper, M., 1965, *They Came to Japan: an Anthology of European Reports on Japan, 1543–1648*, University of California Press.

Cornell, J., 1967, "Individual Mobility and Group Membership: the Case of the *Burakumin*", in Dore, R. (ed.), 1967, *q.v.*, pp. 337–72.

Dalby, L., 1983, *Geisha*, University of California Press.

Dale, P., 1986, *The Myth of Japanese Uniqueness*, Croom Helm, London.

Daniels, G. (ed.), 1984, *Europe Interprets Japan*, Paul Norbury Publications, Tenterden, Kent.

Daniels, R., 1983, "United States Immigration Acts of 1924, 1952, and 1965", in *KEJ*, Vol. 8, pp. 164–5.

Davis, W., 1992, *Japanese Religion and Society: Paradigms of Structure and Change*, State University of New York Press.

de Bary, B., 1997, "Sanya: Japan's Internal Colony", in Moore, J. (ed.), 1997, *q.v.*, pp. 80–95.

Denoon, D., Hudson, M., McCormack, G. and Morris-Suzuki, T. (eds.), 1996, *Multicultural Japan: Paleolithic to Postmodern*, Cambridge University Press.

de Vos, G. and Mizushima, K., 1967, "Organisation and Social Function of Japanese Gangs: Historical Development and Modern Parallels", in Dore, R. (ed.), 1967, *q.v.*, pp. 289–326.

de Vos, G. and Wetherall, W., 1983, *Japan's Minorities*, Minority Rights Group, London.

Dodo, Y., 1986, "Metrical and Nonmetrical Analyses of Jōmon Crania from Eastern Japan", in Akazawa, T. and Aikens, C. (eds.), 1986, *q.v.*, pp. 137–61.

Doi, T., 1973, *The Anatomy of Dependence* (trans. Bester, J.), Kōdansha International, Tōkyō (Japanese original 1971).

Dore, R. (ed.), 1967, *Aspects of Social Change in Modern Japan*, Princeton University Press.

Dore, R., 1984, "The 'Learn from Japan' Boom", in *Speaking of Japan*, 5/47, November 1984, pp. 16–25.

Dower, J., 1986, *War without Mercy: Race and Power in the Pacific War,* Faber and Faber, London and Boston.

Duke, B., 1986, *The Japanese School: Lessons for Industrial America*, Praeger, New York, Westport, and London.

Duus, P., 1995, *The Abacus and the Sword: the Japanese Penetration of Korea, 1895–1910*, University of California Press, Berkeley.

Ehrenberg, M., 1989, *Women in Prehistory*, British Museum Publications, London.

Eisenstadt, S. and Ben-Ari, E. (eds.), 1990, *Japanese Models of Conflict Resolution*, Kegan Paul International, London.

Elison, G. (a.k.a. Elisonas, J.), 1983, "Oda Nobunaga (1534–1582)", in *KEJ*, Vol. 6, pp. 61–5.

Encylopaedia Britannica, 1797, v. IX, Bell and MacFarquhar, Edinburgh.

Esaka, A. and Moroi, K., 1996, "The Coming White-Collar Crunch", in *JE*, Special Issue, 1996, pp. 38–42.

Facts and Figures of Japan, annually, Foreign Press Center, Tōkyō.

Fallows, D., 1990, "Japanese Women", in *National Geographic*, April 1990 issue, pp. 52–83.

Farris, W., 1985, *Population, Disease, and Land in Early Japan, 645–900*, Harvard University Press.

Fields, G., 1983, *From Bonsai to Levis*, Macmillan, New York.

Fowler, E., 1996, *Sanya Blues: Laboring Life in Contemporary Tōkyō*, Cornell University Press.

Frei, H., 1991, *Japan's Southward Advance and Australia: from the Sixteenth Century to World War Two*, Melbourne University Press.

Fukutake, T., 1982, *The Japanese Social Structure: its Evolution in the Modern Century* (trans. R. P. Dore), University of Tōkyō Press (Japanese original 1981).

Fukuzawa, Y., 1872/1969, *Gakumon no Susume*, trans. David Dilworth and Umeyo Hirano as *An Encouragement of Learning*, Sophia University Press, Tōkyō, 1969.

Gessel, V. and Matsumoto, T., 1985 (eds.), *The Shōwa Anthology: Modern Japanese Short Stories*, 2 vols., Kōdansha International, Tōkyō and New York.

Gill, T., 1994, "Sanya Street Life under the Heisei Recession", in *JQ*, 41/3, July–Sept. 1994, pp. 270–85.

Gill, T., 1996, "Kotobuki, Home of Outcasts and Heroes", in *YOKE*, 14/76, March 1996, pp. 6–7.

Gold, S., 1988, "Inside a Japanese University", *Japan Update*, Winter 1988, pp. 3–4.

"Goodbye Japan Corporation", 1996, video produced jointly by Film Australia and NHK.

Goodman, R., 1993, "Education", in *CEJ*, pp. 245–50.

Goodman, R. and Refsing, K. (eds.), 1992, *Ideology and Practice in Modern Japan*, Routledge, London.

Greenfeld, K. T., 1994, *Speed Tribes: Days and Nights with Japan's Next Generation*, Harper Collins, New York.

Guzewicz, T., 1996, "A New Generation of Homeless Hits Tōkyō's Streets", in *JQ*, 43/3, July–Sept. 1996, pp. 43–53.

Hakim, C., 1995, "Five Feminist Myths about Women's Employment", in *British Journal of Sociology*, 46/3, pp. 429–455.

Haley, J., 1991, *Authority without Power: Law and the Japanese Paradox*, Oxford University Press.

Haley, J., 1992, "Consensual Governance: a Study of Law, Culture, and the Political Economy of Postwar Japan", in Kumon, S. and Rosovski, H. (eds.), 1992, *q.v.*, pp. 32–62.

Hall, 1974, Introduction to *Kokutai no Hongi: Cardinal Principles of the National Entity of Japan*, *q.v.*, pp. 1–47.

Hamaguchi, E., 1985, "A Contextual Model of the Japanese: Toward a Methodological Innovation in Japan [sic] Studies" (trans. S. Kumon and M. Creighton), in *JJS*, 11/2, pp. 289–321.

Hanami, M., 1995, "Minority Dynamics in Japan: Towards a Society of Sharing", in Maher, J. and Macdonald, G. (eds.), 1995, *q.v.*, pp. 121–46.

Hanazaki, K., 1996, "Ainu Moshir and Yaponesia: Ainu and Okinawan Identities in Contemporary Japan", in D. Denoon et al. (eds.), 1996, *q.v.*, pp. 117–31.

Hane, M., 1982, *Peasants, Rebels, and Outcastes: the Underside of Modern Japan,* Pantheon Books, New York.

Hane, M., 1988, *Reflections on the Way to the Gallows: Voices of Japanese Rebel Women*, University of California Press/Pantheon Books, New York.

Hanley, S. and Yamamura, K., 1977, *Economic and Demographic Change in Preindustrial Japan, 1600–1868*, Princeton University Press.

Harnischfeger, U., 1993, "Strict Policy Locks Out Most Haven-Seeking Refugees", in the *Japan Times*, Weekly International Edition, 8–14 March 1993, p. 11.

Hasegawa, M., 1984, "Equal Opportunity Legislation is Unnecessary", in *JE*, 11/4, pp. 55–8.

Hashimoto, M., 1995, "Intoxicated Youth", in *JQ*, 42/2, April–June 1995, pp. 136–45.

Hashimoto, M., 1996, "Becoming Aware of Child Abuse", in *Japan Quarterly*, 43/2, April–June 1996, pp. 145–52.

Hata, H. and Smith, W., 1986, "The Vertical Structure of Japanese Society as a Utopia", in Mizuta, N. (ed.), 1986, *Review of Japanese Culture and Society*, Centre for Intercultural Studies and Education, Jōsai University, Saitama, pp. 92–120.

Hayashi, Y., 1992, "Gangsters on Defensive in Japan", in *Yoke*, November 1992, p. 3.

Hearn, L., 1904, *Japan: an Attempt at Interpretation*, Macmillan, London.

Hendry, J., 1984, "Shoes: the Early Learning of an Important Distinction in Japanese Society", in Daniels, G. (ed.), 1984, *q.v.*, pp. 215–22.

Hendry, J., 1989, *Understanding Japanese Society*, Routledge, London.

Hendry, J., 1992, "Individualism and Individuality: Entry into a Social World", in Goodman, R. and Refsing, K. (eds.), 1992, *q.v.*, pp. 55–71.

Henshall, K., 1977, *Naturalism and Tayama Katai*, Ph.D. thesis, University of Sydney.

Henshall, K., 1988, *A Guide to Remembering Japanese Characters*, Tuttle, Tōkyō.

Henshall, K., 1992, "On Japanese Perceptions of their Relationship with Nature", in Henshall, K. and Bing, D. (eds.), 1992, *Japanese Perceptions of Nature and Natural Order,* New Zealand Asian Studies Association, Hamilton, pp. 25–44.

Hoffman, D., 1992, "Changing Faces, Changing Places: the New Koreans in Japan", in *JQ*, 39/4, Oct.–Dec. 1992, pp. 479–89.

Honna, N., and Katō, M, 1995, "The Deaf and their Language: Progress Towards Equality", in Maher, J. and Macdonald, G. (eds.), 1995, *q.v.*, pp. 270–87.

Horio, T., 1988, *Educational Thought and Ideology in Modern Japan: State Authority and Intellectual Freedom* (ed. and trans. Steven Platzer), University of Tōkyō Press.

Hoshino, E., 1983, "Kegare", in *KEJ*, Vol. 4, p. 186.

Howard, K., 1995, *True Stories of the Korean Comfort Women*, Cassel, London.

Igarashi, F., 1986, "Forced to Confess" (trans. McCormack, G.), in McCormack and Sugimoto (eds.) 1986b, *q.v.*, pp. 195–214.

Ikeda, E., 1995, "Society and AIDS", in *JQ*, 42/1, January–March 1995, pp. 21–32.

Inami, S., 1992, "Going After the Yakuza", in *JQ*, 39/3, July–Sept. 1992, pp. 353–8.

"Inside Japan Inc.", in the *Pacific Century* video series, project director Frank Gibney, executive producer Alex Gibney, Jigsaw / Pacific Basin Institute, Santa Barbara, 1992.

Ishida, H., 1993, *Social Mobility in Contemporary Japan: Educational Credentials, Class and the Labour Market in a Cross-National Perspective*, Macmillan, London.

Ishihara, S., 1989/91, *The Japan That Can Say 'No': Why Japan Will Be First Amongst Equals* (trans. Baldwin, F.), Simon and Schuster, New York and

London (orig. *'No' to Ieru Nihon*, with Morita, A., 1989).

Itagaki, T., 1996, "Kan Naoto Stirs the Health Ministry", in *JQ*, 43/3, July–Sept. 1996, pp. 24–9.

Iwao, S., 1991, "The Quiet Revolution: Japanese Women Today", *Japan Foundation Newsletter*, 19/3, pp. 1–9.

Iwao, S., 1993, *The Japanese Woman: Traditional Image and Changing Reality*, Free Press, New York.

Japan: An International Comparison, annually, Keizai Kōhō Center, Tōkyō.

Japan: A Pocket Guide, annually, Foreign Press Center, Tōkyō.

"Japanese Fear Loss of 'Soul' Abroad", *New Scientist*, 2 March 1991, p. 13.

Japanese Women Now, 1992, English Discussion Society, Women's Bookstore Shoukadoh, Tōkyō.

"Japan's *Yakuza* Go Legit", 23 December 1991, Asia Foundation Translation Service Center, Tōkyō, 10 pp. (Japanese original in *Shūkan Tōyō Keizai*, 21 Sept. 91).

JETRO (Japan External Trade Organization), 1993, *Meeting the Challenge: Japanese Kaisha in the 1990s*, Tōkyō.

Johnston, W., 1995, *The Modern Epidemic: a History of Tuberculosis in Japan*, Harvard East Asia Monographs 162, Harvard University Press.

Kalland, A., 1995, "Culture in Japanese Nature", in Bruun, O. and Kalland, A. (eds.), 1995, *Asian Perceptions of Nature: A Critical Approach*, Curzon Press, London, pp. 243–59.

Kamata, S., 1982, *Japan in the Passing Lane: an Insider's Account of Life in a Japanese Auto Factory* (trans. T. Akimoto), Pantheon, New York.

Kaplan, D., 1995, "The Gangster with the Golden Touch: How Susumu Ishii Took the *Yakuza* into High Finance", in *Tōkyō Journal*, Sept. 1995, pp. 32–7.

Kaplan, D. and Dubro, E., 1987, *Yakuza: the Explosive Account of Japan's Criminal Underworld*, Futura Publications, London.

Katayama, K., 1996, "The Japanese as an Asia-Pacific Population", in D. Denoon et al. (eds.), 1996, *q.v.*, pp. 19–30.

Katō, S., 1981, *A History of Japanese Literature: the First Thousand Years* (trans. Chibbett, D.), Kōdansha International, Tōkyō.

Kawamura, N., 1994, *Sociology and Society of Japan*, Kegan Paul International, London.

Kawanishi, H., 1992, *Enterprise Unionism in Japan* (trans. R. Mouer), Kegan Paul International, London.

Kayano, S., 1994, *Our Land Was a Forest: an Ainu Memoir* (trans. K. and L. Seldon), Westview Press, Boulder, San Francisco and London (orig. 1980).

Keene, D. (compiler), 1968, *Anthology of Japanese Literature to the Nineteenth Century*, Penguin, Harmondsworth.

Kitahara, M, 1989, *Children of the Sun: the Japanese and the Outside World*, Paul Norbury Publications, Kent.

Koike, K., 1995, *The Economics of Work in Japan*, LTCB International Library Foundation, Tōkyō (Japanese orig. 1991).

Kojiki—see Philippi 68.

Kokutai no Hongi: Cardinal Principles of the National Entity of Japan, trans. Gauntlett, J., 1949, Harvard University Press, and (this edition) 1974, Crofton Publishing, Massachusetts.

Kondo, Dorihne, 1992, "The Aesthetics and Politics of Japanese Identity in the Fashion Industry", in Tobin, J. (ed.), 1992a, *q.v.*, pp. 176–203.

Kōno, M. and Bowles, T., 1983, "Ainu", in *KEJ*, Vol. 1, pp. 34–6.

Koyama, K., 1987, "Rethinking Education", in *Look Japan*, December 1987, pp. 6–8.

Kumagai, F., 1996, *Unmasking Japan Today: the Impact of Traditional Values on Modern Japanese Society*, with D. Keyser, Praeger Press, Westport and London.

Kumon, S. and Rosovski, H. (eds.), 1992, *The Political Economy of Japan, Volume 3: Cultural and Social Dynamics*, Stanford University Press.

Kunihiro, M., 1976, "The Japanese Language and Intercultural Communication", in Japan Center for International Exchange (ed.), 1976, *The Silent Power: Japan's Identity and World Role*, Simul Press, Tōkyō, pp. 51–74.

Lam, A., 1992, *Management: Discrimination and Reform*, Routledge, London and New York.

Lebra, T., 1976, *Japanese Patterns of Behavior*, University of Hawaii Press.

Lebra, T., 1983a, "*Naikan* Therapy", in *KEJ*, Vol. 5, pp. 310–1.

Lebra, T., 1983b, "Morita Therapy", in *KEJ*, Vol. 5, pp. 253–4.

Lebra, T., 1984, *Japanese Women: Constraint and Fulfillment*, University of Hawaii Press.

Lebra, T. (ed.), 1992, *Japanese Social Organisation*, University of Hawaii Press.

Lee, C., 1983, "Koreans in Japan", in *KEJ*, Vol. 4, pp. 291–2.

Lent, J., 1989, "Japanese Comics", in Powers, R., Katō, H., and Stronach, B. (eds.), 1989, *Handbook of Japanese Popular Culture*, Greenwood, New York, pp. 221–42.

Leupp, G., 1995, *Male Colors: the Construction of Homosexuality in Tokugawa Japan*, University of California Press.

Lincoln, J. and Kalleberg, A., 1990, *Culture, Control, and Commitment: a Study of Work Organization and Work Attitudes in the United States and Japan*, Cambridge University Press.

Linhart, S., 1984, "Some Observations on the Development of 'Typical' Japanese Attitudes towards Working Hours and Leisure", in Daniels, G. (ed.), 1984, *q.v.*, pp. 207–15.

Littlewood, I., 1996, *The Idea of Japan: Western Images, Western Myths*, Secker and Warburg, London.

Macdonald, G. and Kowatari, A, 1995, "A Non-Japanese Japanese: On Being a Returnee", in Maher, J. and Macdonald, G. (eds.), 1995, *q.v.*, pp. 249–69.

Maher, J. and Macdonald, G. (eds.), 1995, *Diversity in Japanese Language and Culture*, Kegan Paul International, London and New York.

Makihara, K., 1992, "Recycling the Mob", in *Time*, 10 August 1992, p. 39.

Matsuzawa, T., 1988, "Street Labour Markets, Day Labourers, and the Structure of Oppression", in McCormack, G. and Sugimoto, Y. (eds.), 1988, *q.v.*, pp. 147–64.

Mayo, M., 1983, "Ogasawara Islands", in *KEJ*, Vol. 6, p. 68.

McCormack, G., 1986, "Crime, Confession, and Control in Contemporary Japan", in McCormack, G. and Sugimoto, Y. (eds.) 1986b, *q.v.*, pp. 186–94.

McCormack, G., 1996, *The Emptiness of Japanese Affluence*, M. E. Sharpe, New York/Allen & Unwin, Sydney.

McCormack, G. and Sugimoto, Y., 1986a, "Democracy and Japan", in McCormack, G. and Sugimoto, Y. (eds.), 1986b, *q.v.*, pp. 9–17.

McCormack, G. and Sugimoto, Y. (eds.), 1986b, *Democracy in Contemporary Japan*, Hale and Ironmonger, Sydney.

McCormack, G. and Sugimoto, Y. (eds.), 1988, *The Japanese Trajectory: Modernization and Beyond*, Cambridge University Press.

McCullough, W. and McCullough, H., 1980, *A Tale of Flowering Fortunes: Annals of Japanese Aristocratic Life in the Heian Period*, 2 vols., Stanford University Press.

McKenzie, F., 1980, *The Tragedy of Korea*, Yonsei University Press.

McVeigh, B., 1995, "The Feminization of Body, Behavior, and Belief: the Cultivation of 'Office Flowers' at a Japanese Women's Junior College", in *American Asian Review*, 13/2 (Summer 1995), pp. 29–67.

McVeigh, B., 1996, "Commodifying Affection, Authority and Gender in the Everyday Objects of Japan", in *Journal of Material Culture*, Vol. 1 No. 3, November 1996, pp. 291–312.

McVeigh, B., 1997, *Life in a Japanese Women's College: Learning to be Ladylike*, Routledge, London and New York.

Miller, R. A., 1982, *Japan's Modern Myth: The Language and Beyond*, Weatherhill, Tōkyō.

Ministry of Foreign Affairs, 1984, *The Dōwa Problem: Present Situation and Government Measures*, Tōkyō.

Mita, M., 1992, *Social Psychology of Modern Japan* (trans. S. Suloway), Kegan Paul International, London.

Miyoshi, M., 1974, *Accomplices of Silence: the Modern Japanese Novel*, University of California Press.

Moeran, B., 1989, *Language and Popular Culture in Japan*, Manchester University Press.

Mogi, T., 1992, "The Disabled in Society", in *JQ*, 39/4, Oct.–Dec. 1992, pp. 440–8.

Moore, J. (ed. for the *Bulletin of Concerned Asian Scholars*), 1997, *The Other Japan: Conflict, Compromise, and Resistance Since 1945*, M. E. Sharpe, New York.

Morishima, M., 1982, *Why has Japan Succeeded: Western Technology and the Japanese Ethos*, Cambridge University Press.

Morita, A., 1987, *Made in Japan* (with E. Reingold and M. Shimomura), Collins, London.

Morris-Suzuki, T., 1996, "A Descent into the Past: the Frontier in the Construction of Japanese Identity", in D. Denoon et al. (eds.), 1996, *q.v.*, pp. 81–94.

Mouer, R. and Sugimoto, Y., 1986, *Images of Japanese Society: a Study in the Structure of Social Reality*, Kegan Paul International, London.

Munakata, T., 1986, "Japanese Attitudes Towards Mental Illness and Mental Health Care", in Lebra, T. and Lebra, W. (eds.), 1986, *Japanese Culture and Behavior: Selected Readings* (rev. ed.), University of Hawaii Press, pp. 369–78.

Murakami, Y., 1984, "*Ie* Society as a Pattern of Civilisation", in *JJS*, Vol. 10, No. 2, pp. 281–363.

Murakami, Y. and Rohlen, T., 1992, "Social-Exchange Aspects of the Japanese Political Economy: Culture, Efficiency, and Exchange", in Kumon, S., and Rosovski, H. (eds.), 1992, *q.v.*, pp. 63–105.

Muramatsu, M., 1996, "The Story of Family Planning in Japan", *JE*, Special Issue, 1996, pp. 30–4.

Murasaki Shikibu, c.1004/1960, *The Tale of Genji* (trans. Waley, A., of *Genji Monogatari*), Random House, New York, 1960.

Murase, T., 1986, "*Naikan* Therapy", in Lebra, T. and Lebra, W. (eds.), 1986, *Japanese Culture and Behavior: Selected Readings* (rev. ed.), University of Hawaii Press, pp. 388–98.

Mushakōji, K., 1976, "The Cultural Premises of Japanese Diplomacy", in Japan Center for International Exchange (ed.), 1976, *The Silent Power: Japan's Identity and World Role*, Simul Press, Tōkyō, pp. 35–50.

Naka, H., 1977, *Japanese Youth in a Changing Society* (trans. L. Bester and S. Amano), Educational Society for Educational Information, Tōkyō.

Nakagami Kenji, 1984/5, "The Immortals" (orig. 1984, trans. Harbison, M.), in Gessel, V. and Matsumoto, T., 1985 (eds.), *q.v.*, Vol. 2, pp. 412–28.

Nakamura, S,, 1996, "Public Pensions for an Aging Population", *JE*, Special Issue, 1996, pp. 48–53.

Nakane, C., 1970, *Japanese Society*, Weidenfeld & Nicolson, London (orig. 1967).

Nakane, C., 1983, "Ie", in *KEJ*, Vol. 3, pp. 259–60.

Nakano, H., 1995, "The Sociology of Ethnocentrism in Japan", in Maher, J. and Macdonald, G. (eds.), 1995, *q.v.*, pp. 49–72.

Natsume Sōseki, 1906/61, *I Am a Cat* (*Wagahai wa Neko de Aru*, trans. K. Shibata and M. Kai), Kenkyūsha, Tōkyō.

Natsume Sōseki, 1914/69, *Kokoro* (trans. E. McClellan, as *Kokoro*), Tuttle, Tōkyō, 1969.

Neary, I., 1993, "Minorities", in *CEJ*, pp. 241–5.

Nihongi—see Aston 1896/1972.

Nihon Shoki—see Aston 1896/1972.

Nippon: a Charted Survey of Japan, annually, Kokuseisha, Tōkyō.

NLSSTSS (National League for Support of the School Textbook Screening Suit), 1995, *Truth in Textbooks, Freedom in Education, and Peace for Children: the Struggle against the Censorship of School Textbooks in Japan*, Tōkyō.

Norgren, T., 1998, "Abortion Before Birth Control: the Interest Group Politics Behind Postwar Japanese Reproduction Policy", in *JJS*, 24/1 (Winter 1998), pp. 59–94.

Nosaka Akiyuki, 1968, *The Pornographers* (trans. M. Gallagher, of *Erogotoshi-tachi*, 1963), Knopf, New York.

Oda, H., 1992, *Japanese Law*, Butterworths, London.

Ogawa, N., 1996, "When the Baby Boomers Grow Old", *JE*, Special Issue, 1996, pp. 17–21.

Ohnuki-Tierney, E., 1984, *Illness and Culture in Contemporary Japan: an Anthropological View*, Cambridge University Press.

Okonogi, K., 1986, "The Japanese Male: Samurai or Wimp?" in *Voice*, December 1986, translation available from Asia Foundation, Tōkyō, 4pp.

Oshimo, S. and Court, B., 1997, "Tamagotchi Gonna Getcha", in *Kansai Time Out*, June 1997 issue, pp. 8–9.

Ossenberger, N., 1986, "Isolate Conservatism and Hybridization in the Population History of Japan: The Evidence of Nonmetric Cranial Traits", in Akazawa, T. and Aikens, C. (eds.), 1986, *q.v.*, pp. 199–215.

Ouchi, W., 1981, *Theory Z: How American Business Can Meet the Japanese Challenge*, Addison-Wesley, Massachusetts.

Pascale, R. and Athos, A., 1982, *The Art of Japanese Management*, Penguin, Harmondsworth.

Paulson, J., 1976, "Evolution of the Feminine Ideal", in Lebra, J., Paulson, J., and Powers, E. (eds.), 1976, *Women in Changing Japan*, Stanford University Press, pp. 1–23.

Pearson, R., 1996, "The Place of Okinawa in Japanese Historical Identity", in Denoon et al. (eds.), 1996, *Multicultural Japan: Palaeolithic to Postmodern*, Cambridge University Press, pp. 95–116.

Pharr, S., 1983, "Women in Japan (History of)", in *KEJ*, vol. 8, pp. 257–63.

Philippi, D., 1968, *Kojiki* (translation and introduction), University of Tōkyō Press.

Philippi, D., 1979, *Songs of Humans, Songs of Gods: the Epic Tradition of the Ainu*, University of Tōkyō Press.

Pineau, R. (ed.), 1968, *The Japan Expedition 1852–1854: the Personal Journal of Commodore Matthew C. Perry*, Smithsonian Institute Press, Washington.

Plath, D., 1983, "Old Age and Retirement", in *KEJ*, Vol. 6, pp. 98–100.

Price, J., 1997, "The 1960 Miike Coal Mine Dispute: Turning Point for Adversarial Unionism in Japan?", in Moore, J. (ed.), 1997, *q.v.*, pp. 49–73.

Rayner, M., 1980, "Women Who Find Dependence Best", *New Zealand Herald*, 20 February 1980.

Raz, J., 1992, "Self-Presentation and Performance in the *Yakuza* Way of Life: Fieldwork with a Japanese Underworld Group", in Goodman, R. and Refsing, K. (eds.), 1992, *q.v.*, pp. 210–34.

Reader, I., 1991, *Religion in Contemporary Japan*, University of Hawaii Press.

Reingold, E., 1992, *Chrysanthemums and Thorns: the Untold Story of Modern Japan*, St. Martin's Press, New York.

"Reinventing Japan", 1992, in the *Pacific Century* video series, project director Frank Gibney, executive producer Alex Gibney, Jigsaw/Pacific Basin Institute, Santa Barbara.

Reischauer, E., 1988, *The Japanese Today: Change and Continuity*, Belknap Press of Harvard University Press.

Reischauer, E. and Craig, A., 1979, *Japan: Tradition and Transformation*, George Allen and Unwin, London, Boston, and Sydney.

"Risen Sun", in the *Nippon* video series, BBC, London, 1991.

Robertson, J., 1992, "Doing and Undoing 'Female' and 'Male' in Japan: the Takarazuka Revue", in Lebra, T. (ed.), 1992, *q.v.*, pp. 165–91.

Rohlen, T., 1983, *Japan's High Schools*, University of California Press.

Rosenberger, N., 1992, "Images of the West: Home Style in Japanese Magazines", in Tobin 92a, *q.v.*, pp. 106–25.

Russell, J., 1991, "Narratives of Denial: Racial Chauvinism and the Black Other in Japan", *JQ*, 38/4 (Oct.–Dec. 91), pp. 416–28.

Said, E., 1978, *Orientalism*, Routledge, London.

Sakai, R. and Sakihara, M., 1983, "Okinawa", in *KEJ*, Vol. 6, pp. 84–91.

Sakamaki, S., 1996, "Fates Worse than Death", in *FEER*, 29 February 1996, pp. 38–40.

Sakamaki, S., 1997, "No, Thanks: That's What More and More Japanese Women Are Saying about Having Children", in *FEER*, 3 April 1997, pp. 36–7.

Sakamoto, H., 1986, "Japan's Conforming Students", in *Yomiuri Shimbun*, 16 June 1986, English translation available as four-page monograph from Asia Foundation, Tōkyō.

Sakurai, J., 1996, "Between a Rock and a Hard Place", in *Tōkyō Journal*, March 1996, pp. 33–7.

Satō, T., 1990, "Tokugawa Villages and Agriculture", in Nakane, C. and Oishi, S. (eds.), 1990, *Tokugawa Japan: the Social and Economic Antecedents of Modern Japan*, University of Tōkyō Press.

Schilling, M., 1996, "Yakuza Films: Fading Cellulose Heroes", in *JQ*, 43/3, July–Sept. 1996, pp. 30–42.

Schodt, F., 1983, *Manga! Manga! The World of Japanese Comics*, Kōdansha, Tōkyō.

Schoolland, K., 1990, *Shogun's Ghost: the Dark Side of Japanese Education*, Bergin and Garvey, New York.

Seigle, C., 1993, *Yoshiwara: the Glittering World of the Japanese Courtesan*, University of Hawaii Press.

Sei Shōnagon, c.1002/1967, *The Pillow Book of Sei Shōnagon* (trans. Morris, I., of *Makura no Sōshi*), Oxford University Press.

Sengoku, T., 1987, "Antiheroes as Role Models", Japanese orig. in *Nihon Keizai Shinbun* of 12 Sept. 1987, available in English as a five-page monograph in the Asia Foundation Translation Series, Tōkyō.

Sethi, S., Namiki, N., and Swanson, C., 1984, *The False Promise of the Japanese Miracle: Illusions and Realities of the Japanese Management System*, Pitman, Massachusetts.

Seward, J., 1972, *The Japanese*, Wm Morrow, New York.

Shida, K., 1996, "A Short History of Weddings in Modern Japan", in *Yoke*, Vol. 14, No. 79, October 1996, pp. 3–6.

Shillony, B., 1990, "Victors without Vanquished: a Japanese Model of Conflict Resolution", in Eisenstadt, S., and Ben-Ari, E. (eds.), 1990, *q.v.*, pp. 127–37.

Shimazaki Tōson, 1906/74, *The Broken Commandment* (*Hakai*), trans. Strong, K., University of Tōkyō Press.

Shimbori, M., 1987, "Japan's Sweat-shop Education", Japanese orig. in *Sankei Shimbun* of 13 February 1987, available in English as a four-page monograph in the Asia Foundation Translation Series, Tōkyō.

Shimoda, T., 1996, "The Role of Women in Japanese Television", in *NZJEAS*, 4/1 (June 1996), pp. 104–15.

Siddle, R., 1995, "The Ainu: Construction of an Image", in Maher, J. and Macdonald, G. (eds.), 1995, *q.v.*, pp. 73–94.

Singer, K., 1973, *Mirror, Sword, and Jewel: a Study of Japanese Characteristics*, Croom Helm, London.

Smart, N. and Hecht, R. (eds.), 1982, *Sacred Texts of the World: a Universal Anthology*, Macmillan, London.

Smith, R., 1983, *Japanese Society: Tradition, Self, and the Social Order*, Cambridge University Press.

Smith, R., 1992, "The Cultural Context of the Japanese Political Economy", in Kumon, S. and Rosovski, H. (eds.), 1992, *q.v.*, pp. 13–31.
Stanley, M., 1994, "Alone on a Wide, Wide Sea", in *Tōkyō Journal*, Dec. 1994, pp. 24–31.
Stanley, T., 1983, "Tōkyō Earthquake of 1923", in *KEJ*, Vol. 8, p. 66.
Stevenson, W., 1989, "The Asian Advantage: the Case of Mathematics", in Shields, J. (ed.), 1989, *Japanese Schooling: Patterns of Socialization, Equality, and Political Control*, Pennsylvania University Press, pp. 85–95.
Strong, N., 1983, "Konketsuji", in *KEJ*, Vol. 4, p. 271.
Sugimoto, Y., 1986, "The Manipulative Bases of 'Consensus' in Japan", in McCormack, G. and Sugimoto, Y. (eds.), 1986b, *q.v.*, pp. 65–75.
Suzuki, K., 1996, "Equal Job Opportunity for Whom?", in *JQ*, 43/3, July–Sept. 1996, pp. 54–60.
Suzuki, T., 1978, *Japanese and the Japanese* (trans. A. Miura), Kōdansha, Tōkyō (Japanese orig. *Kotoba to Bunka*, 1973).
Tayama Katai, 1907/81, "The Quilt" ("Futon", 1907), in *"The Quilt" and Other Stories by Tayama Katai*, trans. and intro. Henshall, K., 1981, University of Tōkyō Press.
Tayama Katai, 1909/84, *Country Teacher* (*Inaka Kyōshi*, trans. K. Henshall), University of Hawaii Press.
Taylor, J., 1985, *Shadows of the Rising Sun: a Critical View of the 'Japanese Miracle'*, Tuttle, Tōkyō.
Thayer, J., 1983, "Yakuza", in *KEJ*, Vol. 8, p. 286.
"The Learning Machine", in the *Nippon* video series, BBC, London, 1991.
Tobin, J. (ed.), 1992a, *Re-Made in Japan: Everyday Life and Consumer Taste in a Changing Japan*, Yale University Press.
Tobin, J., 1992b, "Domesticating the West", in Tobin, J. (ed.), 1992a, *q.v.*, pp. 1–41.
Tobin, J., Wu, D. and Davidson, D., 1989, "Class Size and Student-Teacher Ratios in the Japanese Preschool", in Shields, J. (ed.), 1989, *Japanese Schooling: Patterns of Socialization, Equality, and Political Control*, Pennsylvania University Press, pp. 59–72.
Tokayer, M. and Swartz, M., 1979, *The Fugu Plan: the Untold Story of the Japanese and the Jews during World War II*, Paddington Press, New York and London.
Tsunoda, R., de Bary, W.T., and Keene, D. (compilers), 1964, *Sources of Japanese Tradition*, 2 vols., University of Columbia Press.
Tsunoda, T., 1985, *The Japanese Brain* (trans. Y. Oiwa), Taishūkan Publishing, Tōkyō.
Tsushima, M., 1996, "The Japanese and Religion", *Japan Foundation Newsletter,* 23/5, February 1996, pp. 1–5.
Ueno, C., 1996, "Modern Patriarchy and the Formation of the Japanese Nation State", in D. Denoon et al. (eds.), 1996, *q.v.*, pp. 213–23.
Van Wolferen, K., 1989, *The Enigma of Japanese Power: People and Politics in a Stateless Nation*, Macmillan, London.
Ventura, R., 1992, *Underground in Japan*, Jonathan Cape, London.
Wagatsuma, H. and de Vos, G., 1967, "The Outcaste Tradition in Modern Japan: a Problem in Social Self-Identity", in Dore, R. (ed.), 1967, *q.v.*, pp. 373–408.

Watanabe, H., 1973, *The Ainu Ecosystem: Environment and Group Structure*, University of Washington Press.

Wetherall, W., 1993, "Ethnic Ainu Seek Official Recognition", special feature in the *Japan Times*, Weekly International Edition, 25–31 January 1993.

Whitehill, A., 1991, *Japanese Management: Tradition and Transition*, Routledge, London.

Wilkinson, E., 1981, *Misunderstanding: Europe vs Japan*, Chūōkōronsha, Tōkyō.

Wilson, J., 1986, "Exporting Japan's Aged", feature in the *West Australian*, 29 August 1986.

Woronoff, J., 1981, *Japan: The Coming Social Crisis*, Lotus Press, Tōkyō.

Woronoff, J., 1990, *Japan As—Anything But—Number One*, Yohan Publications, Tōkyō.

Wöss, F., 1984, "Escape into Death: Old People and their Wish to Die", in Daniels, G. (ed.), 1984, *q.v.*, pp. 222–30.

Yamazaki, F., 1996, *Dying in a Japanese Hospital* (trans. Y. Claremont), Japan Times, Tōkyō.

Yashiro, N., 1996, "The Economics of Marriage", *JE,* Special Issue, 1996, pp. 22–9.

Yoshino, I. and Murakoshi, S., 1983, "Burakumin", in *KEJ,* Vol. 1, pp. 216–17.

Index